The Values of Connection

•••••••••••••••••

Robert G. Lee, Editor

....

The Values of Connection

••••••••••••

A Relational
Approach to Ethics

A GestaltPress Book

published and distributed by
The Analytic Press
Hillsdale, NJ

Distributed by: The Analytic Press, Inc.
                    101 West Street
                    Hillsdale, NJ

Library of Congress Cataloging-in-Publishing Data

Lee, Robert G., editor
     The values of connection: a relational approach to ethics
     includes bibliographical references
     ISBN: 0-88163-432-8
     1. Ethics 2. Gestalt therapy 3. Field theory 4. Lee, Robert G.
(Robert Gerald)

Cover Photograph: © Jack Larmour/IStock

Contents

◆◆◆◆◆◆

Theory: From a Field Perspective

Clinical Applications

Widening the Lens

Cultural Reflections

*For my wife Debbie
and for my children and step-children,
Chris, Dina, Pam, Phyllis,
Steve, Schuyler, and Jasmine,
the loves of my life*

Preface

•••••••••••••••

Most of us who work with people in the helping professions do so because we care about others, want to be involved in assisting others, in seeing others grow, and in the process growing ourselves. For myself, I gave up a lucrative career in chemical engineering, some 30 years ago, because being with people in the way that I can as a therapist is so much more fulfilling to me.

So as professionals we want our caring to count, to be effective. Further, we want our caring *not*, in some unintended manner, to come to hurt the people with whom we work. Where do we turn, what guidelines do we have, to assist us in this endeavor? Is this something we have to work out by ourselves? Certainly, our hearts and common sense are major resources. Can our psychological theory of human development, self-organization, and interaction help us here?

These are the questions and the energy from which I started the project of writing this book. For many years, in my early development as a therapist, I had the thought that a direction for how we could best relate to clients/patients, an ethical foundation if you will, must be obtainable from our theory of human nature. I was taken by the position of Thomas Szasz (1961) in which his theory and treatment emanated from his basic ethical belief about who people are:

> Inasmuch as psychiatric theories seek to explain, and systems of psychotherapy to alter, human behavior, statements concerning goals and values ("ethics") will be considered indispensable parts of theories of personal conduct and psychotherapy (p. 8).

Of course, the thrust of ethics in therapeutic disciplines has been to protect the rights of patients/clients, as well as to give guidance to therapists in ethical situations. However, I was looking for more than this. I wanted something on which to build my approach to patients/clients as well as to interact with others. In this regard, I considered the whole activity of working with others in a helping capacity to be an ethical situation.

However, the prevailing thought of the time was that ethics and theory could not be related. I was told by trainers and supervisors that our ethics must be independent of our theory. Still it didn't make sense to me. I was drawn to Gestalt because it made a difference in my own life. And I had found that it had made a difference in how I could be with others as a therapist. So why couldn't it provide us with an ethical statement of how to be with people in general? But because I couldn't find sufficient support for my inquires, I put them aside.

Later in my career, after co-editing *The Voice of Shame* with Gordon Wheeler (Lee & Wheeler, 1996), I discovered that I had the supportive base that I needed to once again pursue this exploration. My interest in the phenomenon of shame and how shame and belonging organize the social field, and how the core of Gestalt theory, with its analysis of contact processes, had long centered on shame and belonging without naming them as such (see also Lee, 1994, 1995), had drawn me powerfully into a sense of the field, intersubjective, interactional, lived quality of human existence as the basis for understanding behavior, development, and psychological phenomena in general. With this field centered theoretical grounding, about eight years ago, I returned to my questions of whether an ethical stance could emerge from our theory.

The result of this exploration, finished about three and a half years ago, is Chapter 1 of this book. In fact, when we turn to a field orientation, an ethics does emerge from Gestalt theory. And it does provide a basis on which to build our treatment of patients/clients and to relate to others. Moreover, Gestalt theory, viewed in this light, offers a new sense of ethics in general. It delineates the difference between an external ethics of rules, as we most commonly think of ethics, and a shared internal ethics which is experienced at a deeper level. The latter forms naturally in the context of a relational field in which people come to have a sense of belonging and trust with one another such that ethical guidelines and implications emerge in each individual from a shared sense of caring and valuing of one another.

In contrast, the former or external form of ethics, which is forged and administered/imposed from the outside, is itself a sign that trust and belonging may not be perceived as possible in a given field. And here as with other endeavors of which I have been a part, as we bring the Gestalt lens more fully to bear on a given topic or phenomenon we not only gain a clearer, broader perspective of that particular phenomenon, but in addition in the process we learn more about Gestalt.

As I approached the end of working on this article, the breadth of possibilities and applications of these discoveries became apparent. Further, this ethics has always been inherent in the Gestalt model. These are the values that originally drew me to Gestalt. The difference here is discovering that they can be derived from our theory instead of needing to import them from other sources. And in discovering their connection to theory, their essence becomes clearer and consequently more available.

Thus about three and a half years ago the project of this book was born. I started thinking about how these values clarify and support my work with clients. I started looking for other authors who had the background to speak further to this subject. And I began noticing practitioners in the field whose work was in consonance with and demonstrated the efficacy of this kind of ethical understanding. My hope has been to cast a different light on the field of ethics and to generate a fresh conceptual and practical starting point for an ongoing dialogue about the nature and utility of ethics as generated by this uniquely Gestalt perspective.

I am delighted by the depth of experience and stature of the authors who have joined me, as well as their enthusiastic creativity in describing their work from this perspective together with the power of the stories they have to tell. It is with honor that I am able to present our collective efforts on the following pages.

The book is organized for your ease of use. Please follow your interest in selecting where to start and how to proceed. Each chapter is complete within itself and is proceeded with an accompanying editor's note, briefly describing how the chapter fits with the themes of the book. We have grouped the chapters into four sections, which is of course a somewhat arbitrary arrangement as the Gestalt lens affords a multifaceted view that always challenges any attempt at rigid categorization. Thus many of these chapters could have been placed in more than one of these sections.

We open the book with a section entitled "Theory: From a Field Perspective," aimed at giving a background for how a field/relational approach enables us to see and fully understand the connective dynamics that are the foundation of growth, fostering the ability to thrive for both the individual and the larger field, and how a set of ethical principles emerges from this ground. This section is headed with Chapter One, "Ethics: A Gestalt of Values / The Values of Gestalt," my initial exploration into this phenomenon, which I have described above. Please consult the Editor's Notes that proceed this and the other chapters for additional framing of the chapters.

Lynne Jacobs, long one of Gestalt's brightest, most grounded, insightful voices, authors Chapter Two, "Ethics of Context and Field: The Practices of Care, Inclusion and Openness to Dialogue." In a piece that cannot be described short of exceptional, Jacobs, as is often her style, graciously shares her own vulnerability as an illustrative foundation from which to explore the multilevel nature of our field and contextual existence. In the process, from a related yet unique perspective, she affirms and enlarges our understanding of relational ethics that we obtained in Chapter One.

In Chapter Three, "Living Ethically in an Interdependent World: Situating Ourselves and Naming Our Values," Deborah Ullman brings her fine intellect, her deft attunement to the condition of others, and her grounding in philosophy and Lewinian thought to focus on the historical development of our current ethical situation and the problem that causes for living in general and for therapists in particular. For many years Ullman has been an editor, whose nurturant and masterful touch has assisted in the birthing of other authors' voices. Thus, it is with all the more pleasure that we present her own voice here.

Next we move to "Clinical Applications," a section which focuses on the use of the ethics that derives from the Gestalt model as a basis for structuring treatment modalities with several different populations. In each case, new relevant theory is visited that has wider applicability. This section opens with Chapter Four, Sandra Cardoso-Zinker's "The Story of Daniel: Gestalt Therapy Principles and Values." Cardoso-Zinker gives us a set of principles which orient her work, and which we may note are grounded in the relational ethics presented in the first section of the book. We then get to follow the course of a master clinician as she shares with us the heartwarming story of how these principles guide her in helping a child and his family attain a level of integrated belonging that fosters their individual growth.

In Chapter Five, "The Relational Ethic in the Treatment of Adolescents," I join Chuck Kanner in presenting a lively account of the relationally based program and approach that he, his wife Cara and their staff employ with troubled adolescents at their institute in Sarasota, Florida. This is an outstanding example of a methodology that is based on and guided by Gestalt's relational ethics.

Chapter Six, "The Ethics of Touch and Imagery in Psychotherapy: A Gestalt Resolution," focuses on what has become a taboo subject in our litigious society. Three theorists-clinicians-academicians, Rebecca M. Murray, James L. Pugh, and Pauline Rose Clance (co-editor of *Touch in Psychotherpy* [Guilford Press, 1998]), who are well-grounded in the research associated with this topic, join in giving us a field based exploration of the importance of touch in a relationally based approach with patients/clients as well as guidelines around the safe and unsafe use of touch and an alternative when it is counter-indicated.

I have always had a special place in my heart for working with couples. Couples possess potential relational resources that most often are unrecognized and untapped when couples are struggling. In Chapter Seven, "Working With Couples: Application of Gestalt's Values of Connection," I present, using case studies, an account of how our derived relational ethics lead not to the individualist oriented tasks of helping couples solve their immediate problems, negotiate better, or become "better" people, but instead to facilitating their accessing their untapped relational resources. This is not a task of their realizing their duty, but instead of establishing sufficient mutual emotional safety so that their understanding and behavior can flow from their underlying relational yearnings.

In Chapter Eight, we are treated to J. Richard White's update of his award winning article "A Special Case for Gestalt Ethics: Working With the Addict." Using a foundation in Linguistics, Existentialism, and the Gestalt field model as well as his extensive experience, White astutely discerns that the ethical basis for working with addicts lies in obtaining an understanding of them and their behavior from within the addict's culture.

Next, in a section entitled "Widening the Lens," we broaden our focus to include a set of chapters that move beyond the boundaries of clinical practice. As with the chapters of previous sections, the richness of these offerings lies not only in what they bring to the topic they address but in addition to their wider applicability. This section opens with Chapter Nine, "The Relational Ethic of Understanding in Groups: A Conversation," in which I interview Lee Geltman, a longtime sensitively attuned, accomplished trainer, therapist and consultant. Geltman shares with us, from his 40 years of professional experience and using his own personal life stories, what he has learned about who people are and what they want when they come to a group, and how he positions himself as a facilitator in their developing self/other process. Additionally, he and I explore nuances of how people acquire and alter their internal sense of ethics.

In Chapter Ten, "On Treating Agents of Oppression," Philip Lichtenberg, renowned for his work on oppression, takes up the sensitive issue of relating to people, whether it be in a therapy session or in our life in general, whose verbal behavior and actions oppress others. He sensitively and insightfully follows our reactions, when confronted in such situations, in what I would term our individualist oriented society, that typically lead to fight or flight. And from a relational ethical perspective gives us an alternative that is grounded in caring and support for the whole field.

The experience of divorce can be cruel and traumatic. Up until relatively recent times it was women who most frequently bore the brunt of such trauma. In Chapter Eleven, "Men's Relational Needs Through the Trauma & Recovery From Adversarial Divorce: A Conversation," I interview Jeff Parks on how the current cultural and legal climate can lead to men being traumatized and on his creative efforts in finding solutions for men and their families. Parks' work is another outstanding example of an approach that is based in the ethics of a relational understanding of the individual and support for the whole field.

We complete the book with three more treasures in a section entitled "Cultural Reflections." The first of these, Chapter Twelve, "Shame and Belonging: Homer's *Iliad* and the Western Ethical Tradition" is a masterpiece by one of the foremost Gestalt theorists of our time, Gordon Wheeler. Through a new reading of Homer's *Iliad*, Wheeler deftly and eloquently traces the roots of the Western ethical dilemma that underpins our conceptualization of human nature and which still so profoundly impacts us in today's world.

Chapter Thirteen, "Finding A Voice: Listening to the Mental Health and Spiritual Needs of the New Communities of East London," highlights the work of Nigel Copsey. From a region that is rich in cultural diversity, Copsey relates a compelling story of developing a department for the National Health Service that listens and responds to the spiritual and mental health needs of the marginalized communities it serves. Once again we find that it is a relational ethic which organizes his program, enabling people of vastly different cultures to learn from and value one another.

The final chapter in the book is another sparkling offering by Gordon Wheeler, Chapter Fourteen, "The Fragileness of Goodness: How the Jews of Bulgaria Survived the Holocaust - A Gestalt Field Perspective." Wheeler gives us the remarkable story of how, astonishingly, none of the Jews of Bulgaria was lost to Nazi concentration camps during WWII. In an analysis that deconstructs the Western notion of heroism as being an individual phenomenon, he examines the fragile field quality that maintains society's goodness, while at the same time bringing us a sense of hope that in our present day world our individual efforts in the service of "goodness" will not be in vain.

The book concludes with a few final words from me in an Epilogue. Again, my hope is that this is not an end but a beginning to a fresh new perspective and ongoing dialogue on ethics in general, articulating and realizing the potential of how a Gestalt relational approach to ethics offers us organizing principles for our treatment of patients/clients and for relating to others in general. Please join us, in what we believe is an exciting and crucial endeavor.

As for myself, this pursuit continually clarifies and transforms my work with clients as well as my interactions with the people in my personal life. It is with these thoughts that I wish you the experience of pleasurable and profitable reading in the company of a select group of authors that I am proud to present to you.

May, 2004   Robert G. Lee
                                             Newton, Massachusetts

References

Lee, R. G. (1994). Couples' shame: The unaddressed issue. In G. Wheeler & S. Backman (Eds.), *On Intimate Ground - A Gestalt Approach to Working With Couples* (pp.262-290). San Francisco: Jossey-Bass.

Lee, R. G. (1995). Gestalt and shame: The foundation for a clearer understanding of field dynamics. *The British Gestalt Journal*, 4(1), 14-22.

Lee, R. G. & Wheeler, G. (Eds.). (1996). *The Voice of Shame: Silence and Connection in Psychotherapy*. San Francisco: Jossey-Bass.

Szasz, T. (1961). *The Myth of Mental Illness: Foundations of a Theory of Personal Conduct*. New York: Dell Publishing Co.

Acknowledgments

•••••••••••••••••••

The ideas in this book are grounded in the notion that support, connection, and belonging bring a shared internal sense of ethics which form the foundation of a healthy ethical field. I was first introduced to this way of being in the world in my early Gestalt training, and I am deeply indebted to my teachers and trainers, over the years, for what those experiences have brought not only to birthing this book but in addition to my life in general.

Further, the ideas in this book have been refined and clarified in many stimulating conversations and interactions with students, patients, colleagues, teachers, and friends. I wish to express my thanks and indebtedness to all those that contributed to my life experience and thinking in this regard. In particular, I wish to acknowledge my appreciation to the following people, whose supportive and at times critical input has more specifically helped to shape the perspective presented in this book: Jack Aylward, Russell Andreason, Isabel Frederickson, Reinhard Fuhr, Les Greenberg, Joseph Handlon, Judith Hemming, Jim Kepner, Ed Lynch, Mark McConville, Joe Melnick, Edwin Nevis, Sonia March Nevis, Brian O'Neil, Malcolm Parlett, Bruce Robertson, Paul Shane, Faye Snider, Sarah Toman, Mike Vickers, Ansel Woldt, and Joseph Zinker. And I wish to thank the authors that have joined me in this venture for both their outstanding contributions and for the rich dialogues that developed between us that has broadened my own awareness and thinking.

A special thanks goes to Linda Knowles for locating the image used on the front cover as well as for her professional skill and generous efforts in incorporating the image into a poignant, artistic, graceful cover design.

Two dear, close, treasured friends, Lee Geltman and Gordon Wheeler, deserve particular acknowledgment and thanks. It is the work that I undertook with Gordon, exploring shame and belonging's regulation of the relational field, resulting in *The Voice of Shame* and other individual endeavors since, that gave me the tools to explore the subject matter of this book. In addition, both Lee and Gordon have been sounding boards and voices of support since my earliest explorations as an author. I am indebted to them for their encouragement, their reading of manuscripts, their creative suggestions, and their friendship in general over the course of this endeavor. I am honored that both of them have also joined me as authors in this collection.

Finally, I want to thank my partner and fellow voyager through this adventure of life, my wife Debbie, for her ongoing support and love throughout this project.

Robert G. Lee

The Editor

••••••••••••

Robert G. Lee, PhD, a psychologist in private practice in Cambridge and Newton, Massachusetts, has written extensively and presented widely about shame and belonging as regulator processes of the relational field. He applies his intersubjective, constructivist insights to a wide range of clinical populations, including individuals, couples, families, children and adolescents, as well as to the topics of self process, development, field theory, ethics, culture, gender, and chronic illness. His research on couples and shame led to a deeper understanding of the hidden dynamics of the intimate couple. His article, "Gestalt and Shame: The foundation for a Clearer Understanding of Field Dynamics," won the 1995 Nevis Prize for Outstanding Contribution to Gestalt Therapy Theory. Bob is co-editor of *The Voice of Shame: Silence and Connection in Psychotherapy*. (Jossey-Bass, 1996). He is a member of the visiting faculty of the Gestalt Institute of Cleveland and teaches and trains nationally and internationally. Other interests in his life include West Coast Swing dancing, snorkeling, and being with and enjoying his wife and their collective children.

The Contributors

●●●●●●●●●●●●●●●●

Pauline Rose Clance, PhD, is co-founder of the Gestalt Institute of GA and faculty member of both the Pine River Psychotherapy Training Institute and A Woman's Initiative of Atlanta, Georgia. She was a professor of Psychology and Senior Faculty Associate for the Advancement of Women at Georgia State University until June 2003. She is the author of *The Imposter Phenomenon: Overcoming the Fears that Haunt Your Success* and a co-editor with Dr. Edward Smith and Dr. Suzanne Imes of *Touch In Psychotherapy.* She maintains a private practice in Atlanta, working with individuals, groups and couples, and provides professional supervision. She has worked on Women and Power issues at the national and international level.

Nigel Copsey, D.Psychotherapy, is the Team Leader of the Department of Spiritual, Religious and Cultural Care in the East End of London UK. The department is funded by the National Health Service to respond to the spiritual and cultural needs of those suffering from mental distress and creating a context where they can be supported. In the last few years he has returned to the early tradition of Gestalt in reaching out into the community to effect change.

Sandra Cardoso-Zinker, MS, Lic, is a Gestalt psychologist from Brazil where she was in private practice for 15 years. She taught Gestalt therapy in work with children and the arts. She has had substantial experience as a child therapist and has written articles about Gestalt therapy in relation to human development and Attachment Theory. At present she lives in Massachusetts with her husband Joseph and teaches Gestalt Couples and Child Therapy in the USA as well as in Europe and South America. She is affiliated with The Gestalt International Study Center and is a faculty member of The Gestalt Institute of Sao Paulo.

Lee Geltman is a psychologist in private practice in Lexington, MA. He is also the President of the Gestalt Institute of New England, where he has conducted training programs for professionals for the last 30 years. In addition, he has provided consulting and training for a wide range of organizations, with a particular focus on non-profit organizations.

Lynne Jacobs, PhD, is co-founder of the Pacific Gestalt Institute. She is also a Training and Supervising Analyst at the Institute of Contemporary Psychoanalysis. She is particularly interested in relational processes in therapy, has authored numerous articles, and co-authored (with Richard Hycner), *The Healing Relationship in Gestalt Therapy: A Dialogic, Self-Psychology Approach.* She teaches and trains nationally and internationally.

Joseph "Chuck" Kanner is the Executive Director of Sarasota Community School, formerly Kanner Academy. SCS is a dynamic therapeutic boarding school for emotionally and educationally troubled children founded by Chuck and his wife Cara in 1997. Chuck is at heart a Gestaltist in life and work and believes in the healing nature of therapeutic community. He was born and raised in New York City, and is a graduate of the University of New Mexico with Honors.

Philip Lichtenberg, PhD, was on the faculty of the Graduate School of Social Work and Social Research, Bryn Mawr College for over 35 years, retiring as Mary Hale Chase Professor Emeritus in 1996. He is the author of six books and many articles. His most recent books, re-issued by GestaltPress are: *Community and Confluence: Undoing the Clinch of Oppression* and *Encountering Bigotry: Befriending Projecting Persons in Everyday Life* (with Janneke van Beusekom and Dorothy Gibbons). He is Co-Director and Principal Faculty with the Gestalt Therapy Institute of Philadelphia, having been with the Institute since its beginning in 1984.

Rebecca Murray, PhD, (formerly Rebecca Terry) is an Associate Professor of Psychology at Georgia Southern University where she teaches undergraduate and graduate courses, and plays an active role in the graduate program in clinical psychology. Her research and publications have been in the areas of woman's psychological development, the process of psychotherapy, media psychology, and child abuse. In addition to her academic career, she maintains a part-time private practice where she works with adult clients using a humanistic and psychodynamic orientation.

Jeffrey Parks, LMFT, LCSW, is an individual and family therapist, trainer, and consultant in private practice in Framingham, MA. A clinician with over 30 years experience, for the last two decades he has specialized in issues involving family losses including death and dying, and separation and divorce. He has worked with children and families in capacities including "play therapist" with children and adolescents, "expert witness" in child custody cases, court-appointed Guardian Ad Litem (GAL) and private and/or court-appointed Parenting Coordinator. In recent years he has focused on helping men recover from the trauma of high-stress, high-conflict divorce.

Jim Pugh, PhD, is a member of the psychology faculty of Georgia Southern University, where he received his degree in 1984. Having worked in mental health settings since 1970, his professional interests have primarily focused on the treatment of chronic pain and the development of stress coping skills.

Deborah Ullman is a Gestalt trained bodyworker, an editor and co-publisher at GestaltPress (previously GIC Press) where she is currently working on a book called *The Healing Field.* Her passionate interests include Buddhist meditation, hatha yoga, holistic healing, music from Mahler to Miles to Makeba to Springstein, and finishing graduate school at Saybrook in San Fransisco. She lives on Cape Cod where one branch of her family washed up almost 400 years ago.

Gordon Wheeler, PhD, is a relational and narrative psychologist, drawing on Gestalt, constructivist, and intersubjective traditions to develop a new model of self, relationship, and experience. He is the author or editor of some fifty articles and over a dozen books in the field, including the recent titles *Beyond Individualism*, *The Heart of Development* (a two volume collection on work with children, co-edited with Mark McConville), and the forthcoming *Love and Play*, a collection of his own essays on psychology, culture, and politics. His recent writing projects include *The Long Goodbye*, a memoir of a family's experience of Alzheimer's disease. Gordon is President/CEO of the Esalen Institute in Big Sur CA, Editor-in-Chief of GestaltPress, and a member of the teaching faculty of a number of post-graduate Gestalt training institutes worldwide. His books have been translated into eight languages. He divides his time between Big Sur, California and Cambridge, Massachusetts.

J. Richard White, MEd, NCACII, is the Center Director of the Gateway Therapeutic Community at the New Castle Correctional Facility in Indiana. For a quarter of a century he has been involved in the development and implementation of treatment programs for under-served populations, and has trained staff in the humanistic approach to treating substance use disorders.

Part I

••••••••

Theory:

From a Field Perspective

Editor's Note:

The first question in our exploration of the existence of a Gestalt ethics is can such an entity be derived from our theory? In quest of the answer to this question, we review here the roots of constructionist, intersubjective Gestalt field theory from Ehrenfels' contribution through those of the Gestalt psychologists, Lewin, Goldstein and Goodman. This journey highlights how person and environment are interconnected. From the theoretical existence and importance of this interconnection, together with an understanding of the field conditions of support and shame, we find that a Gestalt relational ethics does emerge. We learn that ethical solutions must be field solutions, i.e. solutions that further the development of both the individual and the environment. Our theory also informs us that people must be understood from the perspective of their relational strivings and that having *healthy* individuals means having and maintaining a *healthy* environmental field. In the end, we acquire a new, broader sense of ethics in general. We discover that a primary focus of ethics should be the establishment of the conditions that promote the development of a personal, shared, internal ethics that emerges from our sense of interconnectedness and belonging as opposed to relying only on the enforcement of an externally-imposed code, to restrain isolated individuals who are themselves under-supported in the field.

•••••••••••••••••••

Ethics: A Gestalt of Values

The Values of Gestalt

A Next Step

Robert G. Lee

What is a Gestalt ethics? Is it possible for one to exist? If so, can it involve content as well as process? Even more importantly, can a set of ethics of whatever structure be derived from our theory? Or must we carry two unconnected guideposts—a theory that explains and helps us understand human processes, both internal and external, and a set of values of how we want to relate to people in general and clients in particular? Are we left with the position that we must just proclaim our values, perhaps arrived at through our individual experience or through a consensual process, or borrowed from some other theoretical or philosophical position, but *not* derived from our theory? Many have thought this to be true. On the other hand, if our theory offers a theoretically grounded ethical stance, what is a next step in realizing this potential?

Our exploration here is shaped to some degree by how we use terms such as *value* and *ethic*. In one sense, we can talk about instrumental values such as the process values inherent in Gestalt. These are values that have an implicit "IF" preceding them. For example, "knowing a person necessarily includes understanding him/her from the inside, from his/her perspective of the world," which implicitly is preceded by "IF you want to know another person...." Clearly this is a principle and a value of Gestalt, with the "IF" implying the possibility of another, more basic, value. But this is not yet an ethical value. That is, we want something more than situational/conditional ethics here. We want to locate values that don't have an "IF," like the societal value shared by so many cultures, of: "I can't kill you." There may be boundary issues and debates around "I can't kill you," as in self defense and the abortion and assisted suicide debates, but in general there's not an "IF." It is a value we believe in. This is the kind of value we will term an ethical value. But again, are there ethical values of this type, or even instrumental values for that matter, related to our theory and what it says about who we are and how we relate to one another?

This is not a problem particular to Gestalt theory. In fact, since the Enlightenment and the decline of religiously-based definitions of self and human nature, philosophy in general has shown an increasing tendency to split into ethical/moral speculation on the one hand, and analytic/descriptive systems of mind and cognitive process on the other. In the century or so since psychology has emerged from philosophy as a discipline in its own right, this split has been largely carried over and preserved, with attention to ethics in psychology generally being focused on rules for professional conduct, and/or on *how* systems of morality are acquired, completely apart from the content of those systems. In Kohlberg's (1984) scale of moral development, for example, it would seem that any ethical/moral system, even fascism, could conceivably score as the highest level of moral development, as long as it lays out firm and universal principles for right and wrong actions, no matter how repugnant we might find those principles to be. Meanwhile, in philosophy, Russell (1968), taking his cue from his student, Wittgenstein, nearly a century ago announced that in the absence of arbitrary religious guidelines, the philosophy of how the mind works can ultimately have nothing whatsoever to say about ethical choice or moral decision.

Is this a necessary conclusion, or is the separation of psychological theory and ethical concern one of the effects of a somewhat hidden, yet often present, underlying perspective in Western culture, namely the individualist view of human nature?[1] This view of human makeup and interaction embodies a tradition with a long pedigree dating back as far as the early Greeks, a tradition embedded profoundly in the Zeitgeist of each succeeding era as captured and passed on in the works of authors such as Homer and Shakespeare and enunciated so clearly in the early Freudian model, where each isolated human being often seems no more than an "object" to all the others for the mutual discharge of their separate drives and instincts. In short, is this state of affairs the result of the fact that from a grounding within the individualist paradigm it is close to impossible to postulate, let alone describe, how we are interconnected?

If we are merely isolated humans, as the individualist paradigm would have it, then there is no connection between us and thus no theoretical basis for a positive moral stance—that is without an outside influence such as a God. Religion and spirituality can provide a sense of connection and morality within the individualist paradigm. But without an outside influence, such as a God to connect us and to monitor our "sins," we are faced with the dilemma to which Russell (1968) alluded—namely that the individualist paradigm offers no reason within its doctrine for us to be interested in each other's welfare except politically, as a hedge against others taking advantage of us. But even then, if we are only isolated humans, it isn't difficult to deduce, as happens all too often in our individualist oriented culture, that our best chance to survive, and imagine thriving, is to make political contracts with others and then to cheat when we believe we can get away with it. And doesn't this lead us to the uncomfortable, even unbearable, but logical conclusion of Nietzsche —that the ethics of a godless individual paradigm are the pseudo-Darwinian ethics of ruthless competition and might makes right. And, although it makes us yet more uncomfortable, isn't a logical extension of these ethics a little too compatible with the doctrine of Nazism?

Unfortunately, the Gestalt model has at times been taken as

---

[1]See discussion in Wheeler, 2000.

belonging to this individualist tradition, where the goal of development is maximum autonomy and self-support, and maximum differentiation of person and environment—in part the result of Perls' oral aggression contribution to Gestalt theory (In Part I of Perls, Hefferline & Goodman, 1951). This version of the Gestalt model, with its primary strategies for living in the world of a heavy reliance on self and dental aggression as a means of satisfying needs, can stand as a metaphor for one kind of contact process, but it does not serve as well as an organizing image for the whole range of such field/experiential resolutions or mappings. It can be best regarded as a transitional model. Perls gave us, among other contributions, a knowledge of self support. And he gave us, although he did not speak of it in quite this manner, a sense of issues related to a lack of fit between a person and the environment that can lead to dysfunctional, fixed figure formation. We will talk at greater length of this later. But as Wheeler (1991) and others have shown, the oral aggression aspects of Perls' model do not lead to the fullest expression of the potential of Gestalt theory. Rather, refocusing the model on its constructivist, intersubjectivist field theory roots dating back to Lewin, Goldstein, Wertheimer, Kofka and other early Gestalt theorists, restores the larger potential of the Gestalt model. Such a shift leads us away from the individual and his/her internal process only and shifts our focus to the whole field so that we are not only looking at internal processes, autonomy and separation, but we're bringing to life the person/environment field, not just as a transaction but as a holistic, unified field of experience.

More specifically, a field model brings focus to the interconnectedness of person and environment at a deeper level than Perls' model—not to just the transactions but to the intersubjective influences that exist in how people co-construct each other's experience within the transactions. A field model brings focus to how the sense that people carry of themselves and who they are in the world is co-constructed as they and others interact as subjects rather than as passive objects. As such, "self" and "other" are simultaneously defined by the way connection is made or not made in progressive sequences of response following response. In this regard, the degree of fit people experience with others, as well as with non-human aspects of their environment, is crucial in how their co-constructed mapping of their field, their "self-process," develops. Thus we find ourselves particularly interested in the modulation of connection/ disconnection in the field. What kinds of connection/disconnection lead to rich figure formation with possibilities for interconnection in an ever expanding field, and what kinds are experienced as unchosen, undesired ruptures in the field and in turn diminish and hinder self formation and undermine the energy for field resolution and action? Let us call the former the experience of *support* and the latter the experience of *shame* (Lee, 1994a, 1995, 2001; Lee & Wheeler, 1996). The quality of support and shame within a field gives us a reading of the connection/disconnection condition of the field. Together they are our whole field connection/disconnection meter.

Thus, we find that with a field perspective we are able to appreciate how the heart of the Gestalt model, its analysis of contact phenomena, has long included an intuitive understanding of the role of support and shame in governing connections in the field (Lee, 1994a, 1995, 1996, 2001). The question here is whether a field theory model together with a knowledge of support and shame, and the latter's ability to inform us of ruptures in the field, can take us further in deriving a whole field Gestalt ethics? First let us look at what has already been done toward the formation of a Gestalt ethics.

The Existing Foundation for a Gestalt Ethics

Wertheimer (1935) believed that "all values are fundamentally relative, changing with place and times" (p. 353). And thus he warned that the establishment of a Gestalt ethics should be undertaken only with great care. Similarly, most Gestalt Therapy theorists addressing the question of ethics in recent times have asserted that a process-oriented theory such as Gestalt can have little to say about content and therefore values and have had to borrow from other disciplines in an effort to form a Gestalt ethics (Fuhr, 1993; Melnick, Nevis, & Melnick, 1994; White, 1995). These ethical positions, although well constructed, much needed, and highly useful, don't emanate directly from Gestalt theory.

At the same time, the idea that a set of values exists that is compatible with Gestalt theory and practice is not new. Zinker (1998) has given us a taxonomy of process values that he believes are congruent with Gestalt. Gremmler-Fuhr (2001) has noted that as human beings, it is impossible for us not to form value judgements "all the time." She has added her own set of values that she believes are implicitly present within the Gestalt tradition, contextualizing them within a developmental frame. The values that Zinker discusses underlie effective and respectful practice, while Gremmler-Fuhr is interested in the project of supporting the client's clarification of his/her own values, whatever those values may be. Building on both their work, again our interest here is whether such Gestalt values must merely be asserted or whether we can find them in the theoretical terms of the Gestalt matter itself.

We get a hint of that possibility from Hartmann (1935). In a vein similar to that of Gremmler-Fuhr, he states that all perceptions carry a value characteristic that is either experienced as "bad" or "good" which in effect tells us whether we want to move away from or toward something. "Value and being, consequently, are equally real and objective. Ideals of all sort are simply end-goals of dynamic activity..." (p. 209). Moreover, he states that the value qualities of perceptual structures are not purely subjective creations which we "project" into other objects. The value also has something to do with the quality of the environment being perceived. Speaking from a field perspective, he offers:

> The domain of morality has so long been associated with religious instruction that any effort to deal objectively with it is still greeted with suspicion.... yet strangely enough, from the Gestalt point of view, it may represent the culmination of man's rational nature.
>
> The latter position is made tenable by a simple extension of the notion of insight to an appreciation of the social consequences of one's actions. A "good" act is one which takes into consideration all the immediate and long-distance

effects which it may draw after it, and is "performed only if it leads to a better group organization (in the sense of Wertheimer's "good" gestalt). A "bad" act, on the other hand, is one executed out of relation to the setting in which it occurs and thereby inevitably creates tension or conflict between the offender and the society of which he is a "member." Society, however, is not absolved of at least partial responsibility, for there must be something "wrong" with it that one of its parts should react in a way which defeats its own integration (pp. 274-275).

We can gain further support for the existence of a theory-derived Gestalt ethics from Wheeler (1992). In an evocative chapter article he asks many questions which can serve as beginnings in our exploration. Wheeler defines ethics or values as "those habitual preferences, which are *not* governed by perceived outcome, and may quite possibly run counter to some desired outcome state" (p. 115). In this vein, he states that the only satisfaction that necessarily comes from the resolution of an ethical situation is the one that satisfies the ethical or value gestalt. Wheeler says further that "by the use of the words 'ethical issue' or 'matter of principle,' we are signaling that we feel a pull, a desire in the ordinary sense, and that that pull has to do with the satisfaction or resolution of issues of the *organization of the personal ground*, the structured relationship of figures with other figures, and with ground structures themselves" (p.115) (emphasis in original). Wheeler points out that "when we speak of values we are always or nearly always speaking of a situation of *conflict*, or *competition for dominance* (spontaneous or otherwise), of one figure, one desire, over others" (p.115) (emphasis in original).

Is it possible for Gestalt theory to offer anything with regard to one figure, an ethical or even an instrumental value, taking precedence over another, e.g., a personal desire, either intrapsychically or interpersonally, in essence as referred to by Hartmann? Wheeler (1992) suggests that whatever chance exists for this to be true resides in an analysis of the ground—to repeat, in the relationship between figures and between a figure and ground structures themselves as opposed to just the process of a figure emerging from the ground. From such an analysis, Wheeler believes that a concept of health can emerge. And for our purposes here, a theory-derived concept of health could point us in the direction of values that support healthy development. Wheeler offers an example of a too rigid ground producing a constricted figure and a too-loose ground producing an undirected figure.

I believe that this collective information provides us with the basis for a next step. This will become clearer with a brief review of Gestalt theory.

A Brief Review of Gestalt Theory

Our review of Gestalt's intersubjective, constructivistic, holistic, field model starts with Ehrenfels' (1890/1988) who gave Gestalt theory its name with the idea that perceptually we recognize wholes or gestalten.[2] However, he believed that the organization involved in perception is solely a property of the wholes in the "objective environment," not a quality of the people perceiving them. Gestalt psychologists Wertheimer, Kohler, Koffka and others continued the work on perception of wholes establishing evidence for such Gestalt principles as "the whole precedes the parts" and "the whole determines the nature of the parts," and developing a set of "laws" governing the properties of perceptual gestalten. The most important of these laws, and the law from which all of the other laws were derived, was the Law of Praegnanz (Koffka, 1935), postulating that percepts are organized configurations, the quality of which are dependent on prevailing environmental conditions. As with Ehrenfels, Wertheimer believed that perceptual organizational quality was primarily a property of the environment. Still their research produced evidence that people themselves have an active role in what and how information is perceived.

---

[2]See Smith (1988) for a discussion on the history of early Gestalt theory.

Lewin (1935) continued to move this model towards a psychological understanding of the whole person within a contextual field, not just one of perception alone. He saw people as being constantly engaged in solving problems in their life situation, constantly engaged in and moving through or *negotiating* their life field. To this end we use our perceptual abilities to create a "Gestalt map" of our field. More importantly, Lewin (1926/1938) saw that we organize or create this mental/behavioral map based on *our needs in the field*. He gave the example of how a soldier facing the task of survival on a hostile landscape notices and ascribes value to (i.e. maps) different elements of the landscape and/or maps the same elements in a very different manner than a farmer on the same landscape in peacetime, who is more concerned with tending to his crop and raising his family. Thus, not only do our needs influence what we notice in constructing our "Gestalt map," but our needs are also influenced by the nature of our inner and outer environment, which in turn affects the construction of our "Gestalt map." Hence, a hungry soldier on a battlefield may not even notice his hunger until he has reached a place of safety. And when he does eat he most likely will use/develop much different strategies in what, where, and how he eats than would a hungry farmer on the same landscape. Each in his own way balances his own ever changing needs, with even specific needs changing as they interact with other needs and the environment. Notice here the ever present connection and dynamic interplay between organismic and contextual elements of our field in the ongoing, evolving sense of ourselves and the world around us.

Goldstein (1939) brought further clarity to this model. From his work with brain-damaged veterans and other war casualties, he concluded that, as a rule, human behavior is constantly in the process of being organized, and always implicates the whole person—that our only "drive" is to interact and connect with the environment and to organize that interaction/connection into prioritized, interactive patterns based on the perceived greater good of the whole person.

Thus to this point: Gestalt's holistic stance is that people endeavor to unify or map their entire "field," which includes their experience of themselves and their experience of their environment in relation to themselves, organizing their whole context of perceived risks and resources according to their own felt needs and goals (Goldstein, 1939; Kofka, 1935; Lewin, 1935). The organizer of this "field" is the self (Goldstein, 1939; Goodman, 1951[3]). Finally, in our relevant theory here, Goodman (1951) underscored the intimate connection between "self" and "other" with his concept of contact (experience in the "field") and with his metaphor that contact, and self process occur at the boundary between the person and his/her environment. Thus, our organization or mapping of our "field" is an ongoing process that occurs in the context of experience in the "field" (contact). With every instance of contact, or meeting between self and the world, the whole "field" is resolved anew with respect to our relevant felt needs and goals. Now we have a starting place from which to explore our derivation of a Gestalt ethics.

An Emerging Gestalt Principle

Contained in our Gestalt field theory is the theoretical grounding for the instrumental value that understanding someone necessarily includes an understanding of what the world looks like from that person's perspective. That is, in order to understand someone we must understand his/her mapping of his/her "self" and "other" "field." Since each person's mapping of his/her "field" is constructed uniquely in his/her own accumulated contact with others, the only way to understand crucial elements of someone's mapping is to understand his/her perspective. For example, a person's values, those relatively stable preferences we discussed above, are plainly an organized

---

[3] I will refer to Goodman as the author of Part II of *Gestalt Therapy: Excitement and Growth in the Human Personality*. While Perls contributed some initial ideas, From (1978), Stoehr (1994) and Wheeler (1991) identify Goodman as transforming these ideas and bringing them to life in their final form. Stoehr (1994) writes: "It was Goodman who was creating the theory as well as the prose in which it was couched" (p. 87).

feature of the person's perspective.[4] This perspective on value formation process is clearly an implication of our Gestalt self-environment or field organizational theory. Thus we have reached an easily achieved first step in our quest here. On the other hand, this doesn't yet tell us whether we need to understand other people or to take them into account in this way in order to have healthy self processes or to treat people therapeutically. We have a theory-derived principle, but not yet a theory-derived ethic.

Relational Understanding: A Gestalt Principle

Our theory-derived principle can be refined with the help of a previously mentioned Gestalt insight. This is the realization, which flies in the face of our Western individualist tradition, that in constructing my "Gestalt map," both my sense of "self" and my sense of "other" arise, phenomenologically, in the same experiential, interactive act of contact. It is in the experience of contact that the "self boundary" is constructed and continually refined. "Self" and "other" are always interdependent. In fact, from this perspective, the concept of "self" is a misnomer. We cannot have a concept of "self" without an attached concept of "other." In this vein, it is not surprising that DeRivera (1976), continuing Lewin's work in field theory, came to the conclusion in reviewing the phenomena that Osviankina reported in her classic interruption of task study (Rickers-Osviankina, 1928/1976), that the act of engaging in an activity could "only make sense . . . by supposing that the person has entered into a unit with the activity . . . (such that) the person and the activity are joined, so that it is *his* activity—the activity is part of his self" (p. 115) (italics in original). Enlarging on this position, supported by research (e.g., Stern, 1977), if you and I are significant to each other, you are part of my construction of "self" and I am part of your construction

---

[4]Of course we can't equate a person's espoused value system with the actual value preferences of his/her contact process. Part of psychotherapy has to do with exploring discrepancies of this type.

of "self." Beaumont (1993) refers to this *field condition* in a correction he offers to the tendency that has existed in Gestalt practice to embrace an individualist paradigm:

> The continuing tendency of some Gestaltists to continue to understand "contact" in a foreground-bound manner is theoretically unsound. Goodman's interest in overcoming the false organism/environment split remains essential but neglected. Person and environment together are best conceptualized as being a single system. Contact is not the action of one upon the other, but is a mutually creative interaction. Each participates in the creation of the other. . . . [People] define one another in relationship (p. 90).[5]

This points to a corollary principle, another instrumental value, emerging directly from Gestalt theory; a principle that is closely related to the theory-derived Gestalt principle that an understanding of people must include an understanding of them from their own perspective—a principle that is important in a number of ethical situations, particularly the ethics of clinical practice. If, as our theory states, "self process" is essentially relational in nature and if our sense of "self" consists of accumulated, interacting "self/other" units in which "self" and "other" are always bound together by some connective/relational quality, then: *In order to understand another person, we must understand the quality of connections, the relationships, that are part of his/her self/other field. We must understand the parts of the environment that the person has made parts of him/herself and we must understand the quality of the relationships he/she has with those people/things/activities. We must understand the energy invested and the possibilities for connection and life that such an investment represents.*

This is the same as White's (1995) position, stated in a creatively

---

[5]Beaumont is more precisely here discussing how marital partners define one another. The generalization to people in various relationships is completely consistent with his position.

insightful article, where he urges that the drug addict needs to be understood from a position within his/her culture, from a view that appreciates the relationship that he/she is attempting to form with the drug in his/her struggle toward survival. White, finding little support for this stance from within Gestalt theory, came to it by borrowing from linguistic theory.[6] *But as outlined above, this instrumental value emerges directly from our constructivistic/intersubjective Gestalt field theory.* This value differs in an important way from our first theory-derived instrumental value of "understanding people includes understanding them from their own perspective." Focusing on the relational quality of the self/other co-constructed field of the individual takes us out of the individualist paradigm and back into the field perspective emanating from Lewin, Goldstein, Goodman, and others.

Further, if I am part of your "self process" and you are part of mine, then both my external behavior and my internal process, i.e. my intentions, my physical and emotional state, my ongoing mapping of my field, will have a direct or indirect effect on your "self process" and vice versa. Thus *your internal process is an integral part of my internal process and vice versa.* This means that we can no longer speak of "individual" growth. (Growth is defined here as the development of ground structures that support the formation of rich figures with possibilities for interconnection in an ever expanding field.) Instead, we must speak of *growth of the entire individual/ environmental field.* This is undoubtedly why we are born with the capacity to notice and relate to the internal experience of others. Even as infants we help find interactive directions that support both us and the people caring for us (Stern, 1977; Thomas and Chess, 1980).

These formulations take us closer to an ethical value as opposed to an instrumental value. For if it is true that we are connected in this way, that whenever we interact with each other your internal experience becomes part of my internal experience and vice versa so that our mutual growth, the growth of our interconnected fields is dependent on the mutual quality of our experience together, then we

---

[6]White has updated his award-winning article in Chapter 8 of this volume.

have an indisputable reason to understand each other, in which case the instrumental values derived from theory become theory-derived ethics. But let's reserve judgement on this point a bit longer.

However, notice how the direction in which our Gestalt field theory is taking us differs so dramatically from the perspective of the individualist paradigm in which we are seen as separate and autonomous individuals competing with one another to secure our needs. Unfortunately, as we have noted above, the individualist paradigm quickly leads to "I'd best not be aware of your self process, I'd best not care about your experience. For if I do, I will be at a disadvantage when it comes to competing"—the natural conclusion of a zero-sum environmental condition.

The fact that my growth is dependent on your internal process and yours on mine is the theoretical foundation for a third, long-held Gestalt principle that affects clinical practice. *Gestalt therapists are taught that the primary experiment occurring in therapy for the client is the relational experiment between client and therapist. Therefore therapists are taught to apprehend the quality of the intersubjectively developing relationship between themselves and their clients*: They are encouraged to be aware of how they are using themselves, how they join or don't join with their clients, how together client and therapist find areas of connection or disconnection, and how in the process, clients experiment with new ways of being in the world. This of course means that we as therapists are affected also. The underlying theoretical principle here is that the possibilities for change lie in the establishment of a field that will support new awarenesses of self/other, where my internal process will meet yours in some new manner that appreciates both of us.

The next value that emerges when we move to a constructivistic/intersubjective Gestalt field theory has even more ethical/political implications and will give us more information in our quest for an ethical vs an instrumental, theory-derived, set of values. In order to provide a grounding for this value, let us turn to a discussion of what Gestalt field theory can say about health and healthy development.

Is There A Gestalt Concept of Health?

Goodman's (1951) sense of a direction toward healthy development is encapsulated in his observation that optimum field resolution requires the production of a strong figure. This may be a necessary characteristic of healthy figure production; however it is not sufficient for healthy development in itself. As Wheeler (1992) points out, by using this principle alone it is difficult to distinguish healthy figure production from the figure production of someone about to commit suicide or from what is involved in stereotyping or bigotry. Strong figures emerge in each of these examples, but we would not consider them as signs of health.

Remember Wheeler's (1992) insistence that if a concept of health is to emerge from Gestalt theory, it must come not from an analysis of the figure but of the ground and the relationship between ground and figure. In this regard, Gestalt's sense of figure-ground interaction—namely that there is an ongoing simultaneous process of figure testing ground and ground testing figure—might point a way to a concept of health. In order for growth to occur or continue, we must not only be able to use our co-constructed map (our ground) to screen new experience, we must also be able to use new experience to test and modify our ground. In this sense growth refers to our ability to continually maintain a sense of personal integrity, that is, a sufficient set of self/other mappings from the past, while at the same time being able to integrate new possibilities of self/other connection as our needs and environment change.

This of course is field dependent. We will find it difficult to have this level of flexibility between ground testing figure and figure testing ground in areas where significant people or institutions in our environment, i.e. our family, culture, peer group, profession, same or opposite gender or so on, maintain taboos against such flexibility. Thus inflexibility in ground organization may be a sign of lack of health within a particular environmental field. The restriction on testing ground through experience may be necessary in a given field, particularly in the environmental field in which it developed, perhaps because the inability of experience to test ground in specific situations protects a given field from a continuing set of dangers. Or possibly, such inability in these situations has become an expected way to organize for members of a given field, which may provide a sense of belonging and unity for the field's members. However, all this might not fit and thus be dysfunctional in other environmental fields.

Thus, a more accurate statement of health would be something like: in order for healthful growth to occur, we must be able to use our co-constructed map (our ground) to screen new experience, and be able to use new experience to test and modify our ground. Moreover, a ground organization that does not allow experience to test ground or ground to screen experience must be understood in the context of the field conditions in which it developed. This is consistent with our derived Gestalt principle that a person must be understood from the perspective of the relationships of which he/she is a part and which are a part of him/her. Such a condition can be a sign of dysfunction depending on its fit in present field conditions. Here dysfunction is meant to imply a degree of loss of function, a loss of ability to interface with others and the environment within a given field.

But how is it that our mapping process, our flexibility and balance between map testing experience and experience testing map, becomes impaired? Is it that particular ground structures develop that constrict, confuse, or otherwise impair figure development and figure-ground interaction? If so what would be the nature of such ground structures?

Health and Shame

Interestingly, Perls' sense of ill health is fashioned in this manner. In effect Perls' theory implies that the formation of a particular *ground structure*, his "introject," is the basis of neurosis.[7] From our perspec-

---

[7]For Perls, neurosis occurs when a person loses his/her ability to "chew" his/her experience and "swallows whole" an "introject" (standards, attitudes, ways of acting and thinking, which are not truly his/hers). "Introjects" then become the basis for all Perls' "resistances to contact." For example, in projection it is the unassimilated "introject" that is projected.

tive, the formation of this ground structure interferes with healthy figure formation due to the accompanying disowning of parts of self and a resultant inability to form new mappings of the field that are more in tune with one's needs. Thus, this sense of ill health is of the same general form as mentioned above, namely a ground structure that interferes with figure-ground interaction.[8] Does this general approach to an understanding of ill health have merit?

I believe that this approach does have merit, but in order to continue in this direction we need information that Perls didn't have in his awareness—information that is implicitly present in his theory. Although Perls' conceptualization of introjection has significant limitations,[9] including being anchored in the individualist paradigm, it does bring with it an intuitive understanding and appreciation of a phenomenon that can shed further light on our exploration—namely the phenomenon of shame. In fact, I believe that Perls was describing the phenomenon of shame, as best he could, viewing it through an individualist paradigm lens. For example, the ground structure that Perls postulates as interfering with healthy figure

---

[8]Note that Perls' sense of ill health is to some extent situational. Figure formation is constricted in the areas of one's life which relate to the "introjects" (standards, attitudes, ways of acting and thinking, which are not truly the person's), that have been "swallowed whole." Thus a person may be able to produce flexible figures in areas of his/her life that are not governed by the "introjects" he/she has acquired.

[9]Perls' concept of introjection differs in several ways from more current knowledge and thinking in our field of how people take in information. For example, Perls conceived that introjection involves only negative material—positive material is assimilated into the body, according to him. This runs counter to the well-established idea in psychology that introjection is one of the major human learning processes of any kind of material, in which large blocks of information are taken in at once—the major way we learn to walk, talk, relate, and so on. In addition, as Fodor (1996a, 1996b) has been pointing out, whatever information that is taken in about self/other (negative or positive) is not held as a foreign entity as Perls would have it but is integrated into schemas.

formation, again, his "introject," is essentially the same as the ground structure, that the affect theorist Silvan Tomkins (1963) terms a "shame bind," and which another affect theorist, Gershen Kaufman (1980, 1989), describes as the first stage of "internalized shame." [10,11] Viewing what Perls noticed as a sense of ill health from the perspective of shame theory gives us a fuller understanding of health and ill health. At the same time, one of Gestalt theory's strengths is its analysis of contact. With this unique understanding of the nature of self/other process inherent in Gestalt theory, an expanded view of the phenomenon of shame is possible which can inform us even more about the processes of health and ill health. We will refer to the ground structure that Kaufman labels "internalized shame" as "ground shame," thus emphasizing its essence as a ground structure and its relational nature as a self/other mapping tool, given that our ground is our map of our relational field.

In moving to a comprehensive field position, we are not only able to notice shame's intrapsychic function but are also able to notice how this function is tied to a perceived field condition—namely, *a lack of support.* Shame is then useful because it informs us of the perceived condition of connections/disconnections in the field. Shame signals us to pull back when we perceive that our wanting, desire, hope, or the like has insufficient chance of being received

---

[10]The term "internalized shame" was coined by the affect theorist Gershen Kaufman (e.g., 1980, 1989) building on the work of Silvan Tomkins (1963) to denote what he called ongoing shame linkages with affects, interpersonal needs, and the like. Internalized shame, according to Kaufman, is stored in "scenes" or images that have been imprinted with affective, cognitive, and kinesthetic information, which includes acquired messages governing relational interaction.

[11]I have discussed elsewhere the theoretical and circumstantial similarities between Perls' "introjects" and internalized shame (Lee, 1995). One test, mentioned in that discussion, in assessing whether these two constructs are different views of the same phenomenon is: if Perls' "introjects" are indeed internalized shame, then if we look at the transcripts of Perls working with people we would expect to find signs of shame starting to appear whenever Perls gets close to a person's "introject." In fact, this does occur.

(Tomkins, 1963).[12] Said another way, in our ongoing mapping of the field, the experience of shame is in effect an experience that dichotomizes into "this is not my world/not me," which signals us to pull back. The actual experience of shame is felt as information about us as individuals, ranging from a mild sense that our behaviors/ thoughts/hopes/desires are in some way inappropriate, to the extreme experience of corrosive self-examination and judgment that says in effect that something is dramatically and irreversibly wrong with us. From a field perspective we understand that this self-perception takes place when we perceive that there is insufficient support in our field for how we would like to connect. If we extinguish or change our desire to be in accord with the existing support in the field, we won't experience shame. We are only at risk of experiencing shame when our desire continues—that is, when we continue to care about something at a time when we encounter insufficient support.

In many everyday occurrences this sense of the world as not my world/not me, often experienced as shame in the form of shyness, embarrassment, or disappointment, is temporary, telling us to pull back *in the moment* when someone or something is not available. We then have several possibilities. For example, we can wait for a time when we perceive that there is enough support for our desire. Or we can attend to another's need in the moment for support, which might nourish the environment and ultimately make the environment more able to receive our need. Or, we can reshape our approach so that it has a better chance of finding the support that does exist in the field. Again, support means an enabling connection in the self/other field and refers to both internal support as well as external support. In this vein, internal support stems from a previous or ongoing connection or set of connections in the field, i.e. from experience that has been internalized as "me" as opposed to "not me." See Wheeler (2000) for a discussion of how the "hero" draws support from sources such as values derived from previous experience or from identification with figures in history, nature, literature or other print, cinematic, or

---

[12]See Lee (1994a, 1995, 2001) and Lee & Wheeler (1996) for a fuller discussion of understanding shame from this perspective.

electronic media—all of which are connections in the field. In this form, the experience of shame is merely an indication of the perceived lack of fit between a person's wanted, desired, needed connection/reception and what the person imagines he/she will find/is finding in the environment. As such, in this form, shame is a valuable tool that we use in navigating interpersonal situations.

However, with repeated or severe enough instances of missed connection (i.e., consistent or severe physical or sexual abuse, neglect, the experience of being negatively perceived as different because of culture or gender or sexual preference or so on, hardship or loss), my desire, urge, hope, way of being in the world becomes linked with shame, and with the "not me" experience. The experience of shame then no longer serves as an assessment that a desired connection might not be received in the moment. Rather it becomes an enduring *belief*, a fixed gestalt, that my desired connection is not possible in general—a belief that part of me is not wanted and in time a denial that that part of me even exists. As such the whole wished-for person/environment connective unit is shamed and in this way disowned—hardened into what McConville (1995) calls a "ground introject" and into what we call here *"ground shame."*

This form of shame is then a ground structure that inhibits figure formation flexibility. Figures involving the shamed need, desire, way of being in the world can not form. Thus new mappings of self/other involving this desire cannot develop. The more ground shame that develops, the less ability the person has to take in or explore information about self and other and hence the less ability he/she has to meet new situations. Growth is thus impeded.[13] Thus, ground

---

[13]This theoretical position, of ground shame being related to breakdowns in psychological health, is supported by a growing body of research. Remember that ground shame is a Gestalt Field Theory understanding of the affect theorists' internalized shame. My own research found that the presence of internalized shame in one partner of a married couple correlated with lower couple intimacy (Lee, 1994b). Cook (1994), who has compiled a listing of shame research, reports that internalized shame has been strongly linked with depression in a number of studies with populations, including inpatient depressed males, PTSD males, affective disorder or other disorder outpatient

shame freezes self-process.[14,15] And, again, we notice that *this is not just a statement about an individual but about an environmental field.* The development of ground shame corresponds to an inability, lack of energy or resources, or unwillingness in the environment to see/notice someone's need/desire to connect—*the person's internal experience is somehow invisible to the environment.* Thus, *speaking about ground shame is a whole-field way of talking about many instances of frozen/interrupted self-process.* Now we are talking about the field in relationship to health and implicitly about the *field conditions* necessary for healthy self-process. This takes us to the next step in our exploration.

---

psychiatric clients, depressed or anxious private outpatient psychiatric clients, college students, and alcoholics. Cook also reports that in several other studies, anxiety (in clients diagnosed with phobias, panic disorder, obsessive-compulsive disorder, and generalized anxiety disorder) also has been strongly correlated with internalized shame. Likewise, Cook mentions other studies that strongly link internalized shame with the effects of sexual abuse and the presence of eating disorders. In another very interesting study that Cook mentions, with adult outpatient psychotherapy clients with a mean age of 40 years, a structural equation model was used to show that childhood experience with parents only affects psychological stress through internalized shame.

[14]Note that as with Perls' "introjects," ground shame affects figure formation flexibility, to at least some extent, in a situational manner. Although higher ground shame (higher incidence of parts of self/other linked with shame with the accompanying sense of this is not my world/not me) can lead to an overall sense of this is not my world/not me, there can still be areas of one's life where figure formation flexibility is not affected or is less dramatically effected.

[15]Note also that ground shame is not taken as the only source of figure ground interference. Other sources could include biology, neurological injury, learning disability, dietary deficiencies, and so on. However, the effects of these other sources may lead to a severe or consistent enough sense of unreceptivity or lack of support that ground shame develops in relation to them.

Support for the Individual and Support for the Field: Gestalt Values

We have learned that healthy self-process occurs with low levels of ground shame. And low ground shame corresponds to enough perceived receptivity in the field—enough receptivity in a wide range of dimensions in the field. In fact, Wheeler (1994) has written on the necessity of intersubjective reception by others to know self fully. This just repeats the point. What we have developed here supports the adage that "It takes a village to raise a child." However, it applies not only to a child but to everyone across his/her life span. This in itself gives us another instrumental value, namely: *IF we want people to grow in healthy directions throughout their life, then we need to support them sufficiently through our interactions.* And remember that supporting people sufficiently means connecting with them sufficiently, connecting with them in a manner that will offer the least chance to induce ground shame in them or us, namely in a fashion that will offer an opportunity to them and us to meet with mutual respect in accordance with who we each are.

But we have overlooked an important field condition here. Enough receptivity in the field means enough others that are capable of reception, enough of the time, i.e. enough other healthy selves. Thus in a Gestalt field model of contact, self, and development, we find that for self-development and growth to make sense, and for healthy self-process to occur, a condition of the field must exist. This is a condition which the older, individualist model doesn't sufficiently stress and often ignores or denies: in particular, *the development and growth of any healthy self in the field requires a field that includes other healthy (enough) selves.*[16] That is, in order for growth in a healthy direction to occur, people must find, have access to, enough others

---

[16]As ground shame is to some extent situational, even people with high ground shame may be able to be supportive (connect in a manner that others find to be enabling) at specific times and/or under particular circumstances, whereas at other times and/or under other circumstances they will not.

(parents, peers, teachers, lovers, colleagues, etc.) who are capable of providing a receptive intersubjective connection—people who have likewise been able to grow in a healthy direction and who have likewise been able to find/receive enough support in the field. This field condition allows us to move beyond the "immediate ethics, not infallible," which Goodman (1951) suggests can be roughly sketched from "spontaneous dominance" of one figure of interest over another.

Thus our constructivistic/intersubjective Gestalt field theory places a strong value not only on support for the individual but also on *support for the environmental field.* Hence Gestalt field theory provides not only a foundation for the previously mentioned guiding adage, "It takes a village to raise a child," but also for an important modification of that adage: "It takes a *healthy* village to raise a *healthy* child." *Thus for healthy process to exist, there must be enough support for the environment.* This means that proper support for a child includes support for the child's parents as well as for others that relate to the child, e.g., siblings, peers, teachers, babysitters, doctors and so on.[17] This can be generalized to speak to the support requirements of any dependent/ hierarchal relationship—child-parent, student-teacher, supervisee-supervisor, client-therapist, and so on. In each case *pro-viding a primary support for a person in the dependent position (child, student, supervisee, client, and so on) means providing sufficient support for the people/person in the care-taking position (parent, teacher, super-visor, therapist and so on).*

This also means that if we are in each other's field (as friends, colleagues, lovers, spouses, or even acquaintances), then we are each being the person that is contributing to the other's sense of self/other; and thus our best chance for healthful growth, vis-a-vis our experience together, is for those experiences to be mutually perceived as supportive to both you and me. This is the same value we came to earlier. However, looking at our accumulated evidence, there is little doubt left that this is not just an instrumental value but an ethical value. There is no IF here in the general case. If we are connected

---

[17]See Lee, 2000 or 2001, for a case example illustrating the importance of support for a father that turned the tide for his acting-out adolescent son.

in these ways, which our theory says we are, that is, we are part of each other's construction of self and more importantly our inner experience is directly or indirectly part of each other's construction of self, and we are each other's best chance of a healthful experience during our experiences with one another, then *a primary condition for healthful growth is that our interactions are mutually experienced as being supportive* (i.e. offering a connection that fits with us in some manner).

Stepping back and taking a wider view, it becomes apparent that the key theory-derived ethic here is that we can no longer talk about "self vs environment" as the individualist paradigm suggests. We and the environment are interconnected. Thus, the key ethic that emanates from our theory is that *we must find whole field solutions that support both self and environment—that support self/other development.*

There are many instances of how this Gestalt ethic already exists in practice. For example it supports and resonates with Lichtenberg's (e.g., 1994; see also Chapter 10 in this volume) work on social oppression in which he points out that the field is not made healthier by shaming the oppressor. Health in the field comes from supporting the experience, though not the acts, of the oppressor.

Our Emerging Gestalt Field Ethics: The Whole Is Greater Than the Sum of the Parts

Let us reflect a moment on how far our exploration has taken us into the possibilities of a whole field Gestalt ethics. First, we examined the constructionist aspects of Gestalt theory, which gave us the working principle that in order to understand a person we must understand him/her from the viewpoint of the person's own perspective—a tie into the phenomenological approach so closely associated with Gestalt practice. Second, we explored the relational perspective of Gestalt field theory, a perspective with a unique view of human psychological development that clarifies "self" development as being self/other development. The result was the emergence of an instrumental principle on understanding a person's behavior and intent in terms of his/her relational strivings. The value here is not in accepting or not accepting specific behavior, but in where to look for understanding of the essence of people and their development.

In addition, understanding self development as intersubjective self/other development leads us to the awareness that our internal process is a core reflection of the possibilities of connection in the field and is co-constructed as an integral part of each other's experience. This is not to say that we are transparent and anything we think or feel can be known by another. Nor does it mean that we should indiscriminately share our inner thoughts and feelings with others as the self disclosurists suggested (e.g., Jourard, 1959). But it does mean that the way we think, feel, and ultimately act toward one another is not solely an individual phenomenon. Instead, it is a reflection of the condition of the larger field and in turn will have an impact on the possibilities of connection in the field. This highlights the idea that opportunities for change rest in the possibility of one's mapping of the field changing, which is dependent on new intersubjective experience in the field, which in turn means being known and interacted with in some new manner. This is the theoretical grounding for Gestalt therapists' being relational in their interactions with clients.

Next we looked at what Gestalt can say about health and learned that if self is the dynamically derived outcome of whole field process then "it takes a *healthy* field to raise a *healthy* child." More generally, individual health is dependent on the health of the larger field, a sign of which is low ground shame carried by the field's members. This brought us key principles around the notion of support, in the process affirming the nature of support as a beneficial *connection in the field*. Again, the two core values that emerged from our derivation here were first, that people need enough support (i.e. healthy connection in the larger field) in order to develop in healthy directions and second, that the field must have enough support if it is to have the capacity to adequately support its members. It is not surprising that these values have long been an integral part of many Gestalt communities. Personally, they are values I have carried since they were introduced to me in my first Gestalt training program many years ago. What is new is that these values can be derived directly from our theory. We then realized that the accumulated evidence suggests that the last theory-derived value is not just a situational principle but is also an ethical value that is worthy of belief. This took us to the realization that the key ethical value is that we must find solutions to ethical problems that serve both the individual and the larger field, ones that lead to and support healthy self/other development.

Further, such support or connection is possible only to the extent that people within an interaction experience the connection. And again, this means people having a sense that they are being understood sufficiently from their own perspective and from the perspective of their relational strivings. Hence our first two theory-derived principles are in effect a theory-derived ethics as well.

But there is more. In true Gestalt fashion, our set of emerging whole field Gestalt ethics coalesces into a whole that brings with it a larger awareness and potential. With a field in which these ethics are considered by its members to be part of the ground of the field, such that we all understand that my internal experience is part of your internal experience and yours is part of mine, we each feel sufficiently understood, and we can create enough support for the field, won't we find a much different sense of ethics in general?

In such a field, wouldn't there be much less need of an externally enunciated and enforced code of ethics? In fact, couldn't an externally enunciated and enforced ethical code suggest it's up to me and my will power to overcome my nature to take advantage of others? On the contrary, in such a field wouldn't the values we have derived coalesce into a different kind of attitude, a different dynamic? Wouldn't people come more readily to trust that they can rely on one another? Wouldn't they gain a sense that they will be heard in an appreciative manner? And thus they would not have to become isolated, experience their hopes and desires as shameful, and disown significant parts of themselves. Which means they would not have to resort to Herculean applications of will power to hide and control their hopes/desires. Further, wouldn't they learn that their support of others is needed and valued, and wouldn't they come to understand that anything they do to damage the field damages themselves as well as others?

This does not mean that there would be an absence of conflicts and mistakes (or for that matter, some complete absence of human self-centeredness and ethical lapses). However, conflicts and mistakes would be handled with enough support provided by the people involved and the surrounding community, rather than being handled in an individualistically administered process in which participants are seen as adversaries and the name of the game is to discredit, blame, humiliate the other and the most powerful individual or group wins. Instead, in a field of our emerging ethics, there would be significant less ground shame and therefore less need to camouflage shame in general as well as the underlying yearnings. And wouldn't there be much less acting out or "unhealthy" behavior—less of a sense that others are just objects to act on to discharge separate drives and instincts because "that's all you can get from other objects" or because "if you don't you will get left behind." Thus, most importantly, in a field of our emerging ethics, when people find themselves in conflict, when they make mistakes, when ruptures occur, wouldn't there be a value on supporting the people involved and repairing the rupture—a value on repairing the field?

Is this a myth? Does this really happen? In fact, we find an example of this type of field in the research on married couples. In my own research, couples who had developed a high degree of *emotional safety*—such that they felt safe enough most of the time to bring up their deepest concerns, feelings, desires, or problems, had clear expectations of each other, and in general thought of each other as best friends were found to have high marital satisfaction, be affectionate with each other, have a fulfilling sexual connection, exhibit low negativity in their interactions, have good problem-solving capacity, and have *low ground shame* (Lee, 1994b). The opposite was true for couples with a low sense of emotional safety, which corresponded with high ground shame. Gottman (1994), in his extensive research on couples, finds similar groups of couples. The group with skill and success in creating and maintaining fulfilling relationships, which he terms "masters," exhibits the ethics we have derived here. In particular, each couple member's experience is important to the other, and they take care of each other. Gottman reports that in all couples, partners do a high degree of bidding for each other's attention in small ways in everyday interaction. In "masters" couples, the bidding finds reception 96% of the time as opposed to only 36% of the time in couples that do not have successful relationships. Moreover, "masters" couple partners support each other during conflicts. And most importantly, they attend to repairing the damage after conflicts—they support and repair their field.

Thus our emerging whole-field Gestalt ethics predicts the field conditions found in these healthy relationships. Again, note that the old ethics based on "self vs other" have been transcended. In such fields of our emerging ethics, *these ethics become part of the field, internalized in everyone's shared "self process."* As a result, external ethical rules need not be as rigid or as numerous. In fact, a different kind of ethics becomes important—a set of ethics that supports the process of noticing and responding to individuals and of noticing and responding to the larger environmental field. And thus we learn more about healthy fields.

Wrapping Up

Our exploration here, an exploration in progress, takes us an important next step in answering the questions with which we started. When we return to a whole field perspective, a set of whole field key values as well as a direction for a definition of health do emerge directly from our constructivistic/intersubjective Gestalt field theory. These are values that do not need to be overlayed on our theory from our individual or collective wisdom or borrowed from another theory. They stem directly from our Gestalt field theory.

Our theory-derived whole-field Gestalt ethics applies directly to how we want to relate to others. It also brings important implications for clinical practice, implications that parallel and give support to practices that have long been in place in many Gestalt communities. They embody an appreciation for individuals as well as an appreciation for the larger environmental field and in particular place an emphasis on the intimate, dynamic, intersubjective connection between individuals and the environmental field. The environmental field is part of the individual and the individual is part of the environmental field. As seen, Gestalt field theory is built on the existence and importance of this connection, and it is the existence of this connection that brings us the ethical values which we have developed here.[18]

References

Beaumont, H. (1993). Martin Buber's "I-thou" and fragile self-organization contributions to a Gestalt couples therapy. *The British Gestalt Journal*, 2(1), 85-95.

Cook, D. R. (1994). *Internalized Shame Scale: Professional Manual*. Menomonie, WI: Channel Press. (Available from author: East 5886 803rd Ave., Menomonie, WI 54751)

DeRivera, J. (Ed.), (1976). *Field Theory as Human Science/ Contributions of Lewin's Berlin Group*. New York: Gardner Press.

Ehrenfels, C. (1988). On "Gestalt qualities." In B. Smith (Ed. and Trans.), *Foundations of Gestalt Theory* (pp. 82-117). Munchen, Germany: Philosophia Verlag. (Reprinted from *Vierteljahrsschrift fur wissenschaftliche Philosophie*, 1890, 14, 249-292)

Fodor, I. (1996a). A woman and her body: The cycles of pride and shame. In R. Lee and G. Wheeler (Eds.). *The Voice of Shame: Silence and Connection in Psychotherapy* (pp. 229-265). San Francisco: Jossey-Bass.

Fodor, I. (1996b). A cognitive perspective for Gestalt therapy. *British Gestalt Journal*, 5(1), 31-42.

---

[18]The ideas in this chapter have been formed and refined through discussions with and input from a number of people. The chapter was originally presented as a work in progress at the 1996 Gestalt Writer's Conference in Cambridge, MA and presented again at the 2nd Annual Conference of the Association for the Advancement of Gestalt Therapy in San Francisco in 1997. In these and other private communications it has benefited from the input, whether critical or supportive in nature, of Edwin Nevis, Les Greenberg, Reinhard Fuhr, Malcolm Parlett, Mark McConville, Jack Aylward, and Joe Melnick among many others and particularly from the ongoing support of Lee Geltman, Paul Shane, and Gordon Wheeler.

Fuhr, R. (1993). Beyond contact processes: Ethical and existential dimensions in Gestalt therapy. *The British Gestalt Journal*, 2, 53-60.

Goldstein, K. (1939). *The Organism: A Holistic Approach to Biology*. New York: American Book Co.

Goodman, P. (1951). Part II. In F. Perls, R. Hefferline, & P. Goodman. *Gestalt Therapy: Excitement and Growth in the Human Personality*. New York: Delta. (Originally published 1951 by Julian Press)

Gottman, J. (1994). *Why Marriages Succeed or Fail*. New York: Simon & Schuster.

Gremmler-Fuhr, M. (2001). Ethic dimensions in Gestalt Therapy. *Gestalt Review*, 5(2).

Hartmann, G. W. (1935). *Gestalt Psychology: A Survey of Facts and Principles*. New York: The Ronald Press Company

Jourard, S. M. (1959). Healthy personality and self-disclosure. *Mental Hygiene*, 43, 499-507.

Kaufman, G. (1980). *Shame: The Power of Caring*. Cambridge, MA: Shenkman.

Kaufman, G. (1989). *The Psychology of Shame*. New York: Springer Publishing Co.

Kofka, K. (1935). *Principles of Gestalt Psychology*. New York: Harcourt, Brace, & World, Inc.

Kohlberg, L. (1984). *The Psychology of Moral Development, vol.II*. San Francisco: Harper and Row.

Lee, R. G. (1994a). Couples' shame: The unaddressed issue. In G. Wheeler & S. Backman (Eds.), *On Intimate Ground: A Gestalt Approach to Working with Couples* (pp.262-290). San Francisco: Jossey-Bass.

Lee, R. G. (1994b). *The Effect of Internalized Shame on Marital Intimacy*. (Unpublished Doctoral dissertation, Fielding Institute, Santa Barbara, CA.)

Lee, R. G. (1995). Gestalt and shame: The foundation for a clearer understanding of field dynamics. *The British Gestalt Journal*, 4(1), 14-22.

Lee, R. G. (1996). Shame and the Gestalt model. In R. G. Lee and G. Wheeler (Eds.), *The Voice of Shame: Silence and Connection in Psychotherapy* (pp. 3-21). San Francisco: Jossey-Bass.

Lee, R. G. (2000). Honte et soutien: Comprehension du champ d'un adolescent. *Cahiers de Gestalt Therapie*, (7), 9-32.

Lee, R. G. (2001). Shame and support: Understanding an adolescent's family field. In M. McConville & G Wheeler (Eds.), *Heart of Development: Gestalt Approaches to Working with Children, Adolescents and Their Worlds, Vol.II: Adolescence*. Hillsdale, NJ: Analytic Press/GestaltPress.

Lee, R. G., & Wheeler, G. (Eds.). (1996). *The Voice of Shame: Silence and Connection in Psychotherapy*. San Francisco: Jossey-Bass.

Lewin, K. (1938). Will and need. In W. Ellis (Ed.), *A Source Book of Gestalt Psychology* (pp. 283-299). London: Routledge & Kegan Paul, Ltd. (reprinted from *Psychologische Forschung*, 7, 294-385, 1926)

Lewin, K. (1935). *A Dynamic Theory of Personality*. New York: McGraw-Hill.

Lichtenberg, P. (1994). *Community and Confluence: Undoing the Clinch of Oppression* (2nd ed.). Cleveland, OH: GestaltPress.

McConville, M. (1995). *Adolescence: Psychotherapy and the Emergent Self*. San Francisco: Jossey-Bass.

Melnick, J., Nevis, S. M., & Melnick, G. N. (1994). Therapeutic ethics: A Gestalt perspective. *The British Gestalt Journal*, 3(2), 105-113.

Perls, F., Hefferline, R., & Goodman, P. (1951). *Gestalt Therapy: Excitement and Growth in the Human Personality*. New York: Delta. (Originally published 1951 by Julian Press)

Rickers-Osviankina, M. (1976). The resumption of interrupted activities (H. Korsch, Trans.). In J. DeRivera (Ed.), *Field Theory as Human Science/ Contributions of Lewin's Berlin Group*. (pp. 49-110) New York: Gardner Press. (reprinted from *Psychologische Forschung*, 2, 302-379, 1928)

Russell, B. (1968). *Autobiography*, Vol. 2. London: Routeledge, Chapman & Hull.

Smith, B. (1988). An essay in philosophy. In B. Smith (Ed.), *Foundations of Gestalt theory*. Munchen, Germany: Philiosophia Verlag.

Stern, D. (1977). *The First Relationship*. Cambridge, MA: Harvard U. Press.

Stoehr, T. (1994). *Here Now Next: Paul Goodman and the Origins of Gestalt Therapy*. San Francisco: Jossey-Bass.

Thomas, A. & Chess, S. (1980). *The Dynamics of Psychological Development*. New York: Brunner/Mazel.

Tomkins, S. S. (1963). *Affect, Imagery, and Consciousness: The Negative Affects*, (Vol. 2). New York: Springer and Company.

Wertheimer, M. (1935). Some problems in the theory of ethics. *Social Research*, 3, 353-367.

Wheeler, G. (1991). *Gestalt Reconsidered: A New Approach to Contact and Resistance*. New York: Gestalt Institute of Cleveland Press/Gardner Press.

Wheeler, G. (1992). Gestalt ethics. In E. C. Nevis (Ed.), *Gestalt Therapy: Perspectives and Applications* (pp. 113-128). New York: Gardner Press.

Wheeler, G. (1994). The tasks of intimacy: Reflections on a Gestalt approach to working with couples. In G. Wheeler & S. Backman (Eds.), *On Intimate Ground: A Gestalt Approach to Working with Couples* (pp. 31-59). San Francisco: Jossey-Bass.

Wheeler, G. (2000). *Beyond Individualism: Toward a New Understanding of Self, Relationship, & Experience*. Hillsdale, NJ: Analytic Press/GestaltPress.

White, J. R. (1995). A special case for Gestalt ethics: Working with the addict. *The Gestalt Journal*, 18(2), 35-54.

Zinker, J. (1994). *In Search of Good Form: Gestalt Therapy with Couples and Families*. San Francisco: Jossey-Bass.

Editor's Note:

In Chapter Two we continue our theoretical grounding of Gestalt's relational ethics with a sensitive, stunning article by Lynne Jacobs. Using her off-balance mistakes with a client after 9/11, her own childhood experiences of exclusion and drawing on her foundation in Existential, Phenomenological, and Gestalt literature, she takes us on a multilayered journey that mirrors and explicates the contextualized fabric of life experience. She shows us that the ethics that we derived in Chapter One from a field perspective are also true from a contextual perspective, in the process enlarging the definition of those ethics. Jacobs reminds us of our situated, embodied existence and that we swim in contexts from the historic time in which we live to our family, ethnic, national, work and other cultural landscapes to the language we use to express and define our living. We get a felt sense of how our phenomenological field of experience is a shared field with others, what it means to be off-balance because we are excluded, and how caring, inclusion, and openness to dialogue are relational ethics that naturally emerge from our interconnected, shared experience.

2

•••••••••••••••••

Ethics of Context and Field:
The Practices of Care, Inclusion
and Openness to Dialogue

Lynne Jacobs

After September 11, 2001 I became interested in understanding hate and the negation of otherness. I am not trying to guess what the hijackers and planners actually thought and felt, but the effects of their actions could easily be understood as hateful, hostile negation. I became interested in this phenomenon, not to better understand the hijackers, but because the events of that day began to bleed over into my clinical work. I am sickened by the fact that I became hateful and negating towards some of my patients.

After the first week, when I was simply mute, as though words were useless and without meaning, my body and skin felt raw. This rawness became problematic to my patients because I found myself unable to tolerate even the smallest acts of negation, as if the negations were scratches on my raw skin.

Each of us is, I suspect, haunted in particular ways by the events of that day. My nephew, who lost his best friend in the World Trade Center collapse, is haunted by questions and imaginings. What were the last moments of his friend's life? Was he helping others? Was he shocked and paralyzed? Was he on a stairwell, oblivious to the worse horror that was about to engulf him?

Among other things, I am haunted by the image of passengers in the planes that were used as missiles. I imagine the gut-wrenching realization that they were being made involuntary accomplices in terrible mass murder. Such use of them was an ultimate assault on their agency, their dignity. Not only would they die, but they would be used to kill others. An ultimate negation of their will, their ordinary good will.

So in my consulting room, I became highly sensitive to how, at least from my perspective, I was being used and misused. If I had any sense that my patient was engaged in acts of negation, however minute, I reacted. It was as though I had decided that life was not worth living if we engaged in acts laced with contempt, disdain or hostility. I was fighting to make life meaningful again.

I lost my footing and stopped practicing inclusion. I had no inclination to understand from the patient's perspective what was going on. I only reacted to the impact on me. And the "me" here was a person who was desperate to be accorded a dignity that could restore my faith in human connection. My experiential world (or phenomenological field[1]) had been disrupted, even shattered.

Ironically, I became caught up in a spiral of mutual negations. My reactions to being negated were defensive, moralistic, shaming, in other words, negating! So my patients defended themselves by more defensiveness, which I then experienced as further negation. And on and on.

It has taken me a long time to regain my balance with patients. One patient in particular, Isabel, had the bad fortune of beginning to work with me within days of the murderous attacks of September 11. She is a college administrator with a background in linguistics. Her prior therapist had retired suddenly for health reasons. She was very attached to her former therapist, and was enormously distraught over having to leave him before she was ready. He had recommended that she see me, and she agreed, having seen and liked my manner when I gave a presentation at a class she attended. However, she was

---

[1] I will use "experiential world" and "phenomenological field" interchangeably throughout this article.

terrified of working with a woman. She fully expected that a woman therapist would use the power that is inherent in the therapist's position to dominate her. She also dreaded the collapse she would suffer if the therapist got angry with her, and yet she had chosen me in part because she admired and wished to emulate my confident expression of a wide range of feelings, including anger.

Our trouble began within the first few sessions. I quickly found that I was characterizing Isabel in terms of what I saw her "doing to me" rather than in terms of what she was trying to establish for herself. She seemed to ignore or deflect statements I made, and questions I asked. She also acted somewhat imperious, as though she was perfectly entitled to have whatever kind of interaction she wanted with me, regardless of my own inclinations. It was as if I was one of the passengers in the plane, my own agency having no meaning to the patient/hijacker. I felt threatened as I experienced Isabel being subtly demanding and subtly hostile. The subtlety left me at a loss as to how to make these dimensions of our interaction figural.

All of these "mere descriptions" carried judgments I was making, not giving her the benefit of the doubt, but presuming at the outset that her behavior was directed at distancing and negating me. I was assessing her as aiming more at getting her needs met through direct action rather than using the therapy as a place to explore her needs. More disturbingly, I also found myself irritated, annoyed, even righteously indignant that I was being "managed" and "manhandled" rather than being well met and well used by her. And then, more disturbing still, and most crucially, I did not even try to understand what might be going on for her that evoked such noxious (to me) behaviors. I stayed centered in my own negative reactions, and confronted her quite often.

Obviously, human behavior and interaction are inherently ambiguous and open to multiple interpretations. But roughly speaking, beyond the obvious communicative and expressive dimensions, the meta-level of functions of interactions can be usefully looked at as being simultaneously aimed at both self-regulation and at influencing the other. While these two foci are not really separable in action, one or the other of the aims may be more figural at any given moment. Self-regulation involves the task of attempting to maintain one's emotional equilibrium while simultaneously striving to maintain a relatively stable sense of self-esteem. For instance, one may be careful not to interact in ways that increase the chances that one may feel ashamed. One may wish to influence others both to enlist the other in regulating one's own self-states, but also to participate with the other in a way that enhances the other's well being also. These two functions may be operating largely out of awareness. It is often the case that people may attempt to regulate their emotional states with behaviors that shame or in other ways disrupt others, and yet since their intent was so focused on self-regulation, they have little or no awareness that they are doing so by influencing the other to retreat from the interaction. In fact, generally people are only minimally aware of, or interested in, their impact on the other if their self-regulation is jeopardized. I have often found that they cannot make use of exploration of their impact on others until they develop confidence that the therapeutic pair will be able to provide the necessary emotional regulation that they used to rely on themselves alone to provide. My imbalance, motivated by my own jeopardized self-regulatory process, was that I found myself listening and responding too frequently from the following listening stance: "what is the patient doing, or trying to do, to me?" My preferred predominant listening stance is more: "what is the patient trying to do for herself, and how am I expected to contribute?" Is the patient mainly aiming at influencing me by negating me? Or is the patient mainly aiming at regulating her own disrupted emotional process? Buber made this same point by stressing the importance of inclusion, and asserting the necessity for the therapist to know viscerally, bodily, what it is like to be the patient in relationship to the therapist.

I described what Isabel was doing as negating me, and I pressed her to look at what was motivating her to do so. The more I picked up on the negations of me, the more urgently Isabel needed to continue to regulate herself in whatever manner she could muster, thereby foreclosing a chance to learn about mutual regulation. She needed to protect herself in ways that further negated me, because my insistence on being recognized constituted a threat to dominate and negate her. My own despairing "self-regulation-through-blaming" interfered with her chance to develop in such a way that she would have been less likely to negate me!

Our interactions became governed as much by desperation and hate as they were by our therapeutic task. These are shadows that fell over our disrupted connection. Poor contact and connection threatened to impoverish, if not annihilate us, and each of our desperate self-preservative actions became a vicious cycle of further disruption and defensiveness.

I had lost my way as a therapist, and was practically torturing a patient. How was I to find my balance and restore our chances for therapeutic dialogue? In part I turned to meditations on field theory and contextualism for a stabilizing anchor.

I will return to the story of Isabel and me later.

Contextualism

Let us start with a dense statement; one that sets the stage for all that follows. Human subjects are situated, embodied agents, inhabiting, and inhabited by, a non-indifferent world (see Taylor, 1995, p. 22). We are *situated* in that we come into being at a certain time in history, in a certain familial, ethnic, national, and cultural landscape, and within a certain set of language and action practices. As Merleau-Ponty elegantly established, we are *embodied agents* in that our experiential world exists *in relation to us*, and specifically in relation to us as a field of potential actions. That is, our perceptual field has an orientational structure. Things are near, far, up and down, and all in relation to our agentic functioning in a gravitational field. Without gravity, without body, and without agency, the notions of near, far, up and down are without meaning (Taylor, 1995, p. 23). This last statement also points to how our world is a *non-indifferent* one. Figures of interest form. Figure formation is a continual, involuntary process, and figures are emergent phenomena of our situatedness and our agency.

So our existence as human subjects is thoroughly contextual. This is the most fundamental assertion of field theory. All schools of thought that are trying to break free of the atomistic, isolationist legacy of the Cartesian worldview are emphasizing the contextual nature of human existence in one way or another. In Gestalt theory, phenomenological field theory is our particular handle.

Field Theory and Contextualism

There are some valuable aspects of using field theory as our contextual theory, but also some problems. I find valuable some of the principles derived from the amalgam of phenomenology, Lewin's thought, Gestalt psychology, and even, to some extent, how fields are thought of in quantum physics. These include the notions of contemporaneity, horizontalism, and the interrelatedness of phenomena (Parlett, 1991; Yontef, 1993).

One problem is that "field" seems to be defined differently by different theorists. Some people adhere to the Husserlian concept of field as a descriptor of one's experiential world: a phenomenological field (McConville, 2001). That is my preference, as well. An extended quote from McConville's article, "Husserl's Phenomenology in Context," elaborates the phenomenological roots of field theory for Gestalt therapy:

> ...apart from an engaged, bodily perceiver, nothing [no figure] can stand out from anything [ground]. There is no field, in other words, unless we are referring to a field that includes, as a co-constitutive pole, an engaged subjectivity. Writers in Gestalt therapy often leave out this phenomenological rudiment of field theory, speaking of fields as if they existed in themselves...
>
> The point here is that Husserl's phenomenology is...the groundwork, the founding basis for Gestalt therapy's radicalization of field theory. Fields cannot be spoken of properly as existing in themselves, in nature, apart from a co-constitutive human subjectivity (McConville, pp. 200-201; parentheses mine).

Others prefer to define field in more reified terms, as a "thing" that is out there. There are field influences that operate on us, that are beyond us but that are part of the constitution of our experiential worlds, or our phenomenological fields. I think this is better described as our embeddedness in contexts.

We swim in contexts, as I described above. Our phenomenological fields are emergent from these contexts, and are shaped by them. What has the potential to influence us is also at least potentially accessible to awareness, even if that awareness can never be completely fulfilled. And yet it is a bit misleading to refer to "one's" phenomenological field, because that can be easily misconstrued as a solipsistic, subjectivist assertion. Actually, that is far from the case. Our phenomenological fields are also shared fields, despite their uniqueness. This ranges from the most abstract communality of shared language, culture and various "forms of life," as Wittgenstein described, but also more directly, in that my being-in-your-world and your being-in-my-world yields co-constituted and broadly overlapping fields. This is the most basic inclusion.

We are born into historical, cultural, language and action practice contexts, we come into being in them and we also contribute to the shaping of these very contexts. These contexts obviously constitute our experiential worlds, albeit largely without our awareness. They are the necessary pre-condition for the existence of our phenomenological fields. They are the "ground" that makes the "figure" of "experiential world" possible.

A contextual ontology and a contextual epistemology are infinitely regressive. By this I mean that no matter what you may find you know, you can never fully know the preconditions that made such knowing possible. Whatever you are aware of requires a ground from which that figure has emerged, and the ground is necessarily vague, indistinct, and unknowable. All knowledge is therefore partial, incomplete, and subject to continual revision (Wheeler, 2000). Even if you try to study the conditions that give rise to a certain figure of interest by making the conditions figural, those figures will also emerge from an ultimately unknowable ground. It is much like trying to get a fixed and full understanding of the concept of "self." Or more pragmatically, it is like trying to get a fixed knowledge of one's own self. The very act of pointing at it changes it and creates infinitely more to know.

There are also limits to what can emerge and become knowledge, based on the contextual influences at play that shape what figures of awareness may emerge. An obvious example of this is the word, "American." Among whatever other associations and images may be triggered by that word, the white reader likely also imagined a white person. "American" and "white" are intimately linked in white language and culture practices. This, by the way, is a factor in the difficulty people of color have in establishing full presence in our culture. They generally are not held as "dialogical partners" in the ground of white Americans' subjectivity. They become visible only when issues of race or color are raised.

Contexts nest, one within the other, and some also collide. Our immediate history is nested in our less proximal history. Individual history and subjectivity nest inside language practices. One's tennis swing is nested in action practices having nothing to do with sport. Some contexts are incompatible with one another. An abstract example, one which we are all engaged with in present time, is that the current interest in post-modernism, or in post-Cartesian thought, is nested in a long practice of Western philosophy. And much of our theorizing about individual psychology is nested in Cartesian language practices that have influenced every aspect of our lives. On the other hand, a phenomenological world-view, which is also nested in and emergent from Cartesian thought, collides with Cartesianism, giving rise to slippages and disjunctures in philosophical thought that affect us today.

Ethics of Context and Field

As Bob Lee has written so eloquently in the introduction to this collection, there are some ethics that are inherent to a field perspective. I suggest they are intrinsic also to a contextual perspective, in that I believe contexts can be described as organizing along the same principles by which our fields organize. To me, many of the ethics follow from a basic proposition: fields organize according to the principle of Praegnanz. That means that fields organize into figures and grounds in the most sophisticated, complex, differentiated and unified manner, given available resources of our field. In experience-near terms, the quality of your life and mine depends on the richness of the fields of which we are emergent.

In the crude differentiation of "organism/environment field," where I am the organism, the quality of my existence is utterly interdependent with the richness of the environment. My environment is rich if it contains a broad diversity of nourishments and attractions and supports that can allow me increasingly complex, differentiated and satisfying experiences, and if I bring my full richness to the interaction of myself with my environment.

Three major corollaries follow from my proposition. They can be summarized by the practices of care, inclusion, and openness to dialogue. Each of these practices is a manifestation of what Buber called "dwelling in love." Care towards myself necessitates care towards my environment, although that way of phrasing it is not apt. The phrasing I offered is individualistic, atomistic, as if my existence is separable from my environment. Rather, I am trying to convey that care for my environment is also an intimate care towards myself (this conceptualization is very much in line with, and influenced by, Gordon Wheeler's writings, 2000). Also, the quality of my life will influence the quality of my environment. We exist not only in reciprocal differentiation from each other, but also in reciprocal influence. Care, which in the case of interhuman dialogue might mean a respect for, and sensitivity to the dignity of the other, is most likely to be a mutually enriching shared situation, one in which knowing self and knowing another feed upon each other.

Inclusion follows from the idea that the richer my environment, the more possibilities for richness and resources there will be for us all. My description so far sounds like a utilitarian approach to the ethics of care and inclusion. Actually, I am trying to reach for something more than a utilitarian ethic. I am speaking about something more intrinsic to our interrelatedness. That my experience of my personhood is brought into being, and flourishes, when I can participate with others in a way in which we are all enriched. So it is not just that if you are enriched, it increases the possibilities that I can be enriched as well. It is more fundamentally that my enriching influence on you, and yours on me is a defining feature of our humanity, our personhood.

Openness to dialogue is most easily described by looking at the most compelling field for us, our interhuman field. Through the centuries in which a Cartesian model of reality shaped us, and we lived with a split between subject and object, there was a question that seemed impossible to answer: How do we know an "other?" But when Gestalt therapy rode the wave of phenomenology, and the field theory that is intrinsic to it, the emphasis of the question changed. The question is no longer, "how can we know the existence of other subjectivities," but rather, "how, or in what way, will we get to know the other?" The change in emphasis takes for granted that there is no way *not* to know other subjectivities, but it is only through others that we come to have a subjectivity ourselves. Our "how" is meant to ask, "What shall be our approach to knowing another?" Because the "how" of how we approach another will co-constitute the knowing, and it will co-constitute the conditions of our existence. Do we study the other as a specimen? Or do we enter into a "shared situation" (Gadamer, 1975) in which our empathy and theirs together create the knowing?

Dialogue has two faces to it. The first face is the givenness of dialogue as the lived process of coming into being in relationship. We come into being in the irreducible interrelatedness of the organism/environment field, and most importantly in relationship to other people. The other face is that dialogue is also a method, or a means-whereby the ethics of care and inclusion can be brought to life. That is why I called it *openness* to dialogue. Through dialogue with what is new or strange or unknown to us, we expand our experiential worlds to include more and more of the otherness of others, and we can only do that through a commitment to a caring dialogue. But the commitment must be renewed over and over again, because it is always tempting to sink into the comfort of whatever the current language and culture practices may be.

If we accept the idea that various contextual grounds shape our phenomenological field, and that these contexts, while making figure formation possible at all, limit our horizons of experience such that certain realms of knowledge or understanding lie at the edges of, or even outside of, our lived contexts, then it is only through such experiences as confusion, surprise, a sense of nonsense, that our horizons may expand. This becomes possible through dialogue. For instance, one contextual variable that shapes, limits and helps create our knowledge, is the linguistic world we inhabit (and inhabits us). As I pointed out above, if the word "American" becomes synonymous with "white," then there is no place in our context for people of color with whom we supposedly share this American land and idea. So black Americans may exist in our physical, even historical and cultural context as "things," or as factors in our history, but not as "Americans." This, despite the fact that many of their ancestors shaped America long before many white Americans' ancestors arrived here.

If we take a closer look at the context for such a narrow vision, we certainly can discern a history of racism and racial exclusion that has dominated our language and action practices. But we can look even further. We can look beyond the physical boundaries of America, to the *idea* of America. Anglo and European immigrants came to America for a variety of reasons, but few came with excitement about the color and culture mix we are. They came to a "white" country. My point here is that, no matter how thoroughly, broadly, deeply we look at the factors that contribute to the link between white and American, we will never exhaust the exploration.

McConville (1997), a white Gestalt therapist has written beautifully how his own racial ground is illuminated (which then alters his ground, of course) when he experiences moments of bafflement. These are moments when he becomes surprised and confused about the difference between his self-experience and how others perceive him when he is in mixed-race conversations. It is tempting to dismiss such moments, and the people who evoke them. But it behooves us to be open to exploring our bafflement, especially as therapists. It is our chance to encounter something we would never find on our own. Acts of negation, and its hateful effects large and small, are the counterpoint to the values of inclusion and care and openness to dialogue. Clinging to one's narrow horizons excludes and negates otherness.

I have had moments of bafflement and confusion many times myself, and have also had experiences of bafflement when I have been at the effect of the limits of what our language would allow us to conceive.

For instance, when I was about 11 years old I wanted to play baseball in a summer league sponsored by our local Parks and Recreation Department. I was pretty good at first base. I was left-handed, lanky, the perfect body-type. Except, I was female. I wandered onto the playing field with the other players, all boys, ranging in age from 10-12. I thought I fit in perfectly, my own femaleness being of no consequence, as far as I was concerned. What did that have to do with playing games?

I stood at first base and started to participate in the warm up, a ball toss-around, with everyone else. Then we started more serious practice. It dawned on the boys that I was there to join the team, and their looks became hardened as they stared at me. In the practice session they gunned the ball at me as hard as they could throw it. I relished the challenge of catching what they threw my way, and I began also to relish the challenge of proving to them that a girl could play. I assumed that if I played well enough, they would get over their initial distaste and accept me on the team. I ended the day with a sore hand, but I was also excited about the chance to join the team, which I had earned.

I was wrong about the team. The boys did not want me to play. They railed and whined at the coach, insisting that girls are not good enough to play. The coach said I could play, but unfortunately, he had not seen me practice, and had no idea of my skills. He let me play because it was an informal league, and his job was to help all kids use the park facilities. But he too, lacked confidence that a girl could play.

Obviously, this is a tale from the dark ages. At any rate, we went to our first game. The score was close, and in the late innings the coach decided to put me into the game. The boys rolled their eyes. He put me into right field, a position kids are sent to when the coach has no confidence in your ability. I was crestfallen, and felt a shroud of shame and humiliation draped over my shoulders as I slunk out to the field. Two balls were hit my way. I missed them both. I was stiff and uncoordinated, and felt a sense of wretchedness at knowing how unwanted I was.

That was the end of my attempt to play organized baseball.[2]

That experience has given me a profound respect for people who are somehow able to perform well, even in conditions of hostility and negation. I am reminded of blacks who have been hired through affirmative action. Their cohorts often disdain them, expect them to do poorly, and when they do not fare well, the failure is attributed to the idea that they were unqualified in the first place, not to the idea that it is hard to perform well when one's environment is hostile. The shame-evoking nature of such an environment may be just too hard to overcome. It was for me.

The exclusionary attitude I was exposed to meant the resources of my environment were diminished. Support from my teammates was inaccessible. And my teammates each suffered an impoverishment as well, in that my poor play diminished the aesthetics of the game, and contributed to our loss as well. Our reciprocal influence was a cycle of mutual impoverishment and diminished capacity.

What led to such an exclusionary attitude? One factor is that in my childhood, there was no linguistic construct, "girl athlete." Our language and cultural practices did not support the emergence of a figure of a girl athlete. There was no language, no concept that could make sense of who or what I was. This is where openness to dialogue becomes crucial. Dialogue becomes the means whereby care and inclusion become expanded to engage, and eventually include, that which has been beyond one's horizon. There was also no interest in engaging with me in a new discourse, a dialogue, through words and

---

[2]At age 33 I joined an adult women's softball league. I play first base!

actions, that might broaden their capacity to think that a girl could play baseball.

At around that same age I was stunned by another rejection that had nothing to do with what was required for the activity I wanted to pursue. I was passionately interested in politics and government, and I wanted with all my heart to be a US Senate page. Pages were teens that served as messengers in the Senate. I told my parents I wanted to apply for this position and they said it was not possible because only boys were allowed to serve as pages. The bafflement that McConville described radiated through my body like a nauseating shockwave. It was as if I had been running full speed and suddenly careened into a glass wall that I had not seen coming. I could not comprehend what about my gender made me unqualified to be a page. They might as well have said they only accept people who have a birthmark on their right hand. I burned with humiliation and ached for my loss.

From here it is a small leap to understanding why attention to shame is such a central part of the therapy process. Shame is a signifier that an aspect of one's self-experience has not found a welcome reception, perhaps not even recognition, in one's experiential world. The patient's shame can signal the therapist's current limited capacity to receive the patient's experiential world, and it can also signal what has in the past been beyond the horizons of the patient's family and culture.

I think about the notion of internalized homophobia. That concept implies that the self-loathing one finds amongst some gays and lesbians derives from the homophobic context in which their experiential worlds form. Their fields are shaped by (infected by) the homophobic context. I suggest that something even more profound may happen for some. Some gay and lesbian people have grown up in contexts that had no conceptual, language, or action practices at all regarding homosexuality. At least homophobia acknowledges the existence of homosexuality. But in some contexts, the heterosexism is so powerful that the notion of homosexuality exists as a tiny whisper if it exists at all. For the gay or lesbian person who comes of age in that context, they cannot find their existence reflected at all. I think that leaves a huge whole in one's sense of being and belonging. This idea is similar to Wheeler's (2000) assertion that needs are emergent phenomena of the interpersonal dialogue. That is, a patient may not be able to identify a need that has no chance of being recognized by the limited horizons of the therapist's capacity to listen.

Agency and Acts of Conscience

If we are made by our context, then are we merely the passive end-product of the shaping influences of our various contexts? I think we can rightfully assert not. Human being is an emergent phenomenon, meaning that one's thoughts, feelings, attitudes in response to any particular situation can not be predicted in advance, however much they can be read as "obvious" in retrospect. We exist as agents, with choice and responsibility as central dimensions of our selfhood. How do we account for that in a thoroughly contextual ontology?

Our phenomenological field is continually being reshaped by discourse across many contexts. Some of these contexts overlap each other, some are quite separated form each other, some are nested one inside the other. Our agency, limited though it may be, derives from our continual, on-going living amidst multiple contexts. Every time we engage in a discourse across contexts, we open ourselves to difference. With difference comes the possibility for choice, and therefore, agency. However, for choice to be available, one must be open to a dialogue across contexts, one wherein one seeks out the contradictions between contexts. Only then may our horizons expand.

As therapists, we allow ourselves to become deeply immersed in an on-going dialogue that is often intense and absorbing. We can sometimes lose perspective, become unmoored. One way we regain our footing is by reaching beyond our most local and immediate context of the particular dyad, and we bring in a third conversational partner, be it an actual supervisor, or more frequently, our imaginary supervisors, the ideas and sensibilities of our professional communities. Or we broaden our perspective, we re-situate our relationship within the context of the therapeutic task.

For instance, we have all probably had the experience of feeling bruised and abused by patients. Sometimes the relationships we develop with certain patients are volatile, urgent, full of wild mood swings, impelling us towards actions we might later regret. What enables us, calls on us, really, to withstand the surges of emotion, the calls to action, the wishes to retaliate or to rescue? I believe it is that we have a deeply felt commitment to something that is beyond the immediate context of two people in a room, engaged in an intense struggle for psychological life and death (such as the one I describe with Isabel). We are profoundly committed to a task, the task of being a generative influence in the life of the other. Our love of this task is more compelling, most of the time, than are our difficult feelings towards the patient (it may even *allow* us to have certain positive feelings for this difficult patient), and this love of the task pulls us into contact with other contexts beyond the most immediate one of this particular encounter.

I have previously referred to this as taking our task as a "thou." By doing so, one is in dialogue not only with one's patient, but also with one's traditions and generative attitudes as they are embodied in our task:

> It is the dilemma of the therapist that one encounters the patient with the attitude and involvement of dialogue, yet does not seek to be confirmed through the direct human encounter. The therapist's confirmation comes through the expression of oneself in the service of the task. Friedman has suggested, and I agree, that while therapists do not seek confirmation from patients, they must be open to the possibility as inherent in the dialogical relation. In fact, the therapist is confirmed when a patient allows him or herself to receive help (1985, p. 19). Yet ultimately, the therapist's... faith in the "truth" of the task, in the liberation of both people that the task will allow, enables him or her to hold aside the wish to be confirmed by the other, and instead to be

confirmed through knowing that the task is most creatively served in this way (Hycner and Jacobs, p.75).

We are pulled into imaginary and live conversations with our professional ideals, our theories, people who support our endeavor. I remember a time when a patient and I locked horns over whether I would meet with him for 50 minutes or 45 minutes. I experienced him as pushy and demanding. I stiffened my back and resisted. We ended the session with my saying I would think about it, and he said my decision would determine whether or not we could continue together. I walked into a colleague's office to let off steam. She heard my story, and then calmly said that I was letting my pride get in the way, and that the therapy was more important than my hurt pride for now. She was right, and she helped me to re-center in what was important to me, rather than get lost in the immediacy of my reactions (the useful sequel to this interaction is described in Hycner and Jacobs, pp. 136-137).

Return to Isabel

Returning to the story of Isabel that I told at the outset, how were Isabel and I to alter the spiraling negations that had engulfed us? Obviously, the major responsibility falls on the therapist. The key word here is "therapist." That is, there is a certain role I assumed, and that role not only placed me in a position of responsibility, but it opened an avenue for recovery and repair. The role established a different context for me to engage with, one beyond the one I seemed to be operating from, which had devolved into a personal fight for psychological survival. Actually, it seems to me that we became locked in an irresolvable struggle by the fact that I had decontextualized our relationship. I had lost sight of our relationship as residing in the context of a therapeutic endeavor.

What had happened? One way to characterize what had happened is that the two of us had become entangled in our conflicting ways of responding to trauma. The experience of trauma reduces our self-regulatory capacities. We react rather than reflect and respond, we think in simple either-or terms instead of complexly, and we are usually tense and alert for more danger, narrowing the range of interpretive possibilities of our engagement in our world. Isabel had suffered a traumatizing loss of her former therapist. I had suffered the same fate ten years previously, and I had, at the time she entered treatment, just completed writing my own story of loss, which was evoking painful memories. We were both traumatized by the overwhelming violent deaths of so many others, and the sense of loss that flowed through the streets of the country at the time. I needed to withdraw and to be treated gently. She reached for me to attend to her suffering through direct ministration to her needs so that she would no longer feel afraid or pained—a style that I have difficulty responding to even on a good day—so I was brusque, confrontative, and my caring heart was closed off to her. The more I reacted by "digging in my heels," the more insistent she became. Her escalating neediness was a meaningful response to her sense that I was increasingly unavailable to her. She was fighting to have her needs recognized and taken seriously, I was withdrawing and fending her off to protect my raw skin.[3]

By placing our struggle within the larger context of a therapeutic endeavor, I was able to remind myself repeatedly of my task, and by embracing the task with all my heart, I could begin to contextualize our struggles differently, freeing me from my sense of being engaged in a fight for survival. Now, instead of my personal survival being at stake, my love of the task allowed for new figures to emerge. I began to understand how my own traumatized state of mind was playing a much larger role in our interactions than I had at first considered. I renewed my efforts to get the supports I needed to restore my balance emotionally, and to get the supports I needed for understanding Isabel through the practice of inclusion instead of by observing and judging her from a self-protective distance. My esteem for myself, and care for Isabel's development, became attached to doing my task well,

---

[3]I am grateful to Donna Orange, PhD for her insightful comments about the role of my traumatized state of mind in my work with this patient and with others.

whereas when I had become lost, my survival had been defined as getting my patient to see (and stop!) what she was doing to me.

The biggest impediment to acting in a way that reflects the ethics of a field epistemology, I believe, is our immersion in a single, local context such that we have lost touch with anything beyond the most immediate, narrowly proscribed momentary context. We might even say that the problem is that one's sense of one's context has become so narrowed that the context has been lost (as often happens with trauma). The interactions have become decontextualized, much like a figure divorced from its shaping ground[4]. We lose perspective when we do not reach beyond the immediate context for dialogue with something that is beyond the most immediate figure. In moments such as this, the figure becomes all compelling but actually narrow and overly simple. It has lost the quality of "thick presence" which is given to it by our appreciation of it as informed by its most immediate ground, but also by larger contexts. Our openness to examining the contexts that provide the ground for the current gestalt provides a stability that the current moment itself cannot provide.

I believe that hate and negation, the frantic assertions of one whose sense of self is highly threatened, stand in opposition to inclusion, care and dialogue—which can be loosely clustered as love—and are by-products of reduction or decontextualization. A commitment to ever more inclusive attention to the contextual influences shaping any interaction, any language, culture and action practices, is at once the enactment of inclusion, care and dialogue, but is also the ground from which greater inclusion, care and dialogue are likely to emerge.

When we are lost in the most immediate moment, we are most likely to act in ways that are shaming and hateful. This was my problem with my patient Isabel. My slow recovery of my ability to work well with her came from my commitment to keep dialogue as open as possible. That was most difficult for me to do with Isabel, but

---

[4]Frank-M. Staemmler (1997) described this phenomenon as regressive process. I tend to think of it as a traumatized state of mind. Obviously, those two notions bear a family resemblance.

I could more readily engage in useful conversations with colleagues, and with my own reflections on the therapeutic process and my commitment to it. Those cross conversations enabled me to open up a more inclusive dialogue with Isabel, which of course brought me into closer contact with the terrible fears—hers and mine—that locked us in our life and death struggle.

We are faring better now, much to my relief and hers. We have had many conversations about our difficulties, and about her disappointments (and mine) with my reactivity. Recently, Isabel, who knows that I went through analytic training (where I was closely supervised on three "control cases"), was telling me that she had found herself saying to her mother something I had said to her. She wanted to know more about my orientation and my views about therapy so that she could understand better the broader meanings of what she had said. I cringed and laughed and said, "Oh no, don't read my articles or you will see how much my ideas about therapy differ from what I do with you! I am not doing good therapy with you!" She laughed also and said, "aren't you glad I was not a control case for you? You never would have graduated!" Our troubles aren't over, but we are working them out together.

References

Friedman, M. (1985). *The Healing Dialogue in Psychotherapy*. New York: Jason Aronson.

Gadamer, H.G. (1975). *Truth and Method*. Trans. J. Weisheimer & D. Marshall, 2nd ed. NY: Crossroads, 1991.

Hycner, R., and Jacobs, L. (1995). *The Healing Relationship in Gestalt Therapy: A Dialogic/ Self Psychology Approach*. Highland, NY: Gestalt Journal Press.

McConville, M. (1997). "The Gift," in M. McConville (ed.). *The GIC Voice*, GIC, Cleveland.

McConville, M. (2001). Husserl's phenomenology in context. *Gestalt Review*, 5(3), 195-204.

Parlett, M. (1991). Reflections on field theory. *British Gestalt Journal*, 1(2), 69-81.

Staemmler, F-M. (1997). Towards a theory of regressive processes in Gestalt Therapy. *Gestalt Journal*, 20(1), 49-120.

Taylor, C. (1995). *Philosophical Arguements*. Harvard Univ. Press, Cambridge, MA.

Wheeler, G (2000). *Beyond Individualism*. Hillsdale, NJ: The Analytic Press/GestaltPress.

Yontef, G. (1993). *Awareness, Dialogue and Process*. Highland, NY, Gestalt Journal Press.

Editor's Note:

Ethical notions do not exist by themselves. They rest on and reflect an underlying sense of human nature. In the following chapter, Deborah Ullman astutely explores this linkage between the ethics we embrace and what we believe about the makeup of who we are. She then traces the historical development of two differing ethical positions, one being our traditional Western modernist or scientific/ rationalist view, stemming from an individualistic understanding of human behavior, and the other a post-modern perspective, emerging from an interdependent understanding of human experience. Ullman then examines the ramifications of these two perspectives, presenting the contributions of gender research. She concludes with giving us a practical analysis of what this means for therapists and their patients/clients.

3

•••••••••••

Living Ethically
in an Interdependent World
Deborah Ullman

Introduction

At this moment in history unethical behavior is rampant throughout every level of public life, from government to corporate finance, from cover-ups at the Catholic Church to coverage at the *New York Times*. Most of the time we know what we mean by unethical behavior, recognize it when we see it. We share a sense that certain actions, done by us or by others, contradict some more general principle or code—even as we may differ about what exactly that code is. But how do we choose what ethical codes to live by? In our pluralistic world we are surrounded by a noisy multitude of competing standards: how do we choose among them, in our personal relationships, in our lives as citizens, and in our professional behavior?

In Western civilization ethical standards are something applied from the outside, in the way of the Ten Commandments or the code of civil laws. Likewise to Freud, from a psychocultural point of view, ethics are standards of behavior that derive from outside the individual and are superimposed in order to generate socially acceptable behavior. These externally derived standards of our culturally dominant traditions emerge from a worldview based on the individualistic, objective, dualistic view of human experience, one which holds that our basic nature is to be separate, both from our world and from one another. Ethics are then brought in to resolve or pacify the inevitable tensions of putting all these fundamentally separate beings together in a social (and natural) environment.

Here, by contrast, we will explore an interdependent view of human nature, one quite foreign to Western mainstream thinking. In the process we will discover that it leads to quite a different sort of ethics. For example, if I think it is our inherent human nature to dominate wherever possible, to prevail over other species, and for gifted or strong individuals to seek power over other human beings, I will assume certain competitive behaviors are healthy, or at least natural and inevitable. I may even consider this instinct for dominance an ultimate value, as does Nietzsche; and from this perspective I may conclude that unrestrained capitalism with no social safety net is a natural socioeconomic arrangement, and though harsh, is nevertheless the best thing, ethically, and not to be tampered with. If instead I take a traditional Judeo-Christian view, say one that includes ideas about Original Sin, I may decide that a harsh capitalism is natural but evil, and my ethical duty is to supplement it with charity. Or I might be motivated by a Buddhist perspective, or that of the third pillar of Islam, to be charitable, and I might assert that compassion and care of my fellow beings are fundamental to living a healthy life (along with either a quietist or activist stance with regard to the sociopolitical system). In each case, my choice of ethical code will follow from my ideas about basic human nature, whether naturalistic, deistic or spiritual in some other way.

In the same way, if I believe that our basic human nature is that we cannot separate ourselves meaningfully from other living organisms, then I will be led to some other concerns. I may choose not to use toxic pest repellant; nor to wear leather. I may decide it is unethical to drill for oil in wildlife refuges, or to eat meat (or perhaps meat raised in especially cruel conditions). Again, principles of ethical behavior will emerge from our ideas about human nature and our relationships with the world around us (including our relationship with our ideas, if any, of the sacred).

We could continue with elaborations of this general principle. If my ideas about basic human nature (whether God-given or nature-given) include ideas about fixed gender roles, then I may believe it is more ethical for a woman to work at home and a father to invest his energy in workplace pursuits saving little time to spend with his children. Same-sex marriage is an issue loaded with ethical reactivity, while this chapter is being written: either I value equal rights for partners regardless of sexual orientation or I hold to a traditional mainstream view of marriage. Thus, assumptions about values and healthy behavior, ethics and human nature, are always interrelated. When we explore ethics and ethical behavior, we are examining nothing less than our worldview.

For those of us who work with people, as helping professionals, it is important to know what we believe and what our underlying assumptions are about human purpose and healthy behavior. To illustrate and explore this here are two different ethical stances that arise from two distinctly contrasting world views. First, we will present those views and their historic underpinnings, returning later to their implications for ethics and specifically ethical codes for psychotherapists and others in counseling, consulting, training or supervising positions. The first of these two views we will call the modernist or scientific/rationalist view rooted in an individualistic understanding of human behavior. The second will be presented as a deconstruction of this, often referred to as a post-modern perspective, growing out of an interdependent, non-individualistic understanding of human experience.

A Philosophical Sketch of Modernism

Gazing back through the history of Western ideas we see religion, philosophy and science each used as a tool for discovering what is true about our shared human experience. We can trace our way through Christian and Islamic fundamentalism, and then scientific positivism, toward an understanding of the more subtle complexity and pluralism of contemporary human inquiry, by investigating different ways of understanding how we know what we know. Are logic and reason the best tools for the job? Do objective observations in the controlled experimentation of modern science lead to a deeper understanding of the nature of our human experience? Or, as some will suggest, is divine revelation the way to the most all-encompassing truth? If so, whose revelation is true when the particulars differ or collide?

A walk through some major Western philosophical forces might help to orient us. The dominant conceptual framework of the latter European Middle Ages was Scholasticism, an integration of Aristotle's system of nature and the ethical authority of the church as presented by Thomas Aquinas (Taylor, 1998). This institution-alized Christian world view would then prevail in Europe until the 17th century. Philosopher of religion Huston Smith suggests the assumption of this pre-modern time was that "the leviathan of nature was not to be drawn from the great sea of mystery by the fishhook of man's paltry mind" (Smith, 1996, p. 5). And if the mysteries of nature are simply beyond human comprehension by divine intent, then it's a small step to assume it takes hubris, that it is heresy, to try to understand those workings. It was then the questioning of the assumption that "the mechanics of the physical world exceed our comprehension" which marked the shift from the dominantly Christian to the modern world view (Smith, p. 6).

The triumph of scientific rationalism in the seventeenth century developed through the transformational ideas of Bacon, Descartes and Newton. Politically this was a time of growing European nationalism, exploration, and domination of the Western hemisphere. Bacon was an advisor to King James I when he developed the inductive method of reasoning and the systematizing of scientific procedure. This was embraced as a tool for learning to control nature. Newton, using an analytic, deductive mode of investigation, reduced all physical phenomena to the motion of material particles subject to the forces of gravity which he calculated to unprecedented degrees of precision.

Descarte's *cogito* then marks the expression of this same spirit of separation of self from nature, setting modern philosophy on its course by formally divorcing subject from object and body from mind

(Taylor, 1998). The first principle of Descarte's analytic philosophy was "I think therefore I am." This posited two parallel worlds of mind and matter and established mind as more certain than matter. Also his own mind was separate from and more certain than that of others; this suggested an authority for knowledge that was individually based and different for each person (Russell, 1972). Following these seventeenth century ideas, rational modes of thinking grew in science, and spread to government, judicial policy, and public morality[1] (Ingram, 1990).

The eighteenth century's European Enlightenment advanced the program of rationalism by celebrating "the natural light of reason." This further established what we know as modern philosophy (Russell, 1972). Since that time natural philosophy or science has become unglued from moral philosophy or ethics (Wheeler, 1992, 2000). Hume maintained that the truth of the existence of things (scientific knowledge) must be founded in sense experience (empiricism) and not in reason or a priori ideas. This led him to his repudiation of the self as anything but a collection of perceptions experienced. Building on Newton's force of gravity in the material world, Hume suggested association as the central principle in the workings of the human mind—an idea that would dominate modern psychology, at least until the Gestalt model was developed, over a century later. Therefore, Hume concluded, our reasoning was no more determined by cause and effect than by force of habit, ideas having no more validity than impressions (Russell, 1972). Kant, in turn, critiqued Hume's empirical positivism, not on scientific but on

---

[1] The prophet of the Islamic world, Muhammad, received his "commission from Allah" to teach around 610 AD. The content of this revelation appealed to human reason and religious discernment at a time of much societal upheaval in the vast Arabic world. These factors resulted in immediate applications of Islamic law to issues of governance and public policy. (Muhammad himself became a statesman and public official in his own lifetime). This generated an entirely different time line in the Arabic/Islamic world from that of the Judeo-Christian world, including a graduated tax in the 7th century for the purpose of giving back to the poorer members of society from the wealthier ones (Smith, 1991).

moral grounds, by insisting that reason was the sole possible source of all moral concepts (Russell, 1972). In the realm of ethics, Kant offered the categorical imperative as a first principle, suggesting that in every action the ethical course is that which would work if applied as a universal law. Russell reminds us that the interpretation that all men (*sic*) should count equally in determining consequences that affect the community, offers an ethical basis for the democratic movements of the late 18th, and the 19th, and 20th centuries. Here Kant, in attempting to offer an answer to Hume's empiricism, was influenced by Platonic idealism and drew a distinction between the study of "what is" and "what ought to be" (Ingram, 1990). We will see that both the ideas of Hume and Kant were influential in the thinking of a young German philosopher of science, psychologist, and social activist named Kurt Lewin.

While modernism has been characterized by the rejection of the authority of the church and the acceptance of the authority of science, science itself has been regarded as value-free. Again, in this modernist tradition, the realm of nature and the realm of ethics are held rigidly apart. A decline of traditional religion in the West compounded with the reification of positivism and its objective truth have thus left a vacuum of sorts in the place of ethical inquiry. Into this vacuum stepped Nietzsche, a passionate individualist and misogynist, asserting that the human will has ethical primacy: since there is no other standard, might makes right. Nietzsche's position is that each moral or ethical system is actually no more than a disguise for someone's or some group's personal interest. Thus he divides humans into categories of strong and weak: noble-minded aristocrats versus impotent, rancorous masses with bottled-up aggressions, turned against themselves by the ideology of the rulers. He asserts unequivocally that civilization suffered from the populist revolutions of the eighteenth century (Knoebel, 1964). Nietzsche's constructivist thinking planted the seeds for both Existentialism and the subsequent deconstructivism of post-modern philosophy. At the same time he represents the high-water mark of modernist individualism: since there is no divine authority, and since our basic nature is essentially separate and individualistic, there are no moral criteria outside of strength and will themselves. The winners write not only history but the ethical codes of the dominant culture as well (Wheeler, 1992, 2000).

Rumblings of Post-modern Thought

Moving toward the present, contemporary academic discourse revolves around terms like critical theory, deconstructivism, and post-modernism. Although these words mean little to most people outside of academia, the ideas behind them have affected values and standards of human behavior and culture in far-reaching ways. In the 19th century, critical theorists were influenced by the constructivist implications of Hume, Kant and especially Nietzsche's creative power of human willfulness. They were also under the influence of Rousseau's faith in the untaught, natural goodness of humankind and Marx's belief in material laws of historical development. They began to elaborate a program of cultural relativism and perspectival sensitivity. These programs developed initially as a challenge to the value of scientific, reductionistic positivism and Western objectivism in the study of human activity. They were preceded and surrounded by the U. S. abolition and women's suffrage movements and picked up and advanced by the 20th century's civil rights and feminist movements. Critical theory, cultural relativity, and liberation theology and politics, among other movements in literature and the arts, are manifestations of that larger academic movement of the late 20th century known as post-modernism. Post-modernism asserts that absolute objective knowledge is unattainable, since viewpoints are always culturally conditioned; therefore the claims of objectivism are either disingenuous or a result of dangerously delusional thinking (Riebel & Webel, 1998). At its most extreme, and in the words of pop artist Janis Joplin, "nobody knows nothin' more than anybody else" (liner notes to "Janis Joplin—Farewell Song").

While there is a great deal of overlap of modern and post-modern thinking in our current epoch, there are certain principles that distinguish the two historical outlooks. Where the modernist outlook asserts the primacy of the empirical sciences and a positivistic world view, offering empirical, objective truth as its star value, post-modernism introduces and elaborates a perspectival element concerning all human endeavor including the pursuit of knowledge. Contemporary philosopher Ken Wilbur (1995) speaks of the big three distinctions drawn by modernity among science, morals, and art. Max Weber, likewise, identified their disparate value spheres a century ago: science dealing with questions of truth (Wilbur calls this the "it" realm); morals attending to questions of justice (the intersubjective or "we" realm); and art's domain involving questions of taste (the subjective or "I" terrain in Wilbur's construct) (Wilbur, 1995).

From the view of modernism these are separate realms, science, morals and art, and cannot be integrated. This objectivism is a fundamental characteristic of Western dualistic thinking. From this perspective, understanding what it means to be human has been founded in the notion of separate selves, divided from each other and even separate from our own perceptual experience. Systems thinker and deep ecologist Joanna Macy speaks to how "our very perceptions of the world 'out there' distinct from 'in here,' encourage the notion that as selves we are separate and distinct individuals, anchored in separate and distinct bodies" (Macy, 1991, p. 107).

To emphasize the point, this separate self concept is a Western cultural construct, partially built out of the discreet entities of Newtonian physics that act on one another in mechanical, measurable ways. Newton's classical physics is the basis for the behaviorist model of psychology with its mechanistic sequences of conditioned responses that has held such sway in the West throughout the 20th century. To go a step further, according to psychologist James Kepner, "our culture has reified the intellect as the 'self,' leaving emotion and embodiment as distinct and separate realms" (Kepner, 2003, p.7). This way of thinking dominates our Western biomedical ideology and has lead to the loss of the "ability to understand the coordinating activities of the whole system," in the words of physicist and deep ecologist, Fritjof Capra (1982, p. 114, pp.123-163).

The mechanistic thinking influences our very language and, therefore, ways of making meaning from our experience. The limits of this Newtonian thinking have been established concerning the physical universe since the Copenhagen interpretation of quantum theory in 1926[2]. The notion of self as essentially relational and interdependent with others which parallels these ideas of physics[3] remains unintegrated into dominant academic thinking in psychology (Capra, 1982).

Freud, trained as a neurologist, modeled his psychiatry driven by free association on French neurologist Charcot's treatment of neurotics and hysterics (Ellenberger, 1970). Freud's drive theory calls for responding to patients' experiences as not really significant in themselves but surface indications of deep hidden dynamics and, often, as no more than self-comforting fictions (Wheeler, 2000). Freud's developmental theory pits moral and scientific advances against instinctual satisfactions with progress to be made toward civilization only by the repression of human urges (Freud, 1961). In this way, his mode of psychotherapy was the penultimate expression of the modern era's individualistic ideology. The ultimate expression, behaviorism, sees human experience as self-explanatory illusion or side-effects of real stimulus/response conditioning (Wheeler, 2000).

At the same time as these psychological expressions of the dualistic, positivistic world view were prevailing, there were a number of critiques developing. German researcher Christian von Ehrenfels suggested in 1890 that 'gestalts' or patterns of experience be investigated, not just atomized stimuli. Using the example of recognizable melodies, he suggested that 'gestalt qualities' exist rather

---

[2]Werner Heisenberg (1958), building on the earlier work of Planck and the simultaneous work of Bohr, Schrodinger and others, expressed the limitations of Newton's classical physics in a set of formulae. Heisenberg called these "relations of uncertainty" and "principles of indeterminacy" which describe the behavior of sub-atomic material to appear as both particles and waves. What is known about matter is only tendencies to act in certain ways based on observations which themselves necessarily impact behavior.

[3]According to Fritjof Capra (1982, p. 80), "in quantum theory you never end up with 'things;' you always deal with interconnections."

than only sequential elements (Ash, 1995). This, in itself, may seem far afield from questions of human nature, much less from ethical implications. But the challenge to the world view based on discrete particles was fundamental and would have far-reaching consequences. Sigmund Exner built on this in 1894 by writing of unitary impressions from sensory data. These ideas inspired Exner's student Max Wertheimer's careful experimentation on movement perception which opened the way to a whole new school of psychological research that was to become known as Gestalt psychology. This approach carried implications for a radical deconstruction of scientific positivism as expressed in the old world stimulus/response model. While maintaining Hume's insistence on sensory data, Wertheimer altered the meaning of "sense data" to include how perceptions are experienced in whole configurations rather than through sequential associations (Ash, 1995; Wheeler, 1991).

These ideas were applied to ever more practical purposes by Kurt Lewin. In an era when all scientific endeavors, including the budding science of psychology, attempted to emulate classical physics, Lewin built and expanded on the Gestalt psychologists' holistic ideas. As a philosopher of science with an empirical, pragmatic and pluralistic orientation (Ash, 1995), Lewin offered a critique of reductionistic thinking based on a spatial construct of the multiple forces influencing behavior. He called this "topological psychology" and the arena in which behavior and experience unfold he called the "life space." Each of these terms was used in explaining his "field theory" of interdependence among the constructs of life history and genotypes (what we'd now call genetic predispositions), current environmental forces, and intentionality. He also stood for the need to take human research out of the artificial environment of the laboratory and into the real world of human experience. According to Edward Tolman, Lewin ranked alone with Freud in first making psychology a science useful to real human beings and real human society (1947, address to the APA, in Marrow, 1969). Not incidentally, Lewin was particularly motivated to make psychological theory relevant to issues of social injustice.

Lewin's work followed in certain ways that of William James.

James' idea of the individualized self was as part of the world experienced (James, 1912). His radical empiricism was an approach to inquiry that called for working with the multiplicity of relations within human experience and the singularity of knower and known. For James, all knowledge, all science, exist within a relational context of experience (Taylor & Wozniac, 1996). Similarly, Kurt Lewin suggested the need to proceed slowly in the developing of a system of concepts to underpin this newly evolving science of psychology; always paying close attention to both the empirical data as it is acquired, and the theoretical orientation employed in selecting and interpreting the data, shuttling between the parts and the whole. Lewin noted that the data that is attended to is determined (or at least co-determined) by the theoretical orientation of the researcher (Lewin, 1936). Over time Lewin contributed to enormous advances in our understanding of developmental theory, individual behavior, and group dynamics. His was a field-based model of human development that integrates physical, psychological and social factors to account for the enormous complexity of behavior (McConville, 1995). He explained this whole field way of understanding our experiences by suggesting that what we most need at any moment is what organizes the complex field of choices (Lewin, 1936, 1951). This means in the act of forming meaningful sense out of our perceptual and affective experience we notice and prioritize based on what we need most, which in turn is influenced by our contextualized existence.

Neurologist Kurt Goldstein (another of that second generation of German Gestalt psychologists to which Lewin belonged) argued that the drive to make meanings of our experience is the primary universal drive. This need to make meaningful stories of our experience integrates the impact of other selves, internal states, physical environment, and the complex multiplicity of forces and factors in our lives (Van Baalen, 2003). The organizing rubric, the gestalt in all this, is what we need, which in turn determines our choices of what to notice and attend to, and how we make sense of it all in order to survive and feel good. We, and everybody around us, are doing this all the time. Our choice-making will then be further complicated on those occasions when our immediate needs are overridden or contradicted by our values. That moment is the ethical dilemma (Wheeler, 1992).

A further evolution in this line of psychological thought came with Paul Goodman's and Fritz Perls' application of holistic ideas to psychotherapy. Working with Ralph Hefferline, and heavily influenced by Laura Perls, primarily Goodman wrote a foundation for the application of "Gestaltism in psychotherapy" in the book, *Gestalt Therapy: Excitement and Growth in the Human Personality* (1951). One way they defined psychology was as the study of creative adjustments. Creative adjustment is an integration of societal/environmental values with those of the individual in question, an interaction between the person and the surroundings (organism and environment) in which both are changed (Perls, et al., 1951). This concept is how Goodman differentiated the outlook of Gestalt psychotherapy based on the interdependence of the parts within the whole field, from the Freudian notion of adjustment to reality, which implied the individual is to conform to a relatively rigid external system by repressing his/her naturally antisocial behavior.

With this work we have traveled from the different view of perception of the Gestalt psychologists all the way to a different view of human nature and experience based on and extrapolated from that perceptual research: from an individualistic, objective, dualistic world view of psychoanalysis and behaviorism to a holistic, constructivist, participatory, and relational view of human experience associated with the humanistic clinical traditions and exemplified best, perhaps, in contemporary Gestalt practices. This latter is what we are calling a field model and, as with any new view of human nature, it clearly contains implications for a different sort of ethics. The post-mechanical, post-modern view is a constuctivist model with a different position on ethics from that of Nietzsche, who took the constructive nature of our experience to mean that all morality is relative and equal in value. In contradiction to this, new Gestalt thinking joins other contemporary thought by suggesting that the meanings we make and the values we hold do generate an ethical (or moral) imperative to live by—one which tracks the well-being of all parties.

This field theoretical view of human behavior identifies and values how centrally interdependent we are with our environment and emphatically insists that the well-being of the individual cannot be separated from the well-being of the whole field. When relationship and connections are valued over autonomy and separation, synergy over hierarchy or solo heroics, participation over authoritarianism, an ethic emerges with implications for the practices of psychology. If the individual is not fundamentally separable from the social field or the perceptual field, how can we see individual interests as separate from the world around—or stranger still, how can our interests be *inherently* opposed (as in a Freudian or other individualistic system) to those of our neighbors and surrounding environment! This system is built on the relational characteristics of a fulfilling life lived within a healthy society. From this perspective ethical solutions must be field solutions (Lee, 1996/1997/2002; Wheeler, 1992, 2000)

Game Theory, Evolution and Gestalt

Field solutions are ones that advance the well-being of the individual *and* the environment. In the realm of process mathematics called "game theory" this is what we have come to know as win-win, a non-zero-sum game (Wright, 2001). Game theory makes a basic distinction between "zero-sum" and "non-zero-sum" games or activities. In zero-sum games the relative success of each participant is inversely related with any other, as in the wins and losses of any competitive sport: one player's win means the other's loss. In non-zero-sum games this need not be the case and quite possibly one player's success will herald greater success for the other. The two parties will at the very least find that they have some overlapping interests, which will be the non-zero aspects of their activity.

Evolutionary theorist Robert Wright (1994; 2001) maintains that this very non-zero-sum dynamic has informed the unfolding of life on this planet. He proposes that game theory and the language of non-zero-sums offer a logical new way to look at Darwin's theory of natural selection.[4] The object of the game of evolution is genetic proliferation, not necessarily the defeat of other struggling biological entities (which, after all, may be interdependent with one another). Wright also considers how human cultural evolution has been influenced by non-zero-sum dynamics and the particular case of reciprocal altruism (Wright, 1994). However, non-zero-sum game strategy does not always imply cooperation. This will depend on what the prevailing social climate values. Communication and trust, and its complement, trustworthiness, are emphasized and valued highly in Wright's evolutionary framework built on reciprocal altruism. What propels both organismic evolution and human history, according to Wright's theory, is an alternating of zero-sum and non-zero-sum behavior among genes, cells, animals, interest groups, nations, and corporations (Wright, 2001). Wright explains that the direction of human history has brought us into a web of shared destiny where the fortunes of people at great distances from one another are now intricately affected by each other: this puts us all into a non-zero-sum relationship (Wright, 2003). This suggests the need for cultural and ethical value systems with implications for a relational ethics of cooperation that could represent a blossoming of our collective human potential (Wright, 2001).

Fritjof Capra connects with this interdependent or relational view of human functioning when he explains that "ethics refers to a standard of human conduct that flows from a sense of belonging" (Capra, 2002, p. 214). He describes two specific communities to which humans belong in this age of globalization from the standpoint of deep ecology. One community is that of humanity; the other, the global biosphere. A sustainable community, according to Capra, is that one which supports the entire web of life on which our long term survival depends. In the same spirit, Joanna Macy asserts that the reductionism and materialism of the old world view which shaped the

---

[4]In *The Expression of the Emotions in Man and Animals*, 1872/1998, Darwin proposes that universal facial (and other) expressions support the idea that emotional expressions, which are functions of relationships, have been instrumental in the social evolution of the species.

industrial growth society are about as useful for finding our way out of today's ethical dilemmas as the abacus is in helping us understand the universe (Macy, 1998).

Kurt Lewin's field theory of human behavior represents an early attempt to depict this more complex standard. Lewin defines behavior as derived from the totality of coexisting facts that constitute the dynamic interdependence of individuals with each other and their environment (Lewin, 1936). Contemporary extrapolations are offered by a Gestalt model that provides a set of organizing propositions about how our experience comes to be the organized tissue that becomes a useful base for addressing ever wider and more complex life issues (Hycner & Jacobs, 1995; Lee, 1995, 1996/1997/2002; McConville, 2001; Parlett, 1999; Wheeler, 2000, 2002).

This perspective of human nature holds implications for therapy. From this view the psychotherapist offers environmental support to foster the fullest realization of human potential as a co-agent in the co-organization of the client's experience. Obviously the therapist also needs a supportive environment to co-create a healthy life and practice. How does the therapist or any one of us make this happen? Coming from our own culturally or developmentally instilled sense of deficiencies, how do we do this? If we can begin to notice our own habit of regarding struggling behavior as personal deficiency and think of it instead as lack of support, either currently or developmentally/historically, we can take a step toward living this transformational model of human behavior. One characteristic of this dynamic process is the budding awareness that a merciful attitude toward oneself is essential to cultivating resources that can be shared. This approach is one from which ethical behavior emerges organically and contributes to co-creating a more ethically sound interdependent world, one that flows from a sense of belonging, as suggested by Capra. (See also Lee 1996/1997/2002, and Chapter One of this volume.)

Psychology's Dark Continent, Relational Ethics, and Gender

Before the 1970's there had been decades of psychological research studies in which undergraduates, most of them men, served as research subjects and from which conclusions were drawn about human development. In her critique of some of these conclusions, Carol Gilligan asserted (1982) that psychological theory was being written out of these studies without any specific data on women's development and how women might differ from men. She built on Nancy Chodorow's work concerning the cultural constructs of gender that derive from mother-child relationships in cultures where women perform most early child care. The identity of females evolves from sameness or a relationship of connection with the mother, while male identity emerges from differentiation and separation, claims Chodorow. She stresses how girls will emerge from this crucible of confluence with a stronger basis for experiencing another's needs. That is, they will tend to develop empathy (Chodorow, 1978).

Later studies (Bergman, 1991; Bergman & Surrey, 1997; Brown, 1989; Jordan, Kaplan, Miller, Stiver, & Surrey, 1991) look at corresponding but different crises of development for boys (early childhood—mustn't cry!) and girls (adolescence—mustn't disagree!). A body of research has emerged from the Stone Center at Wellesley College that contributes to deconstructing Freudian theories like the psycho-sexual stages of development, the Oedipal complex, and the supposed lack of a complete superego in women. Freud wrote that women's level of ethical functioning is lower than that of men and that their judgments are too often influenced by feelings of affection or hostility (Freud, 1925/1961). So it is, he cast women's experiences and relational lives into "a 'dark continent' for psychology" (Freud, 1926/1961, p. 212), thus reinforcing the notion of male as normal, female as somehow subnormal (African-like, blending the sexism and racism of his time into one phrase). The field-based view of human experience sheds light on gender as, importantly, a cultural construct, a set of differential behavioral expectations and taboos (Ullman & Wheeler, 1998).

Gilligan studied with Lawrence Kohlberg and knew well his six stages of moral development but rejected his assertion that an impersonal principled conception of justice could be equated with the highest level of moral maturity. Instead she saw the narrative of relationship which frequently emerged from investigating women's responses to ethical dilemmas as a high ground that supports an ethics of caring, which closely parallels the field-based ethical views being developed and presented in this chapter.

In the now famous longitudinal study of the voices of adolescent girls at the Laurel School in Cleveland, Ohio, Lyn Mikel Brown, Carol Gilligan, and their research associates discovered the methodological limitations to their initial research design which limited their ability to collect data for their study. In *Meeting at the Crossroads*, Brown and Gilligan (1992) conducted interviews with girls from first, fourth, seventh, and tenth grades looking for information on how they dealt with problems in relationships and how these abilities might change over time. They later looked for connections between the data from their interviews and standard measures of personality development, social, cognitive, and emotional growth. Nothing about the disciplined testing and assessment tools they engaged would have set off an ethical alarm with the American Psychological Association. However, the researchers began to realize at the beginning of the second year that the very act of approaching the girls with prepared questions and staying with the protocol, resulted in loss of connection with the participants. When, instead, they experimented with allowing themselves to respond to the girls dialogically, out of curiosity about what the girls said, the entire process came alive. More authentic relationships developed which generated more breadth and depth of material to work with, a win-win situation. In the words of Brown and Gilligan, "...they often arrived at complex and creative solutions to difficult relational problems. Yet these solutions, although sometimes elaborate, were unknown, and therefore unacknowledged and unappreciated within the public world of the school" (Brown & Gilligan, p. 13). So it was by staying with the complexity of the experiences of the research participants that the researchers moved to a deeper understanding of the lives of the girls, the material they were investigating. As a result of this, a new voice-centered or dialogic research methodology was created. Again, this methodological development both closely parallels the whole-field approach to ethics we are taking here, and also collapses the scientific and the ethical in ways which the dominant scientistic paradigm would not be able to predict or easily accommodate.

Janet Levers, looking at sex differences in the games children play, noted that during grade school girls' games frequently did not survive conflict, whereas boys' games generally did. For girls the relationships were deemed more important than the playing of the game. Boys became engrossed with the legal questions and abstract issues of justice brought up by the disputes. They then proceeded to develop moral judgment through the resolution process, according to Lever's argument. The boys would be practicing here the kind of rules-based ethical thinking, as a conflict resolution mode, which Kohlberg would celebrate, and Gilligan would critique, as the pinnacle of moral development. Traditional girls' games include non-zero-sum games like hopscotch and jump rope, games in which one person's success in no way diminishes the opportunity for another to do well (Gilligan, 1982).

Levers' observations and conclusions point to some important differences in the acculturation of gender which had already been influencing behavior for six or more years before the school yard differences she studied, took place. Contextualizing all these themes, Wheeler explores the many ways stories and understandings of self and relationships are different between various cultures and identity groups. He proposes that just as the Gestalt psychologists found that the construction of meaningful wholes is how we perceive the world around us, so meaningful stories are how we develop a sense of who we are and how we should act. What he calls the most fundamental internal cultural boundary of all is gender, defined as a set of socially constructed meanings that are organized by sexual designation (Wheeler, 2000). Our gender is central to our co-constructed story of who we are from birth, a perspective which fits with the relational field theory we've been exploring here as a basis for a new relational ethics.

If the ethical values of individualism are based on the pseudo-Darwinism of Nietzsche, and ruthless competition is inevitable from that standpoint, a radically different view of who we are as innately relational, men and women, offers the different imperative of generating a healthy society to help us form healthy stories of who we are in dynamic interdependence (Lee, 1996/1997/2002).

Three Principles of Ethics for Psychologists

Turning now to our familiar codes of ethics for psychologists, how will this shift in perspective on human nature affect our understanding and management of ethical dilemmas in professional life? To begin with, we may collect all the codes of professional behavior and organize them under three fundamental ethical constructs: 1) the Hippocratic oath—the principle of doing no harm. This category would include maintaining a high level of competency and understanding the limits of one's expertise (what is customarily known as scope-of-practice issues; 2) acknowledging the issue of "diminished capacity for assent." This means always understanding the position and role of client/patient/student/research participant as one of innately diminished power. This implies the insufficiency of any simple "permission" on the part of the client, to enter into any kind of dual or conflictual arrangement. That is, a psychotherapist, for example, may not use a client's assent, even a written assent, as justification for entering into dual roles such as business, other financial arrangements, research and publishing, romantic or sexual relationships, etc. Since the client is regarded as being in a position of categorically diminished capacity to give informed consent, all such excursions into dual relationship are to be regarded as inherently suspect, at least, and in many cases categorically out of the question; and 3) a requirement for transparency in all financial dealings.

Each of the many specific and complex interactive issues that are explored by Koocher and Keith-Spiegel in their classic and comprehensive *Ethics for Psychologists* (1998) coincides with familiar dilemmas that arise under one of these headings. Here, we touch on the first two topics of doing no harm and acknowledging a diminished capacity for assent, as we compare the ethical issues that come up under the two paradigmatic approaches we have been exploring here (individualistic and field-based).

The question of doing no harm seems pretty straightforward. It includes the need not to represent oneself as qualified to do work for which one is not trained. The follow-up to not misrepresenting one's qualifications, is to refer clients out to better qualified practitioners when appropriate, or to ones with training better suited to the person's needs. These may be cut and dried judgment calls, as with the case of the young man who had never married his daughter's mother and was no longer involved with her except where childcare was concerned. He was looking for a family therapist with detailed knowledge of Massachusetts law as it bore on children's rights and visitation rights, because the mother, who had willingly shared custody for three years, was pulling away. A therapist who had no knowledge of or experience with issues of visitation and custody rights, for instance would be obliged to disclose this, at the very least. Otherwise he/she would be in clear violation of a scope-of-practice issue, under the general injunction of doing no harm, even with the best intentions.

Other instances may be more subjective and therefore call for on-going supervision. The support of a trained supervisor is a critical and central principle of practicing psychotherapy so as to do no harm from any theoretical perspective. For the practitioner who understands human experience as firmly rooted in relationships, this principle of seeking supervision takes on clear ethical, as well as methodological and educational implications. From this field theoretical stance, people, including psychotherapists, are best able to make meanings from their experiences in telling their stories—in the course of shared discourse with others. Supervision is the opportunity to get more understanding about one's own relational dynamics and potential impact on the client (what are called counter-transference issues in the psychoanalytic literature) in the process of sharing the story of one's work with qualified supervisors and professional peers. From the interdependent understanding of experience offered here, the expression 'co-transference' acknowledges that both the client and the therapist are going to be drawing on whole life experiences as they develop this relationship. The therapist, as the paid professional, needs to be very aware of his or her own process dynamics and can best do this with the support of a professional supervisor.

As professionals, our relationship to these ethical considerations is to be mediated by Codes of Ethics—sets of rules for the conduct of all professional and scientific activities of psychologists (and other professions, all with their own variations). The American Psychological Association's official "Ethical Principles of Psychologists and Code of Conduct" offers both standards that apply to the professional and scientific activities of psychologists and general principles for guiding our thinking and behavior in these areas. (Koocher & Keith-Spiegel, 1998). Expressions like exercising "careful judgment" and taking "appropriate precautions," as well as being "honest, fair and respectful of others" give the tone of these principles. There are compliance procedures to enforce the more explicit ethical standards.

These codes are an example of reasonable strictures applied by the community of psychologists on practitioners *from the outside*— again, like the Ten Commandments or like our legal system. They do little to inspire attunement to the subtle, complex interdependence we all share as living, learning members of an ever-changing community of psychological practitioners. It is from this relational view of human experience that supervision emerges, again, as the most essential element of an ethical practice. How can a psychotherapist in New York City in September of 2001 address the post-traumatic stress of her clients without first addressing her own post-traumatic stress and the behavior that stems from it?

A case offered by Koocher and Keith-Spiegel (1998) describes a psychotherapist frequently giving trinkets and substantial gifts to his clients. He also worked out at the gym with some and met others for lunch. Several clients complained for different reasons. Another therapist (Koocher & Keith-Spiegel, 1998) suggested that a patient who jogged join him for the therapy session while they ran together.

In each of these instances the integrity of the therapy session has been compromised by dual relationships in which the client has an inherently diminished capacity for consent.

In the second example it appears that the therapist was exploiting the client who complained to the ethics board that he could not think clearly nor even hear what his therapist said during their running-therapy sessions. By contrast, the practitioner who showered his clients with gifts and attention after hours or between sessions was apparently unconscious of the impact of his generosity. It implied a type of intimacy to certain clients who then felt abandoned. Where the example of the jogging therapist stresses the importance of respecting and prioritizing the client's needs in determining treatment protocol, it also highlights how easily a therapist can take advantage of a client's willingness to trust his judgment and how crucial it is to recognize when self-interest violates the client's best interest. The other case also demonstrates limited self-knowledge on the part of the psychotherapist. The giving of gifts and extra social contacts might indicate a lack of confidence in the therapist's own ability to help his patients by way of the therapy session alone, and it might have been a way to make his clients like him and keep coming. A skillful supervisor will help him learn how his lack of boundaries would confuse his patients about the nature of the relationship. Furthermore, supervision could help him examine whether this behavior indicates that he does not have sufficient support to address needs in other parts of his life. It is when therapists are off balance without sufficient support that they are most likely to make mistakes that can unintentionally affect their clients adversely.

Additionally, from the field-theoretical or interdependent understanding of human experience presented here, these therapists are each engaging in seemingly self-serving behavior that is unethical and ultimately serves no one, as evidenced by complaints to the APA's Ethics Committee. To reexamine these questions in a more subtle way, using this higher or more complex relational standard, if the relational therapist clearly recognizes his or her own interests, is skillful in supporting a mutual relationship, and responding to the client's needs, she or he might determine at an advanced stage of therapy, that it does serve the client to offer an embodied experiment (like the jogging session). But the therapeutic emphasis needs to be on the client's experience of the interaction. Without this focus, this is not therapy.

This example draws attention to certain abilities that the highly attuned therapist must have in order to effectively and ethically work outside the strictures of the old world model. And again, these capacities are most likely to develop within a highly supportive environment, with recurring interactive therapeutic or supervisory feedback for the therapist him or herself (see Parlett, 1999, 2002).

Sexual Conduct

The most publicized violation of the ethical principle for psychologists to do no harm is the transgressing of the APA codes concerning sexual exploitation or harassment (Ethical Standards, 1.11 in Koocher and Keith-Spiegel, 1998). Harassment is defined to include "sexual solicitation, physical advances, or verbal or nonverbal conduct that is sexual in nature." Since sexual issues are frequently part of what patients seek help with in therapy, and any conversation about sex can be construed or experienced as sexual activity, this is sensitive material and calls for considerable awareness and skill on the part of the psychotherapist, far beyond the simple and categorical, behavioral rules. The ongoing challenge comes in evaluating one's own identity and needs, and one's own connection with and response to the client and his or her presenting problem, to moderate the counter-transference issues. The appropriateness (or otherwise) of working with a client whose issues closely resonate with one's own history would depend on how comprehensively the therapist has done his or her own therapy, how adequate is the psychotherapist's supervision, and how experienced the therapist is. Comprehensive clinical training is essential but by no means necessarily enough.

How do we manage to address sexual feelings when they present themselves in therapeutic relationships? The ethical answer must be, with caution and radical respect for the well-being of the client at all times. Leanne O'Shea proposes that excluding or disregarding these sexual feelings is not always beneficial to the client in therapy, partially due to loss of authenticity in the therapeutic relationship (O'Shea, 2000). What then? How do we begin to work with this highly charged material in socially and clinically responsible, ethical ways, in ways that leave room for whole human beings in real relationships but with particular boundaries that create safe space for the sort of exploration that promotes healing? This challenging process has to begin in the teaching and training arenas. Training programs that allow for the safe disclosure of sexual feelings between students and teachers, between students and students, without equating disclosure with the need to act, model ways to work with this sensitive material in therapy. Such a disclosure may not actually happen in the psychotherapeutic dyad later on, but the therapist must be aware of his or her own feelings and be able to acknowledge them in supervision. Without this, the likelihood of unknown, unclaimed erotic feelings is increased, and the likelihood of acting them out is surely increased. With training that addresses this, the therapist is better prepared for dealing professionally and ethically when these issues present themselves, with corresponding benefit to the client.

From a field-based perspective a clinical trainer or supervisor might begin by supporting the acknowledgment of erotic feelings in the teaching or therapeutic environment. The principle here is that we are all living in bodies and engaging through an always potentially erotic field. Research conducted in the late 1980's indicates 86% of psychotherapists surveyed had experienced sexual attraction towards their clients (Pope, Keith-Spiegel, & Tabachnick, 1986). But few therapists reported feeling that they had received adequate training in how to deal with or talk about these feelings. Not to acknowledge sexual feelings between trainers and trainees, or therapists and clients, may serve to fuel the forbidden fantasies. I repeat that the acknowledgment will probably not be from the therapist to the client, but to the supervisor. If the psychotherapist is not comfortable with this terrain, she or he is far more likely to generate feelings of shame associated with sexual attraction, sometimes leading to transgressions, sometimes leading to behavior that diminishes the client, reinforcing her or his own shame issues.

Shame is understood from the interdependent perspective presented here as a break in the field of self-experience, and arises in response to any significant feelings we were or are too alone with (Lee & Wheeler, 1996). From this definition we can see how there is great potential for shame concerning sexual attraction in the therapeutic dyad or in the training dyad. Anything taboo can generate shameful feelings based on the isolation of the one guarding the taboo. Unfortunately clinical training programs which offer no attention to this area contribute to new generations of under-supported practitioners in the field, who in turn may contribute to reinforcing feelings of shame among their clientele. Here is yet another reason why supervision is critically important for working psychologists. Many anti-social behaviors and DSM-IV diagnoses can be seen as shame responses (Kraus & Ullman, 1998; Lee & Wheeler, 1996).

Where the APA offers codes of conduct not to be breached, Koocher and Keith-Spiegel acknowledge some of the complicating characteristics of the therapeutic and teaching environments in which issues of sexual transgressions may arise. People with borderline or histrionic personality disorders have been identified as potentially seductive more often than people with other diagnoses. Psychologists are nonetheless responsible for resisting the temptation to act in response to these perceived overtures and must remain focused on their professional roles. A parallel temptation, of course, when transgression occurs, is to shift the blame to the patient: one psychologist responded to an inquiry from an ethics committee by comparing his client to a black widow spider. He accused her of having worn him down with her low necklines and high hemlines (Koocher & Keith-Spiegel, 1998). Other psychotherapists similarly defend their infractions of sexual codes by characterizing the therapy session as one in which they were "enticed and lured into lustful moments by unscrupulous clients seeking to exploit the vulnerable psychologists" (Koocher & Keith-Spiegel, 1998, p. 209). Because inappropriate or seductive behavior is often the result of childhood sexual abuse, it is essential that the patient be safe enough to revisit the experience without having to revisit the predatory response from the responsible authority figure, i.e., the therapist. Such unethical behavior includes shifting the blame to the client for the failure of the therapist to meet professional standards or expectations.

A structured approach, with less reliance on the unsupported exhortation to "shape oneself up," is offered by Leanne O'Shea (2000, pp. 18-22). A Gestalt training program designed for teaching therapists to deal with the dilemma of sexual attraction between therapist and client or trainer and trainee is proposed and outlined by O'Shea. Her learning conditions include ways to achieve a higher ethical standard, one that addresses the dilemma productively for therapist, teacher/trainer, and client or student, as well as offering insights for the larger culture. Some of these ideas are: that trainees be taught to take responsibility for the power differential in therapeutic relationships; that trainees learn to use various contact skills such as touch, in ethical ways that leave minimal room for misunderstanding; that trainers create an environment where sexual favors do not flow toward trainers or supervisors; that programs offer opportunities for acknowledging and working within the complex web of erotic co-transference; that skill be developed for talking about sexual attraction, sexual pleasure, and problems, with people who are not ordinarily comfortable talking about sex. And perhaps most importantly here: the idea we return to in our argument about the interdependence of individual practitioners—that training programs must stress the critical component of having access to supervision for all professional therapists, counselors, and consultants in order to develop an ethically responsible practice. The possibility of creating therapists and clinical trainers who are able to address sexual issues comfortably could create transformative interventions that serve toward liberating the larger culture from ever more frequent abusive, injurious behavior (O'Shea). If there is a great longing for more meaningful sexual intimacy in this day and age and many people are stuck about how to bring that into their lives, the first step might be an open dialogue with a therapist or trainer or supervisor who her or himself has all the support needed to stay with the struggle and be comfortable, clear, and available to the inquiry (O'Shea).

Conclusion

Martha Nussbaum argues in *Upheavals of Thought: The Intelligence of Emotions* (2001) that for about twenty-five hundred years there have been both ardent defenders and determined opponents of the position that compassion is bedrock of the ethical life. Nussbaum sees the controversy stemming from mainstream attitudes toward emotions as irrational forces. This includes compassion. Looking back over a history of Western ideas about human experience since the Middle Ages, we saw how the mainstream world views of the modern era have advanced rationalism and separated our thinking identities from both our feeling experiences and our embodied lives.

Here, we have suggested that a field-based understanding of human experience advances the cause of an interdependent ethics, an ethics of caring, which calls for ethical solutions which are good for individuals and the entire community of humans, as well as the whole web of life on this planet. When we apply this compassionate ethical standard to the helping professions we find the fatal flaw in the ethical codes of the old system. There, the practitioner is often a lone therapist or consultant functioning in isolation who is exhorted to execute difficult decisions all alone. The alternative ethical standards offered in this essay are woven from the whole cloth of human complexity in relationship and interdependence with the world around. Supervision, support, help are the essential ingredients of a healthy life lived by strong, feeling, insightful people working to generate healthy communities which will, in turn, grow other healthy interdependent individuals.

References

Ash, M. G. (1995). *Gestalt Psychology in German Culture (1890-1967): Holism and the Quest for Objectivity*. Cambridge, UK: Cambridge University Press.

Bergman, S. (1991). Men's psychological development: A relational perspective. (Works in Progress No. 48.) Wellesley, MA: Stone Center Paper Series.

Bergman, S. & Surrey, J. L. (1997). The woman-man relationship: Impasses and possibilities. In J. V. Jordan (Ed.). *Women's Growth in Diversity*. New York: Guilford Press.

Brown, L. M. & Gilligan, C. (1991). Listening for voice in narratives of relationship. In M. Tappan & M. Packer (Eds.), *New Directions for Child Development: Vol. 54 Narrative and Storytelling: Implications for Understanding Moral Development.*, pp. 43-62. San Francisco: Jossey-Bass.

Brown, L. M. & Gilligan, C. (1992) *Meeting at the Crossroads.* New York: Balentine Books.

Capra, F. (1982). *The Turning Point: Science, Society, and the Rising Culture.* Toronto: Bantam Books.

Capra, F. (2002). *The Hidden Connections: Integrating the Biological, Cognitive, and Social Dimensions of Life into a Science of Sustainabiliy.* New York: Doubleday.

Chodorow, N. (1978). *The Reproduction of Mothering.* Berkeley: University of California Press.

Darwin, C. (1998). *The Expression of the Emotions in Man and Animals.* New York: Oxford University Press.

Ellenberger, H. F. (1970). *The Discovery of the Unconscious: The History and Evolution of Dynamic Psychiatry.* USA: Perseus Books.

Freud, S. (1961). Some psychical consequences of the anatomical distinction between the sexes. (Vol. 19, pp. 257-258). *The Standard Edition of the Complete Psychological Works of Sigmund Freud,* J. Strachey (Trans. and Ed.). London: The Hogarth Press. (original work published 1925).

Freud, S. (1961). The question of lay analysis. (Vol. 20, p. 212). *The Standard Edition of the Complete Psychological Works of Sigmund Freud.* J. Strachey (Trans. and Ed.). London: The Hogarth Press. (original work published 1926).

Freud, S. (1961). *Civilization and its Discontents.* New York: W. W. Norton & Company.

Gilligan, C. (1982). *In a Different Voice: Psychological Theory and Women's Development.* Cambridge: Harvard University Press.

Heisenberg, W. (1958). *Physics and Philosophy: The Revolution in Modern Science.* New York: Harpers & Brothers.

Hycner, R. & Jacobs, L. (1995). *The Healing Relationship in Gestalt Therapy.* Highland, New York: The Gestalt Journal Press.

Ingram, D. (1990). *Critical Theory and Philosophy.* New York: Paragon House.

James, W. (1912). *Essays in Radical Empiricism.* New York: Longmans, Green and Co.

Jordan, J. V., Kaplan, A. G., Miller, J. B., Stiver, I. P., & Surrey, J. L. (1991). *Women's Growth in Connection.* New York: the Guilford Press.

Knoebel, E. E. (Ed.) (1964). *Classics of Western Thought: The Modern World.* San Diego, CA: Harcourt Brace Jovanovitch, Publishers.

Koocher, G. P. and Keith-Spiegel, P. (1998). *Ethics in Psychology: Professional Standards and Cases.* New York: Oxford University Press.

Kraus, M. A. & Ullman, D. D. (1998, May). Feminist relational theories and Gestalt therapy: a lively dialogue. Workshop presented at the meeting of the Association for the Advancement of Gestalt Therapy, Cleveland, OH. Also in D. D. Ullman & G. Wheeler (Eds.), *The Gendered Field: Gestalt Perspectives and Readings*. Cambridge: GICPress.

Lee, R. G. (1995). Gestalt and shame: The foundation for a clearer understanding of field dynamics. *The British Gestalt Journal*, 4(1), 14-22.

Lee, R. G. (2002). Ethics: A gestalt of values/ the values of gestalt. *Gestalt Review*, 6, (1), 27-51. (The initial version of this article was first presented at the 1996 Gestalt Writers' Conference, Boston, MA; another version was presented at the 2nd Annual AAGT Conference, San Francisco, CA, 1997)

Lee, R. G. & Wheeler, G. (Eds.)(1996). *The Voice of Shame: Silence and Connection in Psychotherapy*. San Francisco: Jossey-Bass.

Lewin, K. (1936). *Principles of Topological Psychology*. New York: McGraw-Hill.

Lewin, K. (1951). *Field theory in Social Science*. New York: Harper & Row.

Macy, J. (1991). *Mutual Causality in Buddhism and General Systems Theory*. Albany: State University of New York Press.

Macy, J. (1998). *Coming Back to Life: Practices to Reconnect Our Lives, Our World*. Gabriola Island, BC, Canada: New Society Publications.

Marrow, A. J. (1969). *The Practical Theorist*. New York: Basic Books.

McConville, M. (2001). *Adolescence: Psychotherapy and the Emergent Self*. San Francisco: Jossey-Bass.

Nevis, E. (2000). *Gestalt Therapy: Perspectives and Applications*. Cambridge: GestaltPress.

Nussbaum, M. C. (2001). *Upheavals of Thought: the Intelligence of the Emotions*. Cambridge, UK: Cambridge University Press.

O'Shea, L. (2000). Sexuality: Old struggles and new challenges. *Gestalt Review*, 4, (1), 18-22.

Parlett, M. (1999). Creative adjustment and the global field. *British Gestalt Journal*, 9, (1), 15-25.

Parlett, M. (January, 2002). *The five abilities*. A workshop presented at the third annual meeting of the Field Circle Study Group, Esalen Institute, Big Sur, CA.

Perls, F., Hefferline, R., & Goodman, P. (1951). *Gestalt Therapy; Excitement and Growth in the Human Personality*. New York: Dell Publishing Co.

Pope, K. S., Keith-Spiegel, P. & Tabachnick (1986). Sexual attraction of clients: The human therapist and the (sometimes) inhuman training system. *Amer. Psychol. 41*, 147-158.

Riebel, L. &, Webel, C. (1998). *Critical Thinking, the Learning guide*. San Francisco: Saybrook Graduate School and Research Institute.

Russell, B. (1972). *A History of Western Philosophy*. New York: Simon & Schuster.

Smith, H. (1991). *The World's Religions*. San Francisco: Harper Collins Publishers.

Smith, H. (1996). *Beyond the Post-Modern Mind*. Wheaton, IL: Quest Books.

Taylor, E. (1998). History and systems of psychology, learning guide. San Francisco: Saybrook Graduate School and Research Center.

Taylor, E. & Wozniac, R. H. (Eds.). (1996). *Pure Experience: The Response to William James*. Bristol, UK: Thoemmes Press.

Ullman, D. D. & Wheeler, G. (Eds.). (1998). *The Gendered Field: Gestalt Perspectives and Readings*. Cambridge: GICPress.

Van Baalen, D. (2003, March). World War I research: Goldstein and others. In E. Nevis (Chair), European roots of Gestalt therapy. Symposium conducted by the Gestalt International Study Center, Paris, France.

Wheeler, G. (1991). *Gestalt Reconsidered: A New Approach to Contact and Resistance*. NY: Gardner Press.

Wheeler, G. (2000). *Beyond Individualism: Toward a New Understanding of Self, Relationship, and Experience*. Cambridge: GestaltPress/The Analytic Press.

Wilbur, K. (1995). *Sex, Ecology, Spirituality: The spirit of Evolution*. Boston, MA: Shambhala.

Wright, R. (1994). *The Moral Animal: Why We Are the Way We Are - The New Science of Evolutionary Psychology*. NY: Random House.

Wright, R. (2001). *Nonzero: The Logic of Human Destiny*. NY: Random House.

Wright, R. (2003, Spring). Darwin and the Buddha: Does compassion make evolutionary sense? *Tricycle, the Buddhist Review*, 84-87.

Part II

········

Clinical Applications

Editor's Note:

The ethics of connection that emerges from Gestalt field theory provides us with a foundation on which to build our treatment approach. In the following chapter Sandra Cardoso-Zinker shares with us the set of Gestalt principles, honed through her accumulated experience and wisdom and articulated jointly with Joseph Zinker, that guide her work with children and their families. Note how these principles are in sync with the relational ethics that we derived in Chapter One. They are born from a sense that individuals must be understood from the perspective of their relational strivings. Further, it is only in the phenomenology of the field that relational strivings become fully visible. To understand relational strivings, behavior, and development we must look to the field. In addition, the principles that Cardoso-Zinker shares with us reflect Gestalt's relational stance that healthy development of an individual, in this case a child, is dependent on the healthy development of the field. All of which, as she shows us, shapes treatment from diagnoses on. The curative agents are the developing relationships in the field. Thus support for the field is an ethical imperative. She follows her presentation of principles with a heart-warming story that illustrates how these underlying values of connection guide her in noticing, understanding, and supporting both a boy and his family as they experiment with and move toward a more integrated, felt-sense of belonging.

Cardoso-Zinker, whose heritage is Brazilian, writes with a fresh, energetic style. As she likes to say, "working with children takes us to unexpected places. They are in constant movement and transformation. They surprise us with their understanding of the world and introduce us to a different perspective and experience of life. The work is fascinating and sometimes disorienting."

4

•••••••••••••

The Story of Daniel:
Gestalt Therapy Principles and
Values

Sandra Cardoso-Zinker

Working with children has always been an exciting challenge for me as a Gestalt therapist. The young person is experiencing the world with unique perspective, in a process of developing awareness of himself and his environment. He is in constant change and transformation, physically, cognitively and emotionally. She/he[1] is developing her style of communication, learning how to assimilate her experiences, to express her internal world and to make herself present. It is a special experience to witness how the child develops her style of contact[2] and creative adjustments[3] and how she deals with the novelty of the moment. One must be open to the child's

---

[1] To avoid gender bias I will use random "she" or "he."

[2] "Every contacting act is a whole of awareness, motor response, and feeling—a cooperation of the sensory, muscular, and vegetative systems—and contacting occurs at the surface-boundary in the field of the organism/environment" (Perls at al., 1994, p. 34).

[3] "Creative Adjustment is a relationship between person and environment in which the person responsibly contacts, acknowledges and copes with his life space, and takes responsibility for creating conditions conducive to his own well-being" (Yontef,1993, p. 95).

adventure of the unknown, with pure eyes to see what is there. The child's experience is enriched when the therapist sees her, with such eyes, in the moment.

The world of a child is complex and rich. It is important that we pay attention to the totality of the child's existence—to both his individual characteristics and the characteristics of his outer world. Parents, siblings, the extended family, the neighborhood, the school, the social context, the culture[4] in which he lives, the family culture and the therapist culture: all these aspects are interconnected and have an impact on the child's sense of being in the world. We are constantly working with the organism/environment dynamic[5] and with the characteristics of the field[6] in which the child moves, and how these different aspects of his world are interrelated.

Phenomenological - Existential Principles, Field Theory and Values

There are eight principles that I highlight in my work:

1. Everything Is There

In the existential moment where two human beings meet, everything

---

[4] "Culture is the active, interpretive process by which individuals create frames for meaningful relationships. Culture is created in the course of communication between the co-participants: meaning in a culture is just the extent to which communicating communities co-regulate stable themes of information" (Fogel, 1993, p. 161).

[5] "There is no single function of any animal that completes itself without objects and environment, whether one thinks of vegetative functions like nourishment and sexuality, or perceptual functions, or motor functions, or feeling, or reasoning" (Perls, et al., 1994, p. 4).

[6] "A totality of coexisting facts which are conceived of as mutually independent is called a field. Psychology has to view the life space, including the person and the environment, as one field" (Lewin, 1997, p. 338).

exists. In that moment, the potential for change and the infinite possibilities of transformation are there. The present moment contains everything—obstacles to change, the capacity for growth, and the movement toward learning.

I am present—myself, my history, my experience. I am available for contact. The child, the client, is there in front of me with his blockages and his abilities, showing me how he is experiencing his life. He is there in the most competent way that he can be. His competence and his beauty are there, from moment to moment.

When my eyes are genuinely open, I am able to see the subtle movements that reach for contact. I see a gesture, an expression, a smile, a hand that touches my hand. With all his suffering, pain and difficulties, the child is waiting to be seen in his beauty. And everything is there between us.

2. Everything Is In Flow

When we were conceived we started our process of being in constant change. The velocity with which our cells multiplied is fascinating. Nature is in constant transformation: nothing is static.

When we are working with a child, we experience this movement in a very intense way. The child's body is in the process of maturing, in physical, cognitive, social and emotional contexts. The child will experience reality according to his developmental level. And his experience of reality will change as he matures. All aspects of our being are interlaced in synchronized flow.

Being in relation means to be in contact with the unpredictable, being touched and discovering new dimensions of our self. There are no pre-determined levels to reach. At any given moment we can experience the excitement of a new figure that emerges from our field of experience.

The child and his family have the quality of fluidity. There are always new places that they can meet, that they can relate to with each other. The capacity for change is always there, through the dynamic and lively experience of entering contact.

3. Changes and Meaning-Making are Relational

Every change is relational and takes place at the boundary between the child and the environment. The experience that the child assimilates is a process of meaning-making.

An infant experiences the world mainly with his sensory-motor capacity. The development of other abilities will depend on the level of stimulation he receives from the environment. The child needs outside stimuli to grow, to learn and to develop a sense of self. The child needs emotional and social contact.

Touching helps the baby to form an image of his own body. Lack of physical contact and/or being touched in any of the myriad ways that the baby can be touched influences his relation with his body sensations and his sense of physical contact with others. In the process of others talking with him, the baby learns the basic gesture and sound of communication. There is a dramatic change when the baby sees the world from a sitting position and when he stands up, walks and learns to explore and manage his physical space. To walk gives the child the sense of independence and potency especially when the adults in his life respond with signs of affirmation. But insecurity can be experienced by the child when the adults react with anxiety and ambivalence toward this new event.

In each stage of the child's development, he is creating meaning that will constitute the ground for future interactions. At the same time the child is evoking reactions from the environment that he needs to assimilate and to accommodate. His new behavior and attitudes evolve. The environment organizes itself to respond and to influence the child again, promoting new challenges to him. He is learning to make sense of and to assimilate these experiences. Again and again.

Language gives the child the sense of autonomy, differentiation, and impact on the social field. The child has a voice. For the child to grow, his parents must create a "space for his voice to be heard."

This process of giving and receiving will take place continuously: there is a vigorous dynamic between self and environment during the different cycles of life.

4. The Validity of The Process

The work is fundamentally based in the therapist's articulation of what she observes. Movements, gestures, sounds, language, grimaces, mannerisms—these form a rich tapestry for the child's construction of his self.

Before meeting the child it is important to gather information on the significant events of the child's life through conversations with parents. Sometimes we also get information from others such as grandparents, siblings, and doctors.

We are being introduced to the content of the child's life. The information we gather in this way, the "story," has its validity, but it does not define the child. Every person who is talking to us is reporting his own experience in a specific and particular context. While this content is important, it does not describe all the nuances of the child's existence. It is only a partial description of moments gone by. Still, it can enrich the experience of meeting the child if not held tightly, not used to define the child, but used as potential information about the environment as well.

Having received all the information, we need to create a path that cuts through the field of content. Then, we encounter this child in the moment, with fresh eyes. We are open to the child: with full awareness and a sense of wonder.

The emphasis is on process. I see how the child is using his body in the space, how he uses his voice, movement, facial expressions. I am paying attention to the child's energy and how much vitality he is using with me. I pay attention to what is happening with me when I am in his presence. I am open for what is going to happen between us, without an "a priori" agenda. I support the spontaneity created by the moment, and in being with what is there, between us. We co-create our experience.

My openness to the moment and my staying with the process creates a field of acceptance, validation and respect that facilitates the authentic expression of the self, and a positive experience of contact.

When I validate the process, I am validating the child's experience, without judgments, pre-conceptions, criticism or interpretation of what I see. I accept what is there, knowing that it is not the absolute truth, but the child's existence in the moment. It is the most competent and complete expression of his being.

5. The Field Has an Action Potential: Energy

The child integrates the various aspects of his relation with the environment, and the different parts are organized in one field of experience. Each system of the child's field has its own energy.

From the time of birth, the child has been organizing each successive experience and interchange with the outside world. The child builds his psychological field through the inter-relation between the systems (and sub-systems) that are part of his field. Each system has energy to make an impact in the child's development and on his potential actions.

There are many bounded units in his life: an infant and his mother; an infant and his father; an infant and his parents; an infant and his grandparents; an infant and a brother; an infant and the baby sitter... Each one of these interchanges influences the child's creative adjustment to the environment. At the same time the child is actively provoking and evoking changes. As the child develops, her field of experiences becomes more and more complex.

Likewise, the relation that the child has with me has an impact and energy to be integrated in his experience. In the waiting room, for example, there are the client and me, her mother, and a secretary. We make boundaries around the system that is figural at the moment and we establish a relation inside that boundary. The boundaries have different qualities. There are systems where the boundaries are flexible, which facilitates the flow of energy and growth. Other systems have rigid boundaries, closed to perspectives of change. Each one of these relational systems carries energy and impacts the child's assimilation of, or resistance to, the environment and development of the self.

6. The Interacting Fields Drive Changes

In therapeutic work, the interchanges between different relational fields and how each field interfaces with others create change.

We have the child. Her field of experience and unique expression place her in the world in a particular way. The parents also are part of the interactional field and we can establish different boundaries of interventions with them: emphasis on the parental system, emphasis on the couple and family system, or, work with one of the parents. There is also the field of specialists: neurologists, pediatricians, speech therapists and others who are part of the work process.

There is the therapist field: the environment that I create for my clients in my office. My presence, my contact style and the values and integrity of my work are influencing the changes in my clients.

What drives change is the circular dynamic that occurs between all different relational fields where there is a continuous process of interchanging energy. The result of the interventions in each field in a dynamic and circular way transforms the whole field of experience of the client directly and indirectly. We are intervening in the whole culture that surrounds the child, making significant contributions for its development and characteristics.

7. Phenomenological Diagnosis.

The most important information about the client comes from the experience of being in relation with him, listening to his stories, learning about his experience, joining the child in his world, using his language and images. I stay in the moment, attentive and open to follow the child to the places he moves to, respecting his rhythm, competence, vulnerability and how he communicates with the world. I see what is there, with no expectations or interpretation, following and staying in the process.

Phenomenological[7] diagnosis is a set of process observations

---

[7] "The term Phenomenological implies that psychophysiological process that one experiences is uniquely one's own; adding the dimensions of here and now gives these personal phenomena existential immediacy. The ongoing

focused by the therapist on the child's interaction with objects and persons in the field. This kind of perception stems from observing interactional events and how these events express the child's competence or incomplete or unfulfilled development. In the interaction it is possible to identify sensory blockages or uncompleted efforts to connect with the world.

The "diagnosis" is interactional because it factors in resistive response styles created by the whole field within and around the child. A child does not flow or move by herself alone, she moves with the permission and encouragement of the world. A child does not resist by herself, she resists a force that is experienced as pushing against her...or stopping her.

The diagnosis is not static or fixed. It is a moment by moment picture of the child's ongoing flow of interactions in the field. Our hypotheses are in constant transformation and in a dialectic process of continually reconfiguring the experience. I am aware of feelings, sensation, reactions that the child evokes in me. They are important elements with which to understand the attitudes of the persons who are part of the child's life. And they provide a lens through which to view how the child has had to develop his interactional style.

The Phenomenological attitude focuses on observing the client's experience in the field, paying attention to the energy of reaching out for contact. It is the description of how the dynamics of figure-ground[8] and creative adjustments are energetically present in the "stretched flow" of the moment.

8. Awareness of Developmental Issues.

Knowledge of developmental issues enhances the possibility of

---

phenomena (and more) constitute a person's world" (Zinker, 1994, p. 94).

[8] "Contact, the work that results in assimilation and growth, is the forming of a figure of interest against a ground or context of the organism/environment field. The process of figure/background formation is a dynamic one in which the urgencies and resources of the field progressively lend their powers to the interest, brightness and force of the dominant figure" (Perls et al., 1994, p. 7).

interventions that are congruent with the child's emotional, physical, perceptual, neurological and cognitive abilities.

The child needs the stimuli from the environment to develop his abilities and expand his experiential field. This is a relational dynamic: the child assimilates and integrates the stimuli through experience.

For example, as the child develops his muscular and neurological apparatus his relation with the environment changes. Imagine the infant lying down and experiencing the world through his visual, hearing and sensorial-perceptual field. When in a healthy environment the child will be participating in the life of the family, the parents or the caretaker would be touching, talking and moving the baby around his and their world. However there are circumstances where the infant is left too alone and his experience in the world is restricted to the limits of his own abilities. The interaction between infant and environment is poor. The possibility for development is also poor.

But in an adequate environment, the infant's curiosity and excitement are developing at the same time that his muscles and nerves are developing. As his physical development progresses, he is able to move his head toward the sound that he hears. The neurological system is maturing and the muscular responses are getting quicker. Then he can move his body, his arms, and his hands are able to reach for something that is attractive to him. His neck and shoulders can support his head. The muscles in his legs are also getting stronger and soon he is able to stand on his own. At this moment the world changes dramatically for the infant and for the persons in his world. Even the space is not the same when a baby is crawling, exploring the unknown. By then, the baby reaches another important step in the process of becoming a differentiated person: he starts toddling. His presence in the world becomes more influential. He comes and goes. He moves things around. He surprises people with his energy and ability for learning and adjusting to new situations. He is changing and promoting changes around him.

Soon the little boy or girl is walking, running, jumping and dancing. Knowing the moment that the child is developmentally ready to perform each one of these activities is extremely important in the process of diagnosis and therapeutic intervention. With information about development we can empathize with the child's present and past experience, better understanding the impact of his relationship with the outside world.

The knowledge of developmental issues facilitates the use of interventions necessary to stimulate the child in aspects that were neglected at some point in his life. It orients the work, emphasizing competence and the possibility for transformation and thriving.

Then...

There are principles. And there is Daniel—a special young boy whom I met some years ago in my private practice in Sao Paulo, Brazil. He surprised me with his fragility and sweetness. He touched me deeply with his gentle effervescence.

I want to present our story to you. I want to share with you how our lives came together as well as some of our encounters.

Daniel

The first contact was by phone with Daniel's mother. She was referred to me by a pediatric neurologist. She asked for an appointment to get my professional opinion about her son. I asked for some necessary information about the situation and gave her an appointment, soliciting the father's presence in our meeting. She sounded very anxious and in spite of her urgency for me to meet Daniel, I decided to have the first meeting solely with her and her husband.

Meeting with Daniel's Parents

Mother is a 31-year-old obstetrician, working in a hospital. Father is a 32-year-old ophthalmologist, working in private practice and in public service. They were born in Sao Paulo, Brazil. Father is Jewish, and Mother is Catholic. Daniel also was born in Sao Paulo.

They told me Daniel was two and a half years old and

was not able to speak. He would make a very strange sound when he wanted to communicate, but nobody could understand what he wanted. Nothing unusual had occurred during the pregnancy or during or after his birth. He was the only child. Mother was building her career when Daniel was born (to this day work is her priority). At this moment they both work full time. Daniel stays at home with his grandmother (father's mother), a widow with serious back and hip problems that limit her mobility.

Mother had prepared written information for the session about Daniel's development since pregnancy. She was the one who talked about Daniel. Father stayed quiet most of the time, but would speak when invited to.

They had two questions for me: "Is Daniel normal? Why is he making this strange sound?" I did not answer such direct questions, but said that I needed to meet Daniel and spend some time with him. Afterwards I would be able to share some thoughts with them about how I had experienced Daniel during the time we had been together. They agreed and we made an appointment for me and Daniel.

In this interview I learned that he was not breast-fed. He went from the sitting position to standing up, without crawling. He had a very poor diet because he did not accept certain foods (especially solid food). He was still using diapers. He was always a very quiet baby and remains a quiet boy. The parents never worried about him until he started making the "strange sound."

At the end of the session my body was tense. I was impressed by the energy that Daniel's mother invested in writing notes about her child and by her intellectual skills. On the other hand, it was very difficult to interrupt her discourse. She looked worried and had a serious expression when interacting with me. Daniel's father was quiet but physically agitated. He spoke rapidly with a subtle speech distortion. At times I had difficulty understanding him.

As I am processing my thoughts and feelings about being with this couple I am making meaning of my experience with them. In a phenomenological diagnosis my understanding comes from my relational experience with my clients. I listened to the notes that Daniel's mother wrote about him. They were very important in order to locate Daniel in a developmental context, but at the same time I was paying attention to her voice, watching the tension on her face, how she was holding the notebook, and most importantly, how she was avoiding looking at me.

Father's agitated presence and my difficulty understanding his verbal articulation, evoked in me the fantasy that Daniel was expressing the language that he was assimilating from his father. Meaning-making is relational, and the dynamic between Daniel and his family is the ground for his experience and expression in the world.

Paying attention to my sensations and feelings, while in the couple's presence, validating the process, facilitated in me an understanding of how Daniel was expressing his experience of being in the world.

I was left with an intriguing curiosity about Daniel.

Daniel Comes to See Me

I enter the waiting room and see a small boy, white skin, blue eyes, with a slim, slight body. He is holding his mother's hand. She is sitting on the couch and he is standing at her side. He sees me, I come close to them and his mother says I am the doctor she talked about. I smile at him, say my name and how pleased I am to meet him. He nods. I invite both of them to come to my room.

When I work with a young child I invite the mother to be in the room for the first session. The mother's presence gives support. I am inviting her to learn about my work. The level of anxiety and resistance in parents decreases when information is revealed in witnessing the work process. It is also an opportunity to observe the characteristics of the mother-child interaction.

On our way to my room I notice Daniel has a stiff body. It looks like his shoes are "carrying him around." We enter the room; Daniel's mother sits on a chair, looks around holding her handbag and stays quiet. Daniel joins me in looking around the room. His eyes are wide open, his mouth slightly open. He moves his body slowly. He does not touch anything. I talk normally with him, asking questions, showing him the toys; he is looking at me and he sometimes nods his head as if he is agreeing. I continue talking, paying attention to the tiny differences in his expression or his gestures. I show him different objects at a slow pace.

His arm moves very gently and tentatively toward a small wood car without touching it. I smile at him, saying it is a very beautiful car. He smiles back. I am sitting on the floor and he is standing at my side, slightly bending his body forward. He looks inside the cupboard, points to something and makes a sound. After some wrong guesses I get what he wants: a small, colorful wood locomotive. I give it to him. He holds it in his hands with my help. Our fingers touch very gently. He looks at the locomotive intensively ... for a long period of time.

I noticed there are 5 minutes left in the session. I say we will say goodbye in five minutes, showing him my watch. He is very attentive and curious at the same time. The session ends. I say I want to see him again. He smiles agreeing with his head and his body moves with an affirmative gesture. He turns to his mother, she stands up, says thank you. I open the door and they walk away.

Daniel left. I was touched by his delicacy. His gestures were gentle, his blue eyes were soft. He was curious without being agitated. He had a sweet smile. He listened to me and he saw many things. Everything that he held seemed to be heavy and big, but he did not run away. He did not move his hand away from me. He did not forget that his mother was there. He had a very powerful sound coming from his throat. Deep and strong like that of a seal. *Everything was there* in the time that we spent together. A quiet mother, Daniel and me, present in that moment. Daniel and his mother presented a condensation of their lives to me. And I was there, fully absorbed in the energy, grace and stillness of the encounter between the three of us. Everything was there.

Getting to Know Him

Daniel and I were alone in the room. His mother seemed relieved to stay in the waiting room. Daniel remembered many things from the previous session. This time he touched the toys. He liked the small animals, or small plastic figures. He sat on the floor and did not move almost till the end of the session. I sat with him and I was describing verbally what he was doing, movement by movement. I would ask him something or tell him something that I was thinking at the moment. I had not planned any specific activity. I was just looking at him. I noticed he could stay in the same position for a very long time, as if he were imperturbable. It did not make a difference if we were sitting on the cold floor, or on the rug, or on the couch. When he had something in his hand or in focus, everything else disappeared.

My image of the way Daniel was experiencing the world was of taking in a small piece of the world at a time, enjoying it in a solitary way. He seemed to keep things in a special place inside of him, one piece after another, slow and peacefully. Each piece had its importance, but was not connected with another. And he was there: a soft, delicate, fragile presence. I was fascinated by the quality of his presence.

The session that followed had the same pace.

I remembered the session I had with Daniel's parents. He was introduced to me through a notebook. He had spent most of his time with his grandmother who could barely move her body. The family started paying attention to Daniel when he started to make his " "strange sound."

He found a way to make himself present in this family, and I like that.

The parents mobilized when their son's behavior was having a negative impact in their social interactions: the strange sounds coming out of his throat as well his slow body movement. The grandmother was trying to do her best to offer adequate stimulation to Daniel, in spite of her physical disability. Daniel was investing energy to be alive and he found a way to survive. I was present with my personal and professional skills making meaning of my experience with this family. Each one of us was mobilized. *All of our systems mobilized energy to promote change and enrich the field*, for Daniel.

After a few sessions of observation with Daniel, I called his parents to tell them my understanding of the situation. I described Daniel's competence and willingness for contact, and the "sound" coming from his throat was showing that. He needed stimuli from the world around him to further develop. He was alone and the breadth of his experiencing was severely narrower than what was possible for him as a two and a half year old child.

Daniel will be continuing the therapeutic process.

Talking with Daniel's Parents Three Weeks Later

After eight sessions with Daniel I called his parents for a follow-up meeting.

As soon as we sat down, both of them took out their notebooks and took turns asking me questions. For example: "You said that Daniel needs stimulation to develop his body sensation and potency. How much has he developed in the last month? Why is he still making that strange sound? When is he going to start talking?"

I listened to the questions. Then I said they had brought me relevant questions concerning the work. The questions were related to what I had said in our meeting after I had met Daniel. They had heard me and in sharing their worries about Daniel, I could feel how much they cared about him. But I would not answer the questions in this moment. I told them that my work was based in the process of interacting with their son: and it was important to respect Daniel's pace. Together we were creating situations that would help him to expand his abilities, including his vocalizations. I told them that I did not know when the changes would happen, "but they would happen!"

I explained that the development of his speech was one aspect of Daniel's whole being and I was working with the development of his self, in many different aspects.

They were listening to me, quietly looking at me. Then I said: "I need your presence in Daniel's life. You are the most important persons in his life. I spend an important but limited amount of time with him. You are in his daily routine, and I need your help. We need to have periodic meetings to talk about you and Daniel, myself and Daniel, and how together we would help him to grow up."

They were silent, looking to each other, looking at me, and they did not utter a word. Then I told them: "At this moment I see how seriously you are taking this work. Since we started, Daniel never missed one appointment and I know how difficult it is for both of you to create time to bring him to the sessions. I really appreciate your commitment.

They said they needed time to think about what I had said before they could decide to continue, and I supported them. I told them they could call me to communicate their decision. I made one request, that if they decided to stop I would need a last session with Daniel to give closure to our process. I also said that I could refer them to another therapist, if they wished. The session ended and they left promising to give me a call.

Two days later Daniel's mother calls me to say Daniel will continue the sessions with me. I see how much of a struggle it has been for this couple to reorganize their lives to integrate Daniel into their existence. I can sense their suffering and pain of feeling helpless. Intellectual understanding is their strength and I can imagine how difficult is for this couple to have a son whom they see as a "disabled child."

A field perspective does not see the child as the identified patient. The child is just one member of a larger, interconnected system in which meaningful experiences are created jointly among all involved. Meaning-making is relational, so Daniel's assimilation and expression of his being in the world comes from the experiences he has with his mother, his father, his grandmother, and others. The same happens with each one of the members of the family. If one person in this family is not well, the whole family carries the suffering.

The principle that everything is in flow gives me the freedom to make interventions which are different from the family's existing behavior patterns. At the same time that I support their competence and accept their expression in the existential moment, I offer the possibility of contact with new patterns that can be assimilated into their lives. I facilitate a vital dynamic between themselves and the environment. My interventions are focused in the flow of the energy in the whole field of the family's experience (including physicians, teachers, speech therapists, and friends).

The interacting fields drive change. When I make an intervention to the parents saying "I need your presence in Daniel's life," I am reassuring them that they are the best parents for Daniel. I am also teaching them that their son needs to receive impulses from the outside to be able to bring his energy into the world. My message to these parents is for them to make contact with Daniel, their little boy in front of them, instead of relating with their "concept" of what Daniel is or should be. This task involves them learning to use their eyes, ears and feelings to look at and hear their little son, allowing themselves to touch and to be touched by him. Everything is there, and the moment they are able to stay in silence and experience Daniel fully, changes will begin to happen.

During our sessions, every time Daniel experiences the texture of a toy, its weight being absorbed by the strength of his little hands, he will become more aware of his body potency, his sensations and his feelings. He will bring this energy home, evoking in his parents new reactions. He will provoke a disorganization in the status quo of the whole family, promoting growth in all of them.

My energy was mobilized for them. I felt that the parents were validating the process of our work as much as I was. We were learning about each other, building a relationship based in trust, respect and understanding.

I met often with Daniel's parents. Sometimes I would see his mother and grandmother. I gave them information about child development, and they were able to make fundamental changes in their attitude toward children. With Daniel I was working with stimulation and interaction. I joined him where his energy and interest would be moving, and then I would make interventions designed to expand his experience.

Expanding Our Experience

Water:
The baby inside the womb is surrounded by amniotic fluid. The liquid holds the baby's body and facilitates the flow of movements. It provides the first sensations of the skin—the soothing experience of safety.

As I watched Daniel, his presence evoked in me a sensation of delicacy and fragility. He needed to be touched, but in a careful way. I needed to start from the most primitive and safe way to reach him. Then I thought about water...

> First I invited him to put his hands under running tap water. I put a chair by the sink (inside my room), he would stand there. His arms stretched, my arm around his waist, his hands and fingers moving gently under the water. We would stop for a while and then continue.
>
> The next step was to put a bucket with some small plastic figures inside the sink and Daniel would play with them. Then, we would play with a bucket with water while we were seated on the floor. At this point I started to create a context for our playing. If he had chosen animals, I would say: "look how the horse is swimming...it seems that the dog wants to get in the swimming pool also...they can dive...look how fast they are...."
>
> Daniel started making some sounds while moving the figures. I would join him making sounds, exaggerating my facial expressions. Daniel imitated me. His face became relaxed. He started moving his mouth and tongue. My voicing the sounds of the animals and the sounds of the animals diving into the water, helped Daniel to bring out his own voice.
>
> His movements were getting fast. He would carry the bucket, dry the toys, getting more and more objects to put in the bucket. I was constantly calling his attention to

his hands and their temperature, using my hands to help him to experience differences and naming them. He became less worried about getting wet. Sometimes he had to change his clothes before leaving the session. I oriented his mother about the work and asked her to bring some extra clothes. I also made sure not to play on cold days, which are relatively rare in Sao Paulo, or when he was sick. This activity, in its many evolving forms, progressively gave him a sense of the range and elasticity of his mastery.

From undifferentiated sounds, Daniel started to repeat my words. He also learned to say his and other people's names. I was very happy when he learned his first question: "What is this?"

His voice had a unique intonation. He was talking.

Riding a horse:

Daniel always greeted me with a hug, then he would say "bye" to his mother and walk to our room. While I was closing the door he would go to the cupboard, open the door and look inside. I would come close to him, asking if he was OK, and he would say yes, nodding at the same time. He would stand up and take the wood horse to take a ride. While he was going around the room I started making the sound of a horse galloping and he would repeat. Then I would say: "the horse is galloping so fast....Does he know how to go slow"? At the same moment Daniel would slow down...smiling. My answer: "Oh! He knows how to go slow and fast, that is very good, he is a very smart horse." After a while Daniel would stop and say, "Stop."

Noise making:

He was back at the cupboard, next choosing to play with construction blocks. We both had a set of blocks and we were trying to make a big tower. My tower and his tower would fall very often, and Daniel was very comfortable with the sound of the blocks falling on the floor. I would say: "This is such a big noise. Wow!" He would say: "Yes, noise" (his hands touching his cheeks). I would imitate his gesture of surprise saying: "It is true, it is a big noise!!! Lets try again." He would join me, and we would have this dialogue repetitively.

The last five minutes of the session Daniel and I would put away the toys that we had played with, naming them out loud. He would say before leaving: "Bye Sandra, thank you!" My answer: "You are welcome, see you next Friday." Daniel would respond by moving his head and saying: "Friday!" I would open the door and he would walk quickly toward his mother.

With Time, Daniel and His Family Learn to Grow Together

One and a half years had passed. I could hear Daniel's voice from inside the waiting room, telling his mother everything that he would see. The secretary opened the door and Daniel said: "Hi, Neusa, how are you?" Entering the room he saw a bug. He screamed: "Look, a cockroach!" His mother laughed and said: "No Daniel, this is not a cockroach, look how small this bug is...!" Then, turning to me: "He learned this word during the weekend. Since he started talking, we are all talking at home." I smiled.

He looked around the room and saw another client sitting on the couch. He looked at her and said: "I am Daniel, who are you?" I waited for the end of their dialogue and called him. He looked at me and exclaimed, (running toward me and giving me a hug): "Sandra!" To which I replied: "Hello Daniel, what a nice hug!"

Daniel is four years old. He just started speech therapy. He needs specific stimulation in his vocal apparatus to help the articulation of complex sounds (in the Portuguese language there are difficult sounds to pronounce, like nasal sounds). Although he is communicating well he needs to overcome difficulties accentuated by the lack of stimulation during his first two years of life.

He also started going to kindergarten. His mother is three months pregnant. They have been in a new home for 4 months. A babysitter has been taking care of Daniel for a year now.

Much Later

It has been three and a half years since I first met Daniel. He is doing well at school. He likes his new home. He is also enjoying being with his brother, who is 13 months old. He likes to teach his brother how to play. His speech therapist said that his treatment is going to end soon.

The parents still work full time, but the household is well organized with the help of the baby-sitter and a cleaning lady. The grandmother does the cooking for the kids.

Our journey is coming to an end. An important cycle in this family life is completed. They are alive, they have energy, they are relaxed, they are learning how to have fun together. The youngest member of the family, the baby, is very active, moves around the space with joy and is already using language.

Daniel is growing up rapidly. He loves to be outdoors playing, biking, swimming... He loves to go to school. His face has a nice color and his eyes are brilliant with life. And he has sweet blue eyes. His hugs and kisses are gentle. He has a strong fragrant energy.

He is part of a family. He has a potent body. He has a voice.

Creating the Distance: Goodbye

Daniel is 6 years and eight months old. Today is our last session.

When I entered the waiting room, Daniel was sitting at his mother's side holding a bouquet of flowers. His mother had a camera in her hands. He gave me the flowers, a kiss, and was looking at my face, watching my reaction. I thanked him with a big smile, saying that the flowers were beautiful. Looking very happy he smiled back.

His mother said: "I would like to take a photograph of you. It was so important to have met you, to have come here during all these years. We want to make sure to have something to remember this place." I was touched by her request and I agreed to it. She took some photographs of Daniel and myself in different places.

Daniel and I spent some time alone in the room:

> Sandra: "It is very good to see how tall and how grown up you are."
>
> Daniel: "Am I going to see you again?"
>
> Sandra: "Perhaps you will, but it is going to be in a different way. You can come to visit me. You can call me and we will find a time for us to meet. You know we are not going to see each other every week any more..."
>
> Daniel: "Yes, I know. If I don't come here I can stay at home and play with my friends in the afternoon."
>
> Sandra: "Yes, you will have time to do different things. When you started coming and were very young, you needed help to do things, to play, to learn how to talk... But now you can do all those things by yourself..."
>
> Daniel: "I know how to write my full name... and your name also."
>
> Sandra: "You are very smart. I am very proud of you."

There is a moment of silence. We are looking at each other...

> Daniel: "I want you to read one story for me."
>
> Sandra: "Ok, you tell me which one you want."
>
> Daniel: "I want the 'Rainbow.'"
>
> Sandra: "Your favorite... I also like it very much. Where should we sit?"
>
> Daniel: "On the couch."

We sit side by side. The book is open on our laps. I read, following the sentences with my finger so he knows where I am, and he turns the pages. We finish the story and it is time to go. We hug each other, he gives me a kiss, and says: "Goodbye Sandra! I like you, very, very, much!"

*****

Out of the "apperceptive mass" of her own learning and personal development, the therapist enters into the world of a little boy. She has a sense of respect and appreciative observation of this child's phenomenological field. Gradually she builds a supportive environment for him through a variety of experiences in her office and through supporting his family to learn to interact with him as he needs, all of which give him a sense of mastery, strength and belonging.

All of us are proud of Daniel and how lovingly he plays with his little brother.

References

Fogel, A. (1993). *Developing Through Relationships*. Chicago. The University of Chicago Press.

Lewin, K. (1997). *Field Theory in Social Science*. Washington, DC. American Psychological Association.

Perls, F., Hefferline, R., & Goodman, P. (1994). *Gestalt Therapy : Excitement and Growth in the Human Personality*. Highland, NY. The Gestalt Journal Press.

Yontef, G. (1993). *Awareness, Dialogue & Process*. Highland, NY. Vintage Books, Division of Random House.

Zinker, J. (1994). *In Search of Good Form: Gestalt Therapy with Couples and Families*. San Francisco: Jossey-Bass.

Editor's Note:

In this chapter I join Chuck Kanner in describing the creative work that he, his wife Cara, and their staff engage in with adolescents, which is an outstanding example of using Gestalt's relational ethics as a basis for understanding and treatment. Kanner Academy,[1] which began as "The Farm School," was founded by Chuck and Cara Kanner in 1997. Now, in 2003, it serves over 100 students at two locations in and around Sarasota, Florida. The academy addresses the needs of adolescents with emotional, behavioral and educational issues that have led to repeated failure and frustration within both traditional public and private mainstream educational settings.

I have visited Kanner Academy several times. Each time I have been deeply touched to meet these vibrant adolescents and to witness the opportunity given them to become interested in and explore the "foreign" notion that a true relational experience might be possible for them.

---

[1]Presently the Sarasota Community School

•••••••••••••••••••••

5

The Relational Ethic in the
Treatment of Adolescents
Chuck Kanner & Robert G. Lee

When you visit Kanner Academy you are struck by the liveliness of the kids, which belies the struggles they have endured. You might not guess that these are kids whom others have given up on, kids that have stolen cars, used and distributed drugs, aggressively physically injured others, gone after a parent with a golf club, set fires, been social isolates and suicidal, engaged in uncontrollable self destructive behaviors like cutting themselves, been involved in rampant sexual promiscuity (as early as age 12), been labeled with diagnoses such as conduct disorder, attention deficit hyperactive disorder, obsessive compulsive disorder, eating disorders, manic depressive disorder, substance abuse and more.

How do we understand kids who display these behaviors? Are these examples of what might be termed the "bad seed" theory or of other genetic/biological flaws? Or are they examples of a variant of such conceptualizations in which we all are seen as creatures that are innately driven by corrupt aggressive energy, all sinners, who must be controlled by a strong enough physical or moral force, either internally or if needed through outside control? Do these kids thus simply need to come to learn the consequences of their behaviors and/or repent? Or are they machines that have "gone out of whack" and need to be realigned—retrained? Perhaps views such as these hold solutions, but let's consider what can be gleaned from Gestalt field theory, with its understanding of the differences between an individualist paradigm culture and a relational paradigm culture, which offers an alternative perspective.

As Wheeler (2000) points out, how we view development starts with whether we believe a sense of self exists before relationship or whether relationship exists before a sense of self. Are we isolated, separate individuals, similar to Leibnitz' monads (see Boring, 1950), developing our own identity apart from and prior to contact with others? Or is our sense of identity co-constructed in our inter-subjective experience with others? Gestalt field theory supports the latter view.

If as we develop, we learn that others are interested in us, care about us, want to interact with us as we are, and want us to be interested in them, value our nurturance, then we will come to trust our environment. And we will develop what is commonly referred to as "self-confidence," which is in actuality confidence that others will receive us. In short, our experience will be that we belong—that this is our world. And, most importantly, we will have the sense, as part of our ground, that our and others' inner experience is the crux of our collective development.

However, if in our development, we are not received in significant ways, we will develop shame-oriented ground structures that help us disown significant parts of ourselves, protecting us from mobilizing in these directions. These shame-bound ground structures help us negotiate fields, particularly the fields in which they develop, which are not receptive to us in these significant ways. But we pay a large price. The price is that we lose a voice, even an awareness, of our associated underlying needs.

If we are not received enough, and we develop enough shame-oriented ground structures, we are essentially thrown into the assumptions of an individualist paradigm, despite what hopes we might have for a relational paradigm experience. And because of our belief system we will act as if we are in an individualist paradigm culture, again despite how we may hope for a relational existence. We will believe that true relationship is not possible for us. We will assume that people will not be interested in or care about us from a perspective that is important to us, in accord with what we know about who we are. And/or we will assume that people will not want us to be interested in or care about them. And thus we will believe that we don't really belong—this is not our world. Under these circumstances we will feel alone with our own struggle in the world, and we will give up and become depressed or our beliefs will move in the direction that we must aggress on others if we are to get our needs met. In the latter case we must learn to protect our inner experience from view, and to not take in what others say to us that conflicts with our sense of our getting our needs met. We must find a way around rules which only appear to serve others and to block our own need satisfaction. We must learn to not respect others, except as potential hurdles to our needs being met. We must believe that our task is to come to rely solely on ourselves and our own perception, denying even to ourselves any yearnings we have for support. Thus note, parenthetically, that an individualist paradigm is essentially a shamed position, a position in which people have given up on the possibility of intimate relational connection.

This is the position in which adolescents enter Kanner Academy.

It is clear to see in this light that the task with these adolescents is not just controlling their behavior. Instead it is a task that is much more delicate. It is the task of changing their belief system, *challenging their notion that intimate relationship is not possible for them*. It is easy to understand, again in this light, how behavior modification programs and/or medication cannot bring about lasting change in themselves. Asking adolescents to change their behavior is asking them to give up the strategies they have developed for survival in their perceived individualist world. If their beliefs about the possibilities of their connecting in the world don't change, then they may temporarily change their behavior in order to "survive" a time of imposed restrictions, but in the long run they will most often return to the behavior that emanates from their beliefs.

So how do we change someone's belief system? When we are talking about someone's belief system, we are talking about their mapping of their previous experience. And from Gestalt theory, the only way to change mappings of old experience is through new experience. That is, Gestalt field theory tells us that the essence of our co-constructed organization of experience, what we call our sense of self, is not only that we use our co-constructed map to screen new experience, but we also use new experience to test our map. This is the basis of the relational ethic in the treatment of adolescents. *It is the sense that a true relationship is possible, that allows and motivates adolescents to examine their sense of the world and their behavior.*

Surprising as it might be, it is the nature of shame—what happens in the formation of shame-oriented ground structures in the process of disowning unreceived elements of self—that permits the possibility of change. Shame controls our yearnings for connection, helping us to disown them when we perceive that there is insufficient reception for them. But shame does not erase our yearnings; instead they remain with us, camouflaged and hidden. This of course explains the component of the acting out behavior exhibited by these kids that creatively, and otherwise needlessly, draws attention to themselves. And it is this ongoing, camouflaged presence of relational yearnings in these adolescents that provides the primary possibilities for change. Not that it is easy to make contact with these camouflaged, sometimes buried yearnings; still without them there would be no hope for lasting behavioral change.

Let's follow this relational model that emanates from our ethic further. How do adolescents sense that relationship is possible? Let's refer to the relational ethics that derive from Gestalt field theory.[2] Adolescents must get a sense that people are interested in understanding the world from their perspective, interested in their relational strivings. Thus any treatment program must start with people who care about kids and what is important to them.

This is how the Kanner Academy began. Using $10,000 of money

---

[2]See Chapter One in this volume.

they received from Cara's grandmother, Chuck and Cara converted about 1,000 square feet of their garage into a one-room school. The first year they had four students. These are people who understood the experience of troubled adolescents and who wanted to make a difference. Cara had been a speech/language pathologist who noticed that the kids who she served often had a more difficult time emotionally and were often labeled as behavior problems. Chuck was himself once a troubled adolescent and thus knew first hand what it meant to be labeled as a behavior problem. Thus they not only cared deeply about troubled adolescents but they started with an insider's view of what would enable their caring to connect with such kids. Let's hear what Chuck says about the origins of his understanding of and commitment to a relational connection in working with adolescents:

> My own history as a troubled adolescent, and the education I received at the DeSisto School, in Massachusetts, gave me a solid sense early on in my life about what is helpful and what is not helpful in interacting with adolescents. What I remember having the greatest impact on my own development, and on my process of maturation, were the relationships that were personal and intimate. The most important interactions happened when relating to someone who I felt really cared about me and who was willing to share their struggles—someone who was genuinely honest and interested. Let me underline this last statement. The key to these curative relationships was that they were grounded in an honest, caring and equal connection. Responsibility for the honesty, the caring nature, and the feeling of absolute equal investment in the relationship were developed overtime as a joint project of myself and the others involved in those relationships—it was never top-down; it was never one-way.
>
> Being adopted and having fears, stemming from actual life experience, about being left or abandoned was something I have lived with and continue to live with everyday. My adoptive parents were fine people. They loved me and wanted the best for me, but like others in

my world at the time, they had very little idea about what to do with me except punish and try to control me.

The problem was not that they set limits or had ideas about what was best for me. All loving parents, through experience and other acquired knowledge, have a great deal they want to give their children, and mine were no exception. My mother graduated with her Master's degree from Columbia University School of Social Work. My father was an accountant and core member of Democrats for NY. They were educated, competent people. The problem was that they were unable to enter into a truly intimate relationship of mutual responsibility. That is, a relationship in which everyone takes responsibility for themselves, and for how they affect others. My parents saw me as crazy, or something worse, and they saw the task of caring for me as having to fix, explain, and control my behavior. They, of course, were not alone in this kind of belief system. Similar themes on the nature and treatment of adolescents, which are still prevalent today, ran through much of the thinking in the fields of education and psychology. Perspectives such as these are enigmas to me. I don't believe we can fix each other. I have seen no clear convincing evidence that medication in itself, non-relational psychotherapy in the office, better explanations, better facilities to control behavior, or jails have had much meaningful impact on troubled people. At the same time, I don't blame my mother, teachers or therapists for not curing me; they could not.

What my parents could have done, if they knew how, was to be fully invested in being in an intimate relationship with me. A relationship in which they treated me with respect, even when dealing with my disturbing language and actions, and one in which they shared who they were. Instead, when they couldn't figure out what to do about my behavior, they stepped away from our relationship, rather than into it. Psychotherapists and teachers made the same mistake. There was no way I was going to trust and open myself up to someone who was only interested in me for one hour a week and who didn't share any of himself. As simple as it might sound, mutually invested in, intimate relationships were what helped me find my own way. This concept of the power and importance of mutually invested in intimate relationships underlies all that I have to say to you.

This quality, which Chuck refers to, of a relational interest in kids is an ever present characteristic of the staff at Kanner Academy. It is palpable in Chuck's tone of voice and his pet names for the kids that say in effect "you belong here." It is also present in the way that Bruce Robertson, a therapist on staff, can run across the floor in a group meeting to hug a kid who has been out sick for a week, whom he has missed. And it is there in the way that Marie Labriola, a teacher and counselor, looks at kids that clearly says that they matter. And you can hear it in the way that Selah Kelnhoffer, the Director of Residential living, talks about the students like they are part of her family that says that she believes in these kids and will stick out whatever comes up. Chuck's words about relational interest and commitment to these adolescents are not just talk. You can constantly feel the staff's interest in and commitment to these kids. This is where the relational ethic of working with troubled adolescents, or any adolescents for that matter, starts.

However, caring would not go far with these adolescents without a structure that allows the caring to flourish. As Chuck has indicated this structure at Kanner Academy emanates from an understanding of and commitment to relationship, a commitment that supercedes the importance of all other matters. The end result is that the policies and structures developed, as well as the manner in which they are developed, at Kanner Academy do not get in the way of or hinder relationship but instead are centered around relationship.

Two Essential Elements of the Relational Approach at Kanner Academy

Caring is able to thrive at Kanner Academy because all aspects of the program are created and carried out from a relational ethic perspective. Here we would like to focus on two essential elements that are the backbone of that process, namely creating and providing an atmosphere for the birthing/nurturing of adolescents' relational voices, and developing relationally oriented limit setting strategies and structures.

Birthing/Nurturing Relational Voices

One important element in the task of changing adolescents relational belief system is helping them to birth/nurture voices for shamed parts of themselves, parts of themselves that have not been sufficiently received in the past to the point that they have lost hope of the possibility of reception. These emerging voices are expressions of the adolescent's shamed yearnings for connection and belonging, which often lie at the root of their creative acting out attempts to draw attention to themselves. And as such they can embody both shamed desires to be cared about and to care about others. This birthing process can only happen in a relational context. Thus developing a structure in which adolescents may experience a receptiveness to and can experiment with their developing voices for connection is an important part of a relational context.

At the Kanner Academy, the message that the school, staff and other students are interested in and committed to hearing an adolescent's voice starts during the application procedure. Applying adolescents are given a tour of the school in which they sit in on classes and groups and get a chance to meet and interact with staff and students, so that they will understand what happens there. They then are given a choice as to whether they want to attend. Only adolescents who choose to attend are admitted. Given the introduction and the subsequent choice, it is rare that adolescents choose not to attend, an indication that their relational yearnings have not been entirely extinguished. But in terms of the message to them, it is their voice that counts.

Once adolescents are in attendance at the Academy, there are continual opportunities for them to experience that their voices are valued. In fact, kids learn that their voices are necessary for the health and ongoing development of the larger community. A prime vehicle for this is the consensus decision-making process employed at the school, in which every attending adolescent has a voice. This is particularly in evidence within group meetings, which occur daily, last as long as several hours, and which all students are required to attend. The focus of group meetings covers the whole range of life interactions within the school community. This varies from handling community logistics, to establishing and adjusting rules, to processing differences and broadening awareness of other's experience, to processing/supporting/witnessing adolescent's individual life struggles, to addressing disciplinary issues, even deciding when to end the meetings. The staff sets rules concerning health and safety, with student input. However, the adolescents have a much larger role in establishing any other rules. Not only do they have the opportunity and right to initiate discussion and contribute to the awareness of the need for rules and to help shape their form, but in addition they must each give their consent in order for rules to be enacted. And rules and schedules change as the needs of students and staff change, often on a daily basis. Further, the great majority of decisions within the group are determined through this same consensual process in which all students and staff have a voice. Relational awareness, individual responsibility, and the development of intimacy that these facilitate are core themes that transcend group interactions.

Let's look at a simple example of how this network of consensual decision-making provides a forum for adolescents to experiment with voicing their yearnings for connection both in terms of their own needs and in terms of how they want to take care of their community, testing out in both cases whether it is possible that people are interested in what is important to them. This example occurred during the consensus taking to terminate a meeting. The consensus process started as usual with one student saying, "I propose for unanimous consent of the group that we terminate this meeting and maintain confidentiality about all personal matters that were talked about here." He then said, "yes," as his own vote on the issue. Successive students and staff then expressed their "yes" as the process made its way around the circle. About one-quarter of the way around Lisa said, "yes" and with a smile on her face looked at Chuck and said further, "you're a liar." Chuck responded quickly in a curious tone asking Lisa why she had said he was a liar. But she refused to tell him, again with a smile on her face. It appeared that she had risked as much as she could in revealing what was important to her. The consensual process continued to go around the room until another student, Mary said, "No! I've got to find out why he is a liar." Mary said she would not say "yes" to the consensus until Lisa answered. With this support Lisa was willing to say more. She recounted, off-handedly with a smile, that Chuck had told her several weeks ago that he would show her his house but had not done so. Lisa, who will openly tell you that she does not trust adults (understandable considering that she never knew her father, her mother was a drug addict who abandoned her at an early age, and she has been passed from foster home to foster home since then), said that it didn't really matter to her; it was just important that she learned that Chuck was a liar. Of course it is only when something matters that people will feel the sting and experience the shame that goes with not being wanted. But her exposure of her yearning, even in this guarded form, afforded an opportunity for Chuck to apologize and say that he had just been busy and he still wanted very much to show Lisa his house and that he would do that. Lisa seemed markedly relieved.

This is among the lighter moments that occur at the Academy. There are certainly myriad examples that occur in which kids explore whether others are interested in their voice in much more intense ways. But this example illustrates the importance of the subtleties of adolescent's exploration of whether they belong. It illustrates both an adolescent probing as to whether others are interested in connecting with her as a person (Lisa in this example), and an adolescent exploring whether others value her caring of her community (Mary in this example). This example also captures the delicacy of this process, and the energy that the staff at the Academy devote to hearing adolescents' developing voices; the group meeting in this example would not have been adjourned until Mary said "yes." In addition this example portrays the understanding the staff of the Academy possess of the relational balance and interdependence between the individual and the community in which the ability of each to thrive is dependent on the health of the other. Again, this awareness lies at the heart of the relational ethic.

Setting Limits Relationally

Limiting setting is an integral part of running any adolescent treatment program. Adolescence is a time when even "normal" kids experiment with the rules. Adolescents at the Kanner Academy, who all enter with some version of an individualist paradigm belief system, often experiment even more. Remember that these are kids who are in various stages of exploring whether a relational paradigm belief system is really possible. Depending on their progress, they are likely to resort to their individualist paradigm strategies in times of uncertainty, vulnerability or even times that have become habitual, in effect testing out their individualist paradigm assumptions during times of relational uncertainty. Thus limit setting is important. How, when and what limits are set are equally, if not more, important as these determine whether the exercise of limiting setting merely reenforces adolescents's beliefs that the world is unfair and they must continue their survival strategies, only with more camouflage, or whether instead limiting setting becomes an opportunity to touch the camouflaged parts of these adolescents that yearn for a relational field. Let's listen to what Chuck says about his underlying philosophy that guides limit setting at the Academy:

> Kids at school do things I don't like from time to time, things that can be considered disrespectful, inappropriate, or even dangerous for me, the staff, other students or themselves. For example, during the first year of our residential program three students left the dorm in the middle of the night and stole my van so they could go out and find some pot to smoke. A few days later when they told us what they had done, I had many options in dealing with their behavior from throwing them out of school to calling the police. When dealing with any behavior I always try to imagine how I would want to be treated or how I would want to treat my own kids. Not how I actually treat my own child but what I would want objectively. I also try to keep a sense of respect for differences and an

openness to the motivational possibilities behind actions. Each one of us is different, and the possibilities that might answer "why" we do or say certain things are so vast that they are often hard to imagine or to understand. Were these kids rebelling against a sense of authority, or attempting to symbolically get closer to me by using my van, or were they just engaged in an ill conceived joy ride? Again the possibilities are limitless and sometimes unknowable. The only solution is to be in the relationship and work through the situation openly and honestly.

I began the process with these three students feeling angry. They stole my van! That was my reality. I remember at first, one of the student's attitude was summed up in his off hand remark of, "so what," which you will hear a lot from most kids in this kind of situation. It was my response as a kid when confronted with something I did wrong and for which I wanted to avoid responsibility. Still to be on the receiving end of this attitude was even more aggravating. So, I began by expressing how displeased I was that they stole from me when we were developing a sense of mutual trust with each other, when they made certain commitments to me and said they could be trustworthy. These were not new students; they had been in the residential program for about 8 months. I described how I felt hurt and disregarded, and how I wasn't willing to be in a relationship in which I am honest and trusting, and they are not. I reminded them that if they were to get into an accident and hurt someone, just how destructive that could be to them, our community, and me and my family, possibly for the rest of our collective lives. I also explained the reality of stealing in the world, including the societal response to stealing, which of course is jail. They needed to hear my true feelings, the safety issues and also to experience how they affected me and in turn how our relationship affects US. At the same time, although they had done something that was injurious to our relationship, I was not going to take my feelings in the direction of further rupture between us. Radical relational responsibility means moving into the relationship instead of away from it in times of crisis. I take responsibility for trusting them and being hurt and angry.

At this point I stopped and gave time for our relationship to take shape as we sat together. One by one as we sat each became grounded in our relationship and started to figure out how to work things out with me.

The next step is then, what is the consequence? The difference between a punishment and a consequence is that a consequence has a logical connection to the issues at hand. I didn't take Nintendo or their TV privileges from them as that would have no connection to our relationship and what had happened between us. Doing anything that makes them unhappy in hopes it will deter them from acting out in the future is punishment. All parents with troubled kids will tell you punishment does not change their children's behavior.

On the other hand with the notion of a consequence, I try to address what adolescents' actions indicate about their lack of relational competence. What did they not understand about what trust means, what patterns of behavior and disruptions in contact are they experiencing that keep them from feeling good about being responsible for who they are. And instead of just moving on, how do I underline and support the need for that relational learning?

In the end, the consequence I chose for these kids was that they would not be allowed to leave campus at all until I could believe they wouldn't steal or smoke pot. I believed that this goal was within their developmental ability. And I took a privilege from them that would help them focus on this task, one that was directly connected to their actions and to me. There was no arbitrary time limit set for this consequence. I would allow them to go out again when I felt we had worked out our relationships to the point where I could trust them.

At this point I am always asked by parents, "How do you know when it is time to let them move on?" My answer is: when you can look your child in the face, meet in some honest, intimate, relational way, and believe they understand what you want and/or need, when you have built up the relationship, restoring trust and honesty. When adolescents experience a mutual, intimate relationship with you, they will most often feel badly about hurting you, if nothing else. And with the right structure or holding, they will come to address how they have hurt you. This is the core of what we are doing at Kanner Academy. The reason these children never stole from me again was because of the relationship we built together. They didn't want to steal from someone they trusted and loved and who they knew loved them. They had experienced the basis of a mutual relationship, namely the intimate connection between us, and hence they had a basis for developing responsibility. They still may want to go out and smoke pot and steal the van but they won't because of our close mutually invested relationship.

The relational, intersubjective quality of the disciplinary/limit setting process to which Chuck refers here is again something that stands out when you visit the Academy. When Chuck and other staff confront kids about their behavior, it is not a challenge around being bad but around developing an awareness that this is the kid's community. And because the kids sense the possibility of real relationships, you can see them take in the challenges to them, at the pace they can bear, and struggle with how their current experience doesn't fit with the harsh, individualist paradigm lessons of their past. Depending on how well an adolescent has learned the rules of his/her individualist past experience (how strong his/her belief system has become that it is not possible to belong) this may be a slow process. But again, it would not be possible without the present possibility of the real relationships offered at Kanner Academy.

Relational Limiting Setting Structures

In the interest of not having to always start from scratch in responding to an adolescent's off balance condition and behavior, the community at Kanner Academy have forged and adopted a set of structures that stress relational support as well as limits. These structures, which emphasize the Academy's philosophy of relational limit setting, are in a constant state of evolution as the needs of the individuals within the community and the needs of the community at large changes. Let's review a few of these relational limit setting structures.

First, while all adolescents, and staff, are held responsible for their behavior, there is a recognition that these are kids who are in varying stages of developing the ability to respond responsibly. And it is important to have expectations that match an adolescent's ability to respond. Thus there are progressive "levels" of responsibility and privilege through which the students progress during their stay at the Academy. All adolescents are placed in an entry "level" when they enter the Academy, in which they are expected only to be working on being responsible for their own behavior. Elevation to successive "levels" is determined by consensus vote of faculty and students who have attained equal or higher "level" status. As students progress through the levels, they are expected to be progressively more aware of the needs and experience of others and to have this reflected in their interactions and leadership with others. In the final level, students are invited to attend staff meetings and to be a voice for their fellow students' needs and perspectives.

Second, a basic relational structure that supports the students during limit setting is the process of "buddying." From a relational ethic perspective, when an adolescent acts out it means that he/she has lost, for a time, the possibility of relational connection and has moved into his/her individualist paradigm survival strategies. At such times kids need support for the possibility of relational connection, not structures that will isolate them further such as timeouts in a room by themselves. Thus the first part of any disciplinary process at Kanner Academy is for adolescents to be given more relational support, not less. This is often accomplished, in part, through the process of "buddying," in which an adolescent who has acted out must ask another adolescent, of the same or higher level, to "take his/her buddy" (i.e., to be with him/her as a buddy, which means that the adolescent will have a companion of his choosing be within arm's length during his/her time of being off-balance relationally).

A number of the limit setting structures employed at the Academy use "buddying" as a first step. As an example, "expulsion" is invoked when kids resort to physically aggressive behavior such as hitting or kicking, but also might include verbally aggressive behavior such as calling another adolescent a "faggot." Expulsion is an on-campus process. It starts with a staff member or another student bringing an incident to the attention of the group during a group meeting. There must be a consensus from the group, including a "yes" vote by the supposed offending adolescent himself/herself, that "expulsion" is warranted in order for an adolescent to be "expelled." The first consequences of being "expelled" are that the adolescent no longer has a vote in the group, and he/she must be "buddied." Once "expelled," an adolescent is no longer considered to be a regular member in the community. At the same time, expelled adolescents are not separated from the community. They are not deprived of relationship. Instead they are given support in repairing the relational rupture their actions have caused. In fact, one of the main consequences of this procedure is for them to be given more relationship.

When they are ready, "expelled" adolescents must ask for time in their group meeting to talk about what they did. They cannot proceed until the trust of the community is restored in them, until the people in their group come to feel that the "expelled" adolescent will make a different choice in the future around his/her behavior. Once a sense of trust is restored in the community, the "expelled" adolescent then needs to propose a project he/she will complete to give something back to the community and obtain consensus approval from the group for his/her proposed project. The project may be anything from cleaning a room to building something to fixing something. Finally, after the adolescent completes the project, consensus approval must be given by the group in order for the adolescent's group membership and privileges to be fully reinstated.

It is worth mentioning one last limit-setting structure, that also derives from the relational ethic. This is the process of "physical holding." Occasionally adolescents become physically aggressive in a manner in which they can not control themselves. In such instances they need to be restrained, and are held in a position, usually lying on the floor, that is most safe and comfortable for them and others under the circumstances. The Academy adds another dimension to this limit setting structure, a structure that is employed at many adolescent treatment centers. It emphasizes the relational aspects of this process by having other adolescents do the holding. Adolescents are trained in how to hold down a member of their community, who needs such a restraint, in a manner that is safe and caring, of themselves as well as the person being held. Thus off-balance adolescents get to experience the support of their peers in this process and are less likely to project, or to project for as long a time, that the action is simply the result of an unjust authority figure that is taking advantage of them. In addition employment of this structure gives the students that are doing the holding the opportunity to relate to someone who is out of control, in a nurturant manner. This not only is a further message that their nurturance is needed, but it also can facilitate an internal dialogue in them that can have a healing effect on the part of them that could get out of control. This structure is so effective in helping kids calm down that occasionally adolescents ask to be held down in this manner on their own, when they are agitated and do not know how to control themselves.

Again note that, in accordance with our relational ethic, problematic behavior at Kanner Academy results in increased relationship through the exercise of these structures, not decreased relationship. Also remember that these limiting setting structures are an attempt to not always be recreating the wheel. However, they are only as good as they apply to the circumstances of the moment. As such they are not cut in stone and they evolve as needed.

Community in Action - Commitment to Relational Resolution

The heart of this relational building process that we have been describing is community. It is the basic foundation of all that happens at Kanner Academy and the embodiment of the relational ethic in helping the troubled adolescents in attendance there. It is the primary medium through which the birthing of voices occurs, limits are set, connection is made, awareness gained and responsibility built. To get a further glimpse of the interrelated complexity of the community process at the Academy, which can at times appear from the outside to be chaos or anarchy, let's again listen as Chuck recalls a specific group experience:

> It's a Thursday afternoon about 1:30. And 65 of us are sitting together upstairs in the group meeting room. I'm not sure whether you can really imagine a circle of kids and faculty, most of us with our backs pressed to the wall, shoulder to shoulder all the way around the room, which is about 25 ft. by 42 ft. in size. The students range in age from about 9 to 18 years old. There are about six faculty members present, including myself. Some of the younger students are sitting on the floor, facing the center of the circle. A few other students are sitting in front of faculty members. Some of these because they have special needs. For example, the only way Jake, who has experienced extensive sexual abuse, can sit calmly is to have his head rubbed as he sits. But in general, we try to help kids through what can sometimes be very long meetings. And this meeting has already lasted five hours.
>
> At any given moment in school life, things can seem crazy, frustrating and unproductive. This is one of them. The room is noisy, side conversations abound; so it is difficult for even those who want to focus on the dialogue in the main group to do so. Faculty are looking at each other, thinking "do we do something or let the kids figure it out?" And this is always the dilemma. Do we let them struggle or do we be more active. When all of a sudden, Joseph, who is fourteen years old yells, "Quiet! Quiet! Everyone Shut up! I have the floor." Everyone looks at the "Jester," who is the group facilitator for this meeting, a position which changes and which is filled through consensus, every meeting. Joseph continues as the group starts to quiet, "I think if you curse or say anything hurtful you should have to go back to the farm (the residential setting) and spend the night, and your parents will have to come and participate in morning group while you try to get back into school."
>
> Our efforts this day were focused on trying to figure out how to stop the use of the very filthy language that over time had become so commonplace in our everyday

conversations and interaction. I can't really remember how our quest to address this issue started. It could have been a kid who initiated the discussion. Or perhaps a parent complained about his/her child's disrespectful, inappropriate language, or possibly a faculty member brought it up simply because he/she had heard enough bad language and thought it was time to stop school, get together as a community and figure it out. Whatever the path of initiation, the problem had become rampant and we were now facing it, and we had been here for a long time. Everybody was fidgeting--most were talking to their neighbors, feeling overwhelmed. Not that ninety percent of the group didn't get it by this time. They did. After hours of back and forth—"What's bad language?" "What is hurtful?" "Is damn a swear?" And more refined discussions about whether the standard is different for older kids than younger, followed by additional explorations such as—"What if the only way I can express myself is to be profane?" At this point it was not solely the faculty that were drawing the line. Many students had come to understand the seriousness of the issue and also wanted a solution. And students also knew that our time together would be focused on this issue until it was resolved. So there was a growing number who wanted to figure it out simply because they wanted to get out of here and move on, and not be back tomorrow doing it all over again.

This last point is important. Being committed relationally means being willing to spend the time that is necessary for relational resolution. I tell students something Dolores Johnson used to tell me when I was in detention at age 12. I would do my dance and freak out and she would sit me down and tell me, "your time is my time, and my time is your time, and our time is all the time. So whenever you are ready... I'm here for the duration." Thus in meetings such as this, kids know that I and the rest of the faculty are willing to sit here forever until we can come to a consensus about how we are not going to hurt each other.

So here we were frustrated and angry with no real idea of where to go next. After five hours we were all saying things like, "just consenting that we will stop won't change things." My favorite is "we'll expel them persona-non-grata, if they don't stop fuckin' cursing." Of course in that case, the faculty would be there all by ourselves. On the other hand, I'm sure over time every faculty member has also cursed about something. So here we were, stuck. When all of a sudden Joseph shouted his proposal as if it was a proclamation. Now Joseph is one of those really truly sweet kids, who cuddles with his mom at 14, but will ride that edge of misbehaving if it will make him more popular. In mainstream environments he spent most of his time trying to figure out how not to get picked on. However, here where we have a forum to address such interactions, the other kids have come to know him in a fuller way, and in situations such as this they respect him. So when he stands up and speaks, people pay attention. I remember Christine, a level 3, jumping right in, saying, "right on!" It wasn't 15 minutes later that that meeting ended. Joseph invited a final resolution with, "I would like to take a consensus that if you curse or you use your movements or gestures to be hurtful, you'll spend the night... YES!" And around the room it went. "Yes," "yes," "yes," "yes,"... The whole room was in the same place.

The use of filthy language and gestures decreased rapidly in the days following that meeting. I believe that it decreased not just because we had found a consequence that was severe enough, but because the solution came from the community. It is important that we as a community are able to set limits and structures that get followed. However, it is even more important that we help kids become connected, develop an ability to respond to their own and other's needs and in the process develop a sense of their value to others, their relational abilities, and of belonging.

Wrapping Up

Kanner Academy's approach with adolescents is the embodiment of the relational ethics that derive from Gestalt field theory and more. Immersed in an environment that is committed to offering and developing honest, mutual relationships, kids come to understand that they matter and their voices are needed in order for the community to thrive. When they are off balance the community moves toward them rather than away from them, offering more relationship rather than isolation, with help to repair the relational as well as other damage they have caused. This is not an easy process. But the rewards are great.

There is much about the Kanner Academy that cannot be covered in the short space allotted here—such as what a relational approach means for supporting staff or working with parents, or the finer points of dealing with crises, birthing voices, and more. These will be the subject of an up coming book on the relational approach of Kanner Academy. A final word from Chuck:

> I owe many things to those that came before me. Homer Lane (1928) and A. S. Neill (1965) who pioneered the notion that punitive controlling authority would never really control or help troubled children, and that mutual responsibility and community could be healing. These results have also been seen in the "Therapeutic Communities" of Jones (1953) and De Leon (1997). What OUR program is and is becoming has been impacted by the notions contained in "Paradoxical Theory of Change" (Beisser, 1970), and the present moment dialogue and experimentation of Perls, Hefferline, & Goodman (1994). My life and experiences with Michael DeSisto (See DeSisto, 1991, for Michael's description of his work) and the DeSisto School, and the impact of Gestalt principals in my life at such an early age have all helped in forming and creating what Sarasota Community School is today. As we are all impacted by our collective histories and experiences, it would not do justice in describing the process at Kanner Academy to compare it to other programs or try to understand it in terms of past research or theoretical constructions. It is a lively program being recreated in every new moment by those engaged in the process of living it.

References

Bazeley, E. T. (1948). *Homer Lane and the Little Commonwealth*. London: Allen & Unwin.

Beisser, A. (1970). The paradoxical theory of change. In Fagan & Shepherd (Eds.), *Gestalt Therapy Now*. NY: Harper & Colophon Books.

Boring, E. G. (1950). *A History of Experimental Psychology, Second Edition*. NY: Appleton-Century-Crofts, Inc.

De Leon, G. (1997). *Community as Method*. Westport, CN: Praeger Publishers.

DiSisto, M. (1991). *Decoding Your Teenager*. New York: Morrow, William & Co.

Jones, M. (1953). *The Therapeutic Community: A New Treatment Method in Psychiatry*. New York: Basic Books.

Lane, H. (1928). *Talks to Parents and Teachers*. London: Allen & Unwin.

Neill, A. S. (1965). *Summerhill: A Radical Approach to Education*. London: Gollancz.

Perls, F., Hefferline, R., & Goodman, P. (1994). *Gestalt Therapy : Excitement and Growth in the Human Personality*. Highland, NY. The Gestalt Journal Press.

Wheeler, G. (2000). *Beyond Individualism: Toward a New Understanding of Self, Relationship, & Experience*. Hillsdale, NJ: The Analytic Press/GestaltPress.

Editor's Note:

Touch is a major foundational element in our shared human field, a means of communication that offers information unobtainable from other modalities, facilitating growth, stability and ongoing health. Accordingly, the relational messages of interest, caring, comfort, psychological holding, and safety, that stem from our ethical stance, are often best conveyed with the support of some form of touch. However, in the context of our touch-phobic, litigation-prone society, touch in psychotherapy is often considered to be taboo. And, of course, this taboo is not totally baseless as touch can also be injurious if intentionally or unintentionally misused. In the following chapter, Rebecca Murray, James Pugh, and Pauline Clance investigate this dilemma from a Gestalt field perspective, that implicitly contains a respect for the relational strivings of both patients/clients and therapists, restoring a major support for the field in general. They present us with guidelines for when and how touch is useful and warranted in our work with patients/clients, and when and how it is not. And they offer an alternative when the use of touch is not indicated.

6

••••••••••••••••••••••••••

The Ethics of Touch and Imagery in Psychotherapy: A Gestalt Resolution

Rebecca M. Murray

James L. Pugh

Pauline Rose Clance

The phrase "ethics of touch" implies that there are valid reasons both to touch a client in psychotherapy and to refrain from touching. A blanket prohibition requires no ethical guideline; the prohibition is straightforward, uncomplicated, and easily understood. When therapists are surveyed about their practices regarding touch, many report that they do not view touching clients as necessarily unethical (e.g., Pope et al., 1987). Nevertheless, in this age of increased litigation, therapists may be concerned not only about the therapeutic use of touch but about embracing clients or even offering a handshake. Cautiousness is reinforced by liability insurance forms that ask one to indicate whether or not touch is used with clients, and by continuing education in the area of ethics which are essentially "risk management" workshops that discourage therapists from any action that could lead to litigation. Corey, Corey and

Callanan (1998) discuss the present-day concerns about touch in their text on ethics in the helping professions. They note that, "With the current attention being given to sexual harassment and lawsuits over sexual misconduct in professional relationships, some counselors are likely to decide that it is not worth the risk of touching clients at all, lest their intentions be misinterpreted" (p. 256).

In considering an ethics of touch in psychotherapy, we will not directly examine concerns about lawsuits, not because such concerns are not relevant to the practicing clinician, but because self-protection is not at the heart of ethical decision making. The salient *ethical* question at hand is whether touch benefits or harms the client. Nevertheless, we understand the concerns that lead some to avoid touch in order to insulate themselves from legal repercussions, and our hope is that the ethical guidelines we propose here may allow one to engage in the critical thinking necessary to make sound clinical decisions about touch that will withstand malpractice claims.

Instead, we propose that blanket prohibitions against touch in psychotherapy could by themselves be unethical, given the therapeutic value of touch and the ethical mandate to uphold the welfare of the client. The issue of touch deserves thorough ethical analysis, and the Gestalt perspective, in particular, offers a potential resolution to the conflict about whether or not to touch clients. In cases when touch is deemed unethical, we propose an alternative that can harness some of the power of touch while minimizing negative effects. The ethics of this alternative will also be reviewed.

We begin by looking at our culture's attitudes about touch, the destructive impact those attitudes have on all of us, and how such norms influence therapists and clients in psychotherapy. The polarities of ethical positions on touch in therapy include the proscription on the one hand, and the prescription on the other. Hopefully, the resulting dialogue will provide a foundation for a Gestalt ethic of touch.

Society and Touch

An understanding of touch requires recognition of the meaning of touch in a particular society, not just in the abstract. American society can be seen as touch-phobic (Field, 2001). Interestingly, one may argue that a society like ours that allows a very limited range of touch is much more likely to have misunderstandings about the touch that occurs. When sexuality is one of the few situations when people, especially of the opposite sex, touch each other, it is much easier for people to make an attribution (or at least association) of sexuality to touch. Thus the fear that touching increases the risk of sexual stimulation may seem more valid in our society than in one in which people touch more freely in a greater variety of circumstances. Whatever the root of our phobic societal stance, Field speculated (as others have about psychotherapists in particular) that the contemporary anxiety about touch in our culture stems in part from the current trend of litigation over sexual misconduct. As a startling example of this sort of touch phobia, Field described a trend among day care centers to prohibit all touching of children by adults except in cases of obvious need or emergency (and not then unless the touch was unavoidable). Such excessive measures may be enacted more to protect the institution and workers than to protect the children, and Field argues that such measures are an extreme disservice to all of us. She reminds us that insufficient touch is life-threatening to infants, and cites researchers who suggest that a society deficient in touch may be more prone to violence. Additionally, clinicians of all orientations may also speculate about the emotional implications of touch phobia on the development and well-being of people.

Prescriptions for Touch

In a broad sense, touch is often regarded as a basic need that is rarely met to a sufficient degree in our society. Perhaps the most compelling reason for touching is that it is so basic to our well-being. Field (2001) has amassed an enormous amount of evidence of the importance and beneficial effect of touch. She pointed out that people in cultures that touch frequently display significantly less aggression than those in cultures that seldom touch, and she described one study which found significant correlations between lack of physical expression of affection toward the child and later expressions of violence as the child matured. No other cultural difference accounted for this finding. Field stated that "Like diet and exercise, people need a daily dose of touch" (p. x).

Prescriptions for Touch in Psychotherapy

Field's work looked at touch in society broadly, but also addressed the therapeutic value of touch. She and her colleagues noted, for example, a study of massage therapy for adolescents in a psychiatric facility in which those receiving massage showed better adjustment, improved sleep, and shorter hospital stays (Field, et al., 1992). Not surprisingly, the program was discontinued because of fears of sexual improprieties, and the additional concern that the adolescents were more self-disclosing during massage therapy than during psychotherapy. The physical touch seemed to facilitate self-disclosure. Similarly, O'Neil and Calhoun (1975) found fewer symptoms of senile dementia, such as memory deficits, irritability, and carelessness in personal habits, in older people who were touched frequently.

In terms of psychotherapy, there are two general senses in which touch may be prescribed. As a therapeutic intervention, it may be argued that touch can, in the right circumstances, be a powerful and effective intervention. Touch may be used to provide support, acceptance, and encouragement to clients who are confronting difficult or traumatic situations or memories. Raubolt (1985) pointed out that verbal support, in some instances, may be insufficient to help the person who is re-experiencing old hurts and traumas, and the therapist is ethically bound to provide whatever support is needed. Kepner (2001) believes that the therapist's warmth and acceptance may be communicated more strongly through touch than by any other means. He also pointed out that touch may be helpful to the client in integrating material experienced during abreactive experiences. Without the integration that touch can facilitate, a cathartic experience may simply be an isolated event that offers little opportunity for change.

Several therapeutic approaches employ either body work or role plays or both (Smith, 1998; Kepner, 2001). These therapeutic disciplines rely, in part, on the use of touch. Indeed, the role playing that is part of many orientations to group therapy involves touch among members, and perhaps even touch by the therapist. It would tax the imagination of the therapist to devise role plays that never involved touch by anyone. It would be difficult to carry out effectively therapeutic role plays while avoiding the use of touch.

Role plays often are used in expressive therapies, notably in approaches such as Gestalt Therapy, Psychodrama, and others (Kottler, 2002). During role plays, the client may experience having needs met symbolically. Many of these needs are difficult to convey without the use of touch. Indeed, one of the primary strengths of touch in psychotherapy is its power both to elicit childhood memories and ego states, and its ability to communicate powerfully and directly to someone who is in such a child ego state. Many therapists who describe working with the inner child find that touch is often the best way to reach the client who is in a child state. Many of these childhood states may be the remnants of experiences that were pre-verbal and may not be reached through verbal means. These "re-parenting" experiences often require touch if they are to occur at all.

Proscriptions Against Touch

While we emphasize again that therapist self-protection is not an ethical issue, the relation between touch and sexual fears may underlie many proscriptions. We have established that just like those in other sectors of our society, psychotherapists may, in part, avoid or limit touch for fear of sexual misconduct litigation. As we all know, sexual contact is prohibited by the ethical guidelines of the various mental health professions and if we adopt sanctions about touching there is, in effect, a double protection against sexual contact. Physical touch may lead to sexual arousal on the part of the therapist, the client, or both; so touching may very well be prohibited partly in an effort to preclude the arousal. Such a prohibition also offers a much clearer defense in legal situations; if you did not touch the client, you surely did not have sex with the client. Furthermore, while touching might be interpreted as sexual behavior, lack of touch makes it difficult to prove a case against the clinician. Other forms of behavior, especially body language (smiling, eye contact, tone of voice) may be considerably more flirtatious than many forms of touch, but they are much harder to prove in court.

According to Pope, Keith-Spiegel, and Tabachnick (1986), many therapists acknowledge that sexual interest between therapist and client occurs, and yet over half of the respondents in their study reported never having received any training in how to deal with sexual attraction in therapy. We speculate that this lack of education and awareness may lead to unnecessary sanctions against touch. Pope, Sonne, and Holroyd (1993) pointed out that it is difficult for therapists to appropriately address sexual feelings in therapy if those feelings are forbidden and misunderstood. Indeed, therapists interviewed for their study indicated that they responded to sexual feelings in therapy with (among other reactions) shock, guilt, anxiety, confusion, and fear of losing control. In contrast, O'Shea (2000) found that when therapist trainees were given support to voice their sexual feelings toward each other, they became much more comfortable with such feelings in general, and there was much less sexual acting out in the training program.

The therapist has the responsibility of maintaining boundaries and insuring that sexual feelings do not lead to sexual behavior, and it may be the presumed link between sexual feelings and behavior that makes touching seem so risky. The reality of this risk has not been adequately demonstrated. It is certainly counter to what O'Shea found with trainees. In the only study of this kind we are aware of with practicing therapists, Holroyd and Brodsky (1980) found that older and more experienced therapists were less likely to engage in touch that leads to intercourse. Additionally, an analysis of therapist responses to Holroyd and Brodsky's questionnaire indicated that touch itself did not lead to sexual misconduct, but therapist who made a practice of touching only opposite-sex clients were at risk of sexual impropriety.

Part of the concerns about sexual arousal may derive from the ease with which touch can be misunderstood. Touch is a very powerful form of communication, but it is much less precise than verbal communication. When you touch someone, you communicate something very strongly, but what (Smith, 1998)? Clarity of communication is increased by timing (Geib, 1998), context (Geib, 1998; Horton, 1998; Kertay & Reviere, 1998; Smith, 1998), and by linking the touch with verbal communication (Geib, 1998; Horton, 1998; Smith, 1998), and especially by getting informed consent to touch (Geib, 1998; Smith, 1998). There is no doubt, though, that touch by itself does carry some risk of miscommunication.

Aside from sexual concerns, touch may be proscribed because of the fear that it will arouse strong emotions. On the one hand, it is argued that touch can arouse powerful emotions in the client. Touch may also be used to *soothe* a client's intense feelings, Kertay & Reviere, 1998). Triplett and Arneson (1979) found that children given verbal and physical comforting were better comforted than those receiving verbal comforting only. In adults, it has been argued that touch may afford the client relief from intense feelings without the client's having to grapple with those emotions (Smith, 1998). The issue of soothing emotions seems related to the concern that touch would gratify the client and encourage dependency, although Milakovich (1998) cites the need for gratification in some clients, stating that for clients with deficit-based pathology, gratification of previously unmet needs may be therapeutic. Other clinicians, however, regard their task as one of discouraging any dependency on themselves and encouraging the client to learn how to satisfy their own needs. Perls (1969) described the importance of frustrating the client's efforts at manipulating the therapist into taking care of her. The ideal was to help the client to stand on her own two feet, to learn to meet her own needs through direct contact with the environment.

Many of the sanctions associated with touch have more to do with how one touches than with whether one touches. One particular danger can occur when the therapist touches in a way that treats the client as an object rather than as an individual person. Touching the client in a "matter-of-fact" way can be an unpleasant, even traumatic experience for the client. Kepner (2001) pointed out that to touch the client in a way that objectifies the body can lead the client to experience alienation from his own body. Even though the therapist may have had the best of motives in touching the client, in such an instance the effect of the touch could be quite destructive. Geib (1998) found that therapists who had experienced negative touch in their own therapy reported that their therapists had been insensitive to clients' reaction to the touch and had failed to discuss the touch with the clients. Geib also reported that some of the therapists interviewed said that the touch was inappropriate to where they were in the therapy process, again suggesting insensitivity, lack of communication, and poor timing. Horton (1998) surveyed clients about their experience of touch and found a great deal of overlap with the results of Geib's work.

The Dilemma

We all face a social dilemma, and therapists face an additional practical dilemma. The social dilemma is that an enormous body of evidence supports the importance, even necessity of touch for human communication and well-being. Yet American society traditionally has been touch phobic and appears to be becoming more so. This trend toward less touch exists despite the inclusion in this country of people from cultural backgrounds who touch naturally and without concern. It should be noted, as do Clance and Petra (1998), that for clients and therapists who are not "Anglo," touch in therapy may not necessarily pose a dilemma. For example, a Latina therapist they interviewed noted that to not touch her Latino clients would be odd and likely perceived negatively.

Nevertheless, for the majority of therapists, using touch is challenging the social norms. To change our perception and use of touch would be to change the society in which we live. Not to touch is to give tacit support to the touch fears and touch deprivation that characterize our society. As we raise our clients' awareness of their need for touch, we also raise their awareness of our society's limitation. This consciousness-raising is a political act.

The therapist faces the additional practical dilemma that touch can be a useful and powerful intervention. Touch, which has the power both to arouse and relieve strong emotions, would seem to be more of an asset than a liability. Yet, as we have discussed, touch also carries with it considerable risk for both the client and the therapist. Risks related to miscommunication, unwanted sexual arousal, objectification, dependency gratification and the like should not be ignored. The dilemma is perhaps best summarized as involving the violation of social norms and the risks of therapeutic error on the one hand, counterposed with the desire to facilitate change via an extremely powerful method on the other. Simply to dismiss an intervention of the magnitude of touch would seem to be a great loss.

The Gestalt Resolution

It would seem that use of touch should be encouraged rather than prohibited if the clinician can use touch with the right people, at the right time, in the appropriate manner. Avoiding touch with clients is an unfortunate stance to adopt not only because physical contact can be so therapeutic, but also because it is quite possible to engage in critical thinking about the use of touch such that the decision to touch a client can be theoretically and ethically grounded. The Gestalt perspective, which provides a guideline for how this might be accomplished, can be summarized as follows.

Positive touch is a very basic need (Harlow, 1959). Infants who do not receive adequate touch may have impaired attachment to their caregivers, and may fail to thrive (Field & Schanberg, 1990). The need for touch remains powerful throughout life, and Field (2001) has described evidence for the beneficial effects of touch throughout the lifespan. Our society is touch-deprived and seems to be growing increasingly so. As a result, most of us have difficulty meeting our touch needs adequately. Lack of touch may become a powerful form of unfinished business for many people, but it is also a source of conflict because of the powerful social prohibitions against touch. The need may therefore fail to become figural for many. Those individuals who do succeed in becoming aware of the depth of this need may then seek out therapy or other experiences to rectify this deficiency, but many are likely to remain unaware of their touch needs (Geib 1998; Milakovich,1998). Touch by a therapist may help this need to become figural, enabling the client to move forward in the contact-withdrawal cycle in order to meet this need. If other blocks occur in this cycle, other interventions may be necessary, but if the need fails to become figural, no movement will be possible.

Gestalt field theory recognizes that any organism and environment are interrelated. I am not the air that I breathe, but at any time that air is, in fact, a part of my biological organism, and without that air I would cease to exist. Breathing also illustrates another characteristic of field theory, the notion that the field always is in flux. My relation to the air around (and within) me is changing perpetually; in fact, stasis would result in death. Both of these principles apply to human relationships within the field as well. As Lee (lead chapter in this book) puts it, "'Self' and 'other' are always interdependent. In fact, from this perspective, the concept of 'self' is a misnomer. We cannot have a concept of 'self' without an attached concept of 'other'" (pp. 13-14). In Gestalt theory, the contact boundary is where exchanges occur between "self" and "other," allowing the individual to organize her field, which is the totality of "self" and environment. In breathing, the primary contact boundary is in the lungs, where oxygen and carbon dioxide are exchanged. In human relationships, several different contact boundaries are possible, including the purely symbolic boundary of language. However, the very term "contact boundary" suggests the possibility of physical contact, with the boundary being the skin, which as Field (2001) pointed out, is the largest organ of the body. If, indeed, we do organize our self system through contact with the other, then physical contact can play a very powerful role in that process. Lack of touch could contribute to a person's sense of self as "untouchable," leading to what Smith (1998) has described as the development of character, a static perception of self, in this case as negative, undesirable, and unlovable. While it is possible to help the client to de-construct this self-concept through purely verbal means, a more direct approach would be to offer a new kind of contact at the boundary that would necessitate reorganizing the field, primarily through physical contact.

An Ethical Taxonomy

Gestalt therapist and theorist Edward Smith developed a taxonomy to guide therapists who wish to use touch through an ethical decision-making process regarding the merit of such action (Smith, 1998). Smith's model begins with an acknowledgment of the sort of therapist touch that is clearly taboo (i.e., sexual and hostile/aggressive touch), and then focuses on the many forms of touch that can take place between therapist and client that are not explicitly prohibited. Such touch may range from inadvertent physical contact with a client to the intentional use of touch as a therapeutic technique.

Smith (1998) emphasized that the ethical therapist must consider three important factors when deciding whether or not to touch a client. First, the long-known wisdom that the message sent is not necessarily the message received. Second, that one must understand the cultural relativity and meaning of the touch; and third, that one should bear in mind that communication through touch is more ambiguous than verbal communication and generally more powerful. With these factors in awareness, the therapist must then base the decision to touch a client on both theoretical and ethical considerations. From a theoretical perspective, Smith asks us to question whether or not our orientation supports the use of physical contact or offers a rule or guideline against such action. Ethically, he challenges us to consider: 1) whether or not we have adequate theoretical grounding and training in the technique of touch we wish to employ; 2) if the touch is ego-syntonic with us; and 3) if our best judgment indicates that the touch is congruent with the client's therapeutic needs at this time.

Evoking elegant decision-making paradigms such as this, coupled with informed client consent, allow the therapist to engage in touch with clients that is ethical and therapeutically valid. Following is an example of the therapeutic use of touch with a client for whom touch was deemed ethical.

A Case Example of Ethical Touch

Olivia began the session lamenting her ongoing depression,

explaining, "I have everything I've ever wanted, in abundance, and yet I can't feel it. I feel locked out of the joy of my own existence." As she spoke she gestured in front of herself, put her hands out and said, "It's as if the beauty of my life is out there, just out of my reach, and I'm stuck back here unable to touch it." As the session progressed, and Olivia spoke more about being unable to "feel and touch" her life, she continued to put her hands out like a mime delineating a wall. Her therapist, responding to Olivia's hands pushing against empty space, considered the possible benefit of touching Olivia's hands with his own. He wanted to allow her to more fully explore the action and energy in her hands, arms and body, and to give her interaction and engagement in the field.

Making the Ethical Decision to Touch

Harkening back to Smith's (1998) taxonomy, Olivia's therapist decided to initiate touch. This decision was founded on Gestalt theory and training, coupled with the judgment that such touch would be beneficial at the moment and comfortable to initiate (i.e., *ego-syntonic*). The therapist asked Olivia if she would like to try touching the palms of his hands with her own (*informed consent*). She considered this invitation for a moment, began pushing with energy against the empty space in front of her and responded, "Yes, I'd like to try that." Their hands made contact. His touch was solid but gentle, and as she pushed he provided a flexible limit. Their contact became a sort of fluid dance, with the therapist responding to her need for coming forward and pulling back.

The therapist conceptualized Olivia's depression as stemming from self-interruption in the contact/withdrawal cycle (Smith, 1985). Olivia was aware of her desire for contact with her environment, but tended to block and retroflect her arousal and emotion, thereby fueling the longing, despair and sadness she had felt for many years. Working from this frame of reference, her therapist tailored his touch (pressure, resistance, push) to metaphorically mirror the emotional and physical contact Olivia craved. Touching between them allowed Olivia to experience being met, engaged, and allowed to explore without being stifled or forced to conform.

While continuing the touch experiment, they explored her experience. Olivia began to cry without knowledge of what induced her tears. Eventually she began to articulate the pain she felt at feeling blocked from making full emotional contact with her self and her life. She sobbed as she was flooded with memories of being "under Mother's thumb," and taught to disconnect from all intense feelings. As Olivia spoke, she enacted the content of her memories with her hands. She continued to test the experience of touching, becoming more playful and enjoying the freedom of expression. Suddenly Olivia's tears began to flow again, and she said, "I wish I could live my life like this, being able to push out and have someone there to push back without pushing me over or forcing me to push harder than I want to."

Olivia was expressing the motivation behind her self-interruption and the satisfaction she felt in making contact. Only providing insight about this pattern is not likely to facilitate change in Olivia as dramatically as enactment and corrective experience. Her therapist's touch provided the experiential component necessary for a powerful therapeutic exchange. The interplay of hands allowed Olivia to more fully express her (largely unconscious) conflict of needing and wanting contact but interrupting her desire. The intentional, theory-driven, touch intervention on the part of her therapist heightened Olivia's conflict and then provided her a corrective experience.

Indeed, at the beginning of the subsequent session Olivia said, "The memory of moving my hands with yours has stayed with me. That interaction with you says it all. I stifle myself from fully experiencing my life because I fear that I'll either reach out to find nothing or that when I reach out I'll get dominated and pushed back. Moving my hands with yours was a wonderful, deeply emotional, experience for me. I remember the initial fear, and then the pleasure of being able to have my power while you had yours too." While this insight and experience could conceivably be facilitated without touch, it is difficult to imagine a more expedient and powerful intervention.

A Case Example of Touch Deemed Unethical

Despite the creative and dynamic potential for the successful and ethical use of touch in psychotherapy there are times, such as with the client we'll call Connie, when touch may be counterproductive and therefore unethical.

Connie first initiated therapy when she was 23 because she recognized that the sequellae from the childhood sexual abuse she experienced by her father were greatly impairing her functioning. She had the classic symptoms of posttraumatic stress disorder (PTSD) related to sexual trauma. After six years of individual and then group therapy, Connie was relatively symptom-free and had established a life she enjoyed. Four years after the termination of treatment, Connie was robbed at gunpoint. The circumstances and aftermath of the traumatic experience were in many ways a recapitulation of her earlier trauma. Her PTSD symptoms returned and she again entered therapy, this time not only to address the experience of the robbery, but to work through the unmanageable abuse flashbacks, feelings and memories that had resurfaced.

As therapy progressed, Connie focused more and more on her original trauma. She gradually began to integrate the affect associated with being a traumatized, lonely, desperate child who would try to escape her father by spending as much time as possible in an abandoned shed on her parent's property. As Connie adopted more of a child ego state in session, she struggled with the intense guilt and indefatigable self-hatred so common in survivors. Connie would frequently see the image of herself as a young girl hiding in the shed. She reported that, in the image, the girl was huddled in a corner, frightened and crying. Connie was captivated by this image but unable to engage in any sort of experiential enactment, in large part because her self-loathing prevented her from being able to tolerate any contact with the girl in the image. Connie would make remarks such as, "She's disgusting, I don't want anything to do with her."

Making the Ethical Decision to Avoid Touch

Touch with people whose childhood experiences included physical or sexual abuse is controversial. Many therapists report that they never touch clients who suffered such abuse, and the fear that is often expressed is that touch by the therapist may re-traumatize the client. Milakovich (1998), however, surveyed therapists about their use of touch in therapy and found that many who had themselves experienced childhood abuse deliberately sought therapy experiences involving touch and reported that being touched by their therapists was a significant part of the healing experience. Many expressed their sense of yearning for safe, appropriate touch and the relief they felt when that need was met. Traumatic touch in these cases seemed to be healed by therapeutic touch. In summary, touch in therapy with abuse survivors is not strictly taboo, yet extreme caution and careful decision making are required before touch is broached (Geib, 1998; Horton, 1998; Milakovich; Smith Lawry, 1998).

In the case of Connie, her therapist determined that to touch the client would be detrimental, and yet the client (in both her adult and child ego state) clearly needed contact, nurturance and containment. The power of literal touch cannot be equaled, yet under circumstances like that with Connie, touch would be unethical. Following Smith's (1998) taxonomy, touch with Connie would be risky since she: 1) may not have the ego strength to receive the message as it was sent; 2) seemed immersed in the experience of an abusive "culture" where touch has a largely pejorative meaning; and 3) was therefore quite likely to misinterpret the communication intended by the touch. Despite the therapist's theoretical grounding and training, and her ego-syntonic wish, she judged touching to be incongruent with Connie's therapeutic needs at the time. In summary, literal touch was deemed unethical. Yet, not to facilitate contact in the field was also judged to be counterproductive. As an alternative, Connie's therapist stayed at the level of imagery and facilitated contact in the image.

Imagery: The therapeutic alternative

Virtually every form of psychotherapy incorporates the use of imagery, ranging from such techniques as cognitive/behavioral desensitization and performance enhancement to Gestalt dialoguing and psychodynamic techniques for working with memories (Arbuthnott, Arbuthnott & Rossiter, 2001a). The use of imagery has, however, been examined recently by researchers such as Paddock, Noel, Terranova, Eber, Manning, and Loftus (1999) who question the ethics of imagery and guided visualization in therapy. They presented laboratory evidence to suggest that imagery is a powerful technique that can easily lead to the phenomenon of imagination inflation (i.e., false memories).

Paddock, et al. (1999) asked volunteers to rate their confidence about whether or not various events on an inventory had happened to them prior to age 10. A week later, participants engaged in a guided imagery exercise in which selected events from the inventory were embedded. Afterwards, participants were again given the inventory of life events and asked to rate their confidence about each event having actually happened to them as a child. Results indicated that the guided imagery experience tended to increase participants' confidence that certain events had taken place in their childhood, even when they had previously denied having experienced those events. Paddock et al. acknowledged that their work is laboratory based and not necessarily analogous to clinical practice, but nevertheless conclude that their results "should give clinicians considerable pause" (p. 590). They ended their article with the following statement:

> The central finding of this study, a reminder once again about the malleability of memory and individual differences in susceptibility to suggestion, should encourage psychotherapists of all theoretical outlooks to proceed in a scientifically informed manner. Psychotherapy may well be an art, but it must be informed by research on basic psychological processes (p. 591).

Paddock et al. (1999) suggested directions for future research into imagination inflation. Arbuthnott et al. (2001b) and Enns (2001) acknowledged the importance of laboratory findings and the ethical implications of imagination inflation, but emphasized that abandoning or unnecessarily curtailing imagery techniques that have been shown to be effective would also be unethical. To summarize the debate, the therapeutic use of imagery appears to be most problematic when used to uncover or resolve traumatic memories. It is generally recommended that clinicians avoid or cautiously use this application of imagery (Enns, 2001). Furthermore, when using imagery for other purposes it is recommended that the clinician take precautions to minimize imagination inflation and memory misattribution. Such precautions include: informed consent about memory and memory fallibility; considering client factors such as level of suggestibility and tendency to dissociate before engaging in imagery work (Enns); and using metaphorical imagery and fantastical elements in the imagery so real and imagined events can be more easily distinguished (Arbuthnott, Arbuthnott & Rossiter, 2001b).

Reviewing the laboratory research and ethical implications of those findings is clearly important to an ethical discussion of the use of imagery. Additionally, the fervor about imagery work underscores one of the points we wish to make, which is that imagery is an extremely powerful technique. As Arbuthnott et al. (2001a) noted, imagery techniques focus attention of sensory modalities such that the experiences had in imagery are quite similar to real events. While the power of imagery may be an ethical liability in terms of memory distortion, it is also a clinical blessing in terms of its potential for providing a therapeutic experience of great impact.

Many Gestalt therapists have successfully capitalized on the impact of guided imagery. For example, Crocker (1984) induces in her clients a state of deep relaxation and from this "alpha state" proceeds with guided imagery. She provides a number of case examples illustrating the use and benefit of imagery work with clients. In one example, an adult client imagined a scene of herself as a child with her mother. The client experienced sitting on her mother's lap and being held, and afterwards concluded, "The past really can be changed" (p. 17). Perhaps the potency of imagery like this lies in the link between the mind and body. Baker (2000), a Gestalt therapist who blends energy healing, touch, and imagery in her work, attributes the power of guided imagery to such a link. She asserts that, "Images are experienced as actual events in the body" (p.280), and that, "The body does not discriminate between sensory images in the mind and an actual event on the outside" (p.280). In support of the mind-body link, Baker explains that images produce detectable physiological changes in the body, such that aggressive images may, for example, actually increase adrenalin production.

Revisiting the Case of Avoiding Touch

Returning to the case of Connie, imagery is a suggested technique for the treatment of childhood sexual abuse. Pearson (1994) reviewed the empirical, case study, and conceptual literature related to abuse treatment. Guided imagery was among the 11 techniques covered in this critique. When done responsibly, so as to avoid memory distortion, imagery can be a very effective therapeutic tool with adult survivors. Connie's therapist used imagery as a means to provide Connie with healing physical contact when literal touch was deemed unethical.

Specifically, Connie and her therapist made contact with the child-Connie who was huddled in a corner of the shed, frightened and crying. The adult Connie, overwhelmed by repulsion for her child-self, could not imagine making physical contact with the child. She allowed the therapist, however, to enter the image and sit next to the child as Connie explored both the needs of the child and her avoidant stance toward the girl. Gradually Connie became more and more receptive to having her therapist hold and soothe the suffering child in imagination. Over a series of sessions, and with the therapist's imagined touch and physical support of the child in place, Connie was then able to engage in dialogues between her adult and child. Awareness and insight aroused compassion in Connie, who ultimately integrated the projected child-self with her current adult-self. The termination process was initiated shortly after the point when the adult Connie, in imagery, embraced her child-self and began to provide the emotional and physical contact needed for healing.

Summary

Psychotherapists have become, like our society, touch-phobic. This fear of touching clients is based partly on the risks associated with touch as a therapeutic technique, and this is a legitimate ethical concern. However, many therapists refrain from touching not for ethical reasons but for reasons of self-preservation in this age of increased ethical misconduct charges. Despite these fears associated with touch in psychotherapy, the use of touch has clearly been established as a powerful and often unsurpassed tool for change. To summarily abandon touch because of its risks would, from our perspective, be unethical.

Instead, we propose a Gestalt resolution. From the perspective of Gestalt field theory, touch is a form of contact that is basic to communication, support, acceptance, growth, and health. Touch has no verbal substitute. Refusal to touch clients would, therefore, be an unfortunate stance to adopt not only because physical contact can be so therapeutic, but also because it is quite possible to engage in critical thinking about the use of touch such that the decision to touch a client can be theoretically and ethically grounded. Every decision to touch or not touch carries the potential for risk and benefit. The mandate of the ethical therapist is to make sound clinical decisions. To this end, we suggest that one evoke taxonomies such as that developed by Smith (1998) to guide decision making about touch with clients.

When touch is deemed unethical, much of the potential benefit of touch can be realized by employing the technique of imagery. Imagery itself carries potential risks and also requires ethical awareness. Nevertheless, when used properly, the therapist can "touch" the client through imagery. In this way, one may retain the benefit of touch while avoiding the risks that would make touch unethical if done literally.

References

Arbuthnott, K.D., Arbuthnott, D.W. & Rossiter, L. (2001a). Guided imagery and memory: Implications for psychotherapists. *Journal of Counseling Psychology*, 48(2), 123-132.

Arbuthnott, K.D., Arbuthnott, D.W. & Rossiter, L. (2001b). Laboratory research, treatment innovations, and practice guidelines: A reply to Enns (2001) and Courtois (2001). *Journal of Counseling Psychology*, 48(2), 140-143.

Baker, F.S. (2000). Healing in psychotherapy: Using energy, touch, and imagery with cancer patients. *Gestalt Review*, 4(4), 267-289.

Clance, P. R. & Petra, V.J. (1998). Therapist's recall of their decision-making process regarding the use of touch in ongoing psychotherapy: A preliminary study. In E.W.L. Smith, P.R. Clance, & S. Imes (Eds.), *Touch in Psychotherapy: Theory, Research and Practice* (pp.92-108). New York, NY: Guilford Press.

Corey, Corey & Callanan (1998). *Issues and Ethics in the Helping Professions* (5ᵗʰ ed.). Pacific Grove, CA: Brooks/ Cole Publishing.

Crocker, S. F. (1984). Gestalt and deep relaxation. *The Gestalt Journal*, 7(2), 5-30.

Enns, C. Z. (2001). Some reflections on imagery and psychotherapy implications. *Journal of Counseling Psychology*, 48(2), 136-139.

Field, T. (2001). *Touch*. Cambridge, MA: The MIT Press.

Field, T., Morrow, C., Valdeon, C., Larson, S., Kuhn, C., & Schanberg, S. M. (1992). Massage therapy reduces anxiety in child and adolescent psychiatric patients. *Journal of the American Academy of Child & Adolescent Psychiatry*, 31, 125-131.

Field, T. & Schanberg, S. M. (1990). Massage alters growth and catecholamine production in preterm newborns. In N. Gunzenhauser (Ed.), *Advances in Touch*. Skillman, NJ: Johnson & Johnson.

Geib, P. (1998). The experience of nonerotic physical contact in traditional psychotherapy. In E.W. L. Smith, P.R.Clance, & S. Imes (Eds.), *Touch in Psychotherapy: Theory, Research, and Practice* (pp. 109-126). New York: The Guilford Press.

Harlow, H. F. (1959). Love in infant monkeys. *Scientific American*, 200, 68-74.

Holroyd, J.& Brodsky, A. (1980). Does touching patients lead to sexual intercourse? *Professional Psychology*, 11(5), 807-811.

Horton, J. (1998). Further research on the patient's experience of touch in psychotherapy. In E.W. L. Smith, P. R. Clance, & S. Imes (Eds.), *Touch in Psychotherapy: Theory, Research, and Practice* (pp. 127-141). New York: The Guilford Press.

Kepner, J. (2001). Touch in gestalt body process psychotherapy: Purpose, practice, and ethics. *Gestalt Review* 5(2), 97-114.

Kertay, L., & Reviere, S. L. (1998). Touch in context. In E.W. L Smith, P.R. Clance, & S. Imes (Eds.). *Touch in Psychotherapy: Theory, Research, and Practice* (pp. 16-35). New York: The Guilford Press.

Kottler, J. (2002). *Theories in Counseling and Therapy*. Boston, MA: Allyn & Bacon.

Milakovich, J. (1998). Differences between therapists who touch and those who do not. In E. W. L. Smith, P. R. Clance, & S. Imes (Eds.), *Touch in Psychotherapy: Theory, Research, and Practice* (pp. 74-91). New York: The Guilford Press.

O'Neil, P. M., & Calhoun, K. S. (1975). Sensory deficits and behavioral deterioration in senescence. *Journal of Abnormal Psychology, 84*, 579-582.

O'Shea, L. (2000). Sexuality: Old struggles and new challenges. *Gestalt Review,* 4(1), 8-25.

Paddock, J.R., Noel, M., Terranova, S., Eber, H.W., Manning, C. & Loftus, E.F. (1999). Imagination inflation and the perils of guided visualization. *Journal of Psychology, 133*(6), 581-595.

Pearson, Q.M. (1994). Treatment techniques for adult female survivors of childhood sexual abuse. *Journal of Counseling and Development, 73*, 32-37.

Perls, F. (1969). *Gestalt Therapy Verbatim*. Moab, Utah: Real People Press.

Pope, K.S., Keith-Spiegel, P. & Tabachnick (1986). Sexual attraction to clients: The human therapist and the (sometime) inhuman training system. *American Psychologist, 41*(2), 147-158.

Pope, K.S., Sonne, J.L., & Holroyd, J. (1993). *Sexual Feelings in Psychotherapy: Explorations for Therapists and Therapists-in-Training*. Washington, DC: American Psychological Association.

Pope, K.S., Tabachnick, B.G. & Keith-Spiegel, P. (1987). Ethics of practice: The beliefs and behaviors of psychologists as therapists. *American Psychologist, 42*(11), 993-1006.

Raubolt, R. R. (1985). Humanistic analysis: Integrating action and insight in psychotherapy. *Journal of Contemporary Psychotherapy 15*(1), 46-57.

Smith, E.W.L. (1985). *The body in psychotherapy*. Jefferson, NC: McFarland & Company, Inc.

Smith, E.W.L. (1998). A taxonomy and ethics of touch in psychotherapy. In Smith, E.W.L., Clance, P.R., & Imes, S. (Eds.), *Touch in Psychotherapy: Theory, Research and Practice* (pp.36-52). New York, NY: Guilford Press.

Smith Lawry, S. (1998). Touch and clients who have been sexually abused. In Smith, E.W.L. Clance, P.R., & Imes, S. (Eds.), *Touch in Psychotherapy: Theory, Research and Practice* (pp. 201-210). New York, NY: Guilford Press.

Triplett, J. & Arneson, S. (1979). The use of verbal and tactile comfort to alleviate distress in young hospitalized children. *Research in Nursing and Health, 2*, 22.

Editor's Note:
In this chapter, I take up the question of how the relational perspective on human nature and process that we developed in Chapter I, which included both methodological implications and a derived ethics as well, can be applied to working with couples. Recall that in this perspective, we see people as best understood in terms of their relational strivings, and we argued that their individual growth is ultimately supported only by supporting the health and development of the whole field. Thus the answer to this question lies in supporting the unique relational resources within a couple system. Hence, our derived relational ethic leads us not to solving the immediate problems with which couples are struggling, to helping them negotiate better, nor to becoming "better" people in general—the tasks that stem from an individualist perspective. Instead, we are drawn to a much more profound underlying task: facilitating couple members' process of understanding and using the relational perspective developed here—both ethically and as a process skill—with its natural imperatives for connection and growth. This is a task of establishing emotional safety and birthing voices that have no permission or ability to exist in an individualist system.

7

••••••••••••••••••

Working With Couples:

Application of Gestalt's

Values of Connection

Robert G. Lee

I have a favorite story that I often share with my couple clients. It is a metaphor of how I do therapy with couples. In my mid teenage years I tried my hand at surf fishing. I had an older cousin, whom I looked up to, who loved fishing in the surf off the coast of California. He was an important figure to me in my adolescent years, like a nurturant older brother, and a number of times he took me with him on his trips to the beach, trying to teach me the art of bait casting. I loved to be with him, and I loved being at the beach with its crashing waves, endless sand, salt air breeze, and squawking seagulls. But I and the bait casting rod that he introduced me to did not take well to each other. I would heave a cast, trying to duplicate my cousin's graceful form. The line would go sailing seaward and I would get a rush of excitement. But very shortly, in a sudden backlashing jerk, the line would come to a halt in midair with the reel becoming one mass of snarled knots. My cousin, in his kind manner, would tell me it was useless to try to untie such a snarl of knots and invariably suggest that I cut it out of the reel. But there was something about such a snarl of knots that intrigued me. While I never became a very good bait caster, I did become quite an expert at undoing those knots.

I discovered that if I tried to pull hard on the line, the snarl would only become tighter. But if instead I slowly and persistently attended gently to the many knots within the snarl, the knots would gradually soften, although it was difficult to tell that any progress was being made for considerable time. However, with enough time, the snarl would all of a sudden just fall away. It was like magic to me.

I have often had that same experience in working with couples. And I realize now that the small, soft working of knots within the snarl in the metaphor is analogous to helping couples tolerate and undo their shame cycles a little bit at a time. And the relational ethics, derived in Chapter One, of noticing and understanding, in this case, couple members' relational strivings and supporting the health of the whole system, are the basic tools in this endeavor.

As discussed in Chapter One, it is couple research that tells us that the ethical values that we have derived from Gestalt field theory do in fact exist in healthy systems. In successful marriages, these ethical values are part of the couple's shared ground. And further this is what distinguishes successful couples from unsuccessful couples. Thus the main task in working with couples is to help them internalize these values. That is, *the job of couples therapy is done when couple members become as interested in the quality of their partner's experience as they are in their own, when in times of conflict in particular they monitor that there is sufficient support for both of them, and when they repair ruptures that do occur, finding solutions that work for both people. These are the caretakers of the emotional safety that is needed for ongoing intimacy and growth within a couple.*

So how do we go about helping couples internalize these values? First, these values can't be imposed from the outside. Gestalt field theory tells us that the only way that any values become part of someone's map of possible connections is through experience. Couple members must experience the effect of these values in their own lives. And that requires helping them build enough emotional safety. This must start with the therapist employing these values when he/she relates to each couple member. For couples therapy to work, each couple member must come to feel that the therapist is genuinely interested in the quality of his/her experience. And each partner must feel that the therapist is equally concerned with providing support for both him/herself and his/her partner. Thus listening to the experience of each partner, in particular the yearnings of each partner, providing sufficient support for both couple members, and noticing and repairing any ruptures that occur between therapist and couple members are the embodiment of Gestalt's ethics of connection for the therapist.

Jean and John:
An Example of Listening to Yearnings and Providing Sufficient Support at the Beginning of Therapy

Midway through Jean and John's first session with me, Jean leaned forward as she started to speak to her husband, who was sitting at the other end of the couch. Although she was leaning forward and her left hand was stretched out toward John, moving in slow circles in a caressing fashion on the fabric of the couch, her voice was hesitant and her face wore an unsettled look. In fact she was starting to say to her husband that she did not know whether she could depend on him. The couple had been separated since she had asked him to leave, about five months previously, after he had told her of an affair he had had a number of years before. For her that was the last straw, in spite of how much they loved each other, their marriage had been filled with disappointment, fights, yelling, distance, criticism, and disconnection.

John did not let her finish. In a soft but critical voice he interrupted, "that's the trouble with you, 'J.' You don't know your-self. You never know when to let well enough alone, and you're constantly looking for trouble even when there is none."

At this point, it appeared to me that neither Jean nor John was experiencing sufficient support. My guess was that they were both off-balance, John more so than Jean because he was more involved in trying to knock Jean off-balance. It was likely that Jean's talking about whether she could depend on John had shamed John.

More importantly it didn't appear that either of them knew much about how to get support. In particular John seemed to be trying to get support by criticizing Jean. If his attempt worked and he managed to knock Jean off-balance, they would then be in the middle of a couple shame cycle. Neither couple shame cycles nor individual shame cycles lend themselves easily to obtaining support. But when both couple members are reacting out of an experience of shame, the foundation for supporting one another has been lost. Sometimes I will let couples continue into their shame cycle as a way of setting ground—later exploring with them the ways the interaction supports and doesn't support each of them and at what price. But in this case Jean and John both appeared too fragile to endure such a "failure." So I intervened at this point, and I intervened with John because he appeared to be the most fragile.

I said to John that he looked like he was off-balance and might need some support, and that he did not seem to know how to get support for himself. I asked if that at all resonated with what he was experiencing. He sat for a moment with a look of astonishment on his face. Finally, he said, "Yeh, but you're speaking Greek. How is that possible?" I asked him if he wanted a suggestion. And with a look of curiosity mixed with scepticism he said he did. Whereupon I suggested that he might tell Jean that he was feeling a little off-balance and ask her if she would be willing to tell him something that she liked about him. He looked even more stunned and said that he couldn't do that. When I asked why, he said that she wouldn't be interested in doing that. Sensing the yearning and fragility in both of them I graded down the experiment, asking him if he would like me to ask her for him. Hesitantly, he said that would be OK. When I asked her, a smile came over her face and she said that she would like to do that. After thinking a bit, she said in a warm tone, "I like your ears." He blushed!

After a moment I asked him if it helped to hear her say something she liked about him. And he said that it did. Again, after awhile I asked him if he could listen to Jean continue, but listen with a sense of what she was saying was not a condemnation of him but an indication of the support that she needed. And I asked her if she could talk more from her sense of her experience and needs as opposed to just John's behavior. With that Jean and John were able to negotiate this interaction successfully. Jean said that she was feeling fragile in regard to their connection and she could not handle any more surprises from him. John said that he understood, and the good part of his telling her what had happened in the past was that there were no more surprises.

This example illustrates the importance of listening for yearnings, providing sufficient support, and in essence finding ways to undo the smaller knots as they occur. Like in my bait casting metaphor, in all couples, couple members frequently cast lines to each other for connection. Jean's leaning forward and moving her hand toward John in caressing circles appeared to be such an attempt, as did John's soft voice as he spoke. While all relationships develop tangles from time to time, when relationships are struggling as much as this one was, these attempts at intimacy too often end in a snarl of frustration, pain, shame, and ultimate disconnection.

The same trap exists for us as therapists. Focusing on what goes wrong in a couple interaction, instead of bringing to awareness, modeling and helping to create the support that the couple needs, can reinforce the sense of criticism and shame that they already carry.

As in the above example, the best way to provide support for couples is to help understated, camouflaged or unnoticed/ unresponded to yearnings have a chance for connection, by noticing signs of their possible existence, inquiring about such signs and exploring with the couple whether there might be a reception for a yearning when one is found. At the same time it is important to monitor whether there is enough support individually and in the system for any particular yearning to emerge and to flow. More fragile yearnings will not emerge or flow until sufficient emotional safety is established. However, as in the above example, when yearnings have sufficient support in the couple system to emerge, although not recognized by the couple because of their shame cycles, the therapist can often facilitate their becoming clearer and flowing by bringing his/her own supportive focus to such yearnings and adjusting the safety (grading up or down) of the experiment as needed.

The snarl for couples is a snarl of shame (Lee, 1994a, 1994b,

1996), a snarl that signifies a complex system of beliefs around the underlying, often unawares, perception that it is not possible to be received as a person, or that reception brings too much pain and shame, thus carrying too high a price. This is often experienced as: my spouse/partner does not understand me, does not care about me, isn't interested in me, only thinks about him/herself, just wants his/her own way, is self centered, is inadequate, is mean and so on. And it is accompanied at some level by a self perception which can vary from an associational judgement such as "what kind of a dunce am I if I'm with this kind of person" to a much more self focused judgement such as I am foolish, stupid, inadequate, ugly, too much or too little in some manner, interested in dumb things, inappropriate, wrong, weak and so on. The combination of these self/other perceptions leaves one with the fundamental sense that *this is not my world, I don't belong*—an isolated, hopeless state.

When these sorts of perceptions are triggered without sufficient support, people become guarded, hide their true yearnings for connection which they experience as shameful and resort to strategies such as blame, control, rage, withdrawal, self contempt, stonewalling, attacks on the character of their partner, sarcastic humor, perfectionism, addictions, and so on. In short their process becomes adversarial either directly or silently. And at some point along the line these strategies have a high risk of triggering similar perceptions and strategies in their partner. In which case both people will be shamed and off-balance and not have the ability to hear, see, or understand the other and will also be incapable of exposing (or even being aware of) their true yearning for connection. Instead couple members' yearnings for connection will become disguised and/or transmuted into attacks on the other or on the self. Such is the legacy of shame. Again this is what happens in couples when there is insufficient support. Couple interactions become a win-or-lose exercise in a zero-sum game rather than a situation in which they both can flourish and grow.

Thus when people are off-balance, they have very little ability to make decisions that will lead to them obtaining the connection they desire. So the relational ethic in working with couples starts with an emphasis on constantly monitoring the level of support for both people.

Jean & John: An Example of Insufficient Support

Let me give an example of what can happen when there is not enough support. This example occurred further along in therapy with Jean and John. To set the stage, as their therapy progressed, sessions focused on the possible signs of yearning that were usually somewhat camouflaged and went unnoticed by the other, helping them develop a clearer voice where appropriate, and helping them test out whether that voice could be heard by the other. After a number of sessions they started to build some trust that there were times that they could connect. During this period it was also important to support their verbal and nonverbal resistance to getting back together too quickly. They both had strong yearnings to get back together, as well as an equally strong dread of returning to their old situation—although the latter was voiced mostly by Jean and the former was voiced mostly by John. At this stage, they still could not manage on their own anything but short interactions without falling back into their shame cycles. With my support to go slow around even thinking about getting back together, they continued to progress in making connection during their therapy sessions.

At about the eighth meeting, they took a week off for Thanksgiving. Jean drove to Connecticut to be with their 21-year-old daughter, and John flew to Minnesota to be with his brother. She had a good time while he was miserable negotiating a strained relationship with his brother and was missing seeing their daughter. When I next saw them, there were signs right away that there was not enough support between them, especially for him. When I greeted them in the hall outside my office, John, although smiling, made an off hand, subtle comment complaining about Jean, and then a slightly more despairing comment about a current event. While I usually notice in detail the quality of how people say hello to me in the waiting room, which gives me an indication of the state of their current self/other organizational process, I did not sufficiently attend to those subtle signs that morning:

Once in the session, John had more trouble than usual listening to Jean's experience. Jean had brought a small present back from Connecticut for John that symbolized her hopes for them as a couple. She gave him the present, describing what it meant to her with regard to her hopes. John received it politely, though perfunctorily. Again, I did not grasp how needy and off-balance he must be. As Jean proceeded to another topic, John had difficulty following what she was saying. Somehow I was still naively absorbed in the progress they had made before their Thanksgiving trips. And I tried to work with John's not listening in that light. But I was clearly not hearing John's underlying experience. Nor was he in a state where he could let much of it show.

About twenty minutes into the session, out of the blue, John suddenly became very angry. He laid into Jean harshly saying, "this has got to stop! You have got to take some responsibility for what you are doing! You are just out of control with the way that you hurt others. And it has just got to stop! I have taken enough! You have to understand how hurtful you are." He then took the present that she had given him earlier in the session and with an air of indignation flipped it back to her, contemptuously explaining that he could not accept anything from someone so hurtful. At this point he was close to yelling. Jean got up, saying that she could not take any of this and left the room and the session. I was glad that she could protect herself, in the absence of my providing the support they both needed.

It was now clear to me how off-balance John was, as well as the fact that I had missed seeing it. After a moment to collect myself, I apologized to John, empathizing with how he had carried his experience alone in the face of my not being available. This seemed to both surprise him and also calm him. I then listened to him talk in detail about how difficult it had been for him to be with his brother and how much he missed seeing his daughter. I didn't do anything of a confrontational nature with John as I believed that he was too vulnerable. And although I still needed to repair the rupture that my inattentiveness had caused with Jean, I did not need to do anything to help protect her in this session. What was figural to me in the moment was the importance of doing what I could to repair the rupture that I contributed to with John—again an application of the ethics of support and connection that we derived in Chapter One.

At the end of the session I suggested to John that I see him alone the next session, pending agreement by Jean. There are significant reasons not to see one member of a couple individually when doing couple therapy. The balance of favoritism and the sense that you are able to fully understand the struggle and point of view of the couple member that is not seen can be easily disturbed. These considerations of course fit in general with the ethics of attending to the experience of and supporting both couple members. However there are occasional times when supporting the couple is best served by attending to the couple-related needs of one couple member individually. In this case my assessment was that, while I still needed to repair the damage that I had contributed to with Jean, she had a strong sense that I understood and appreciated her struggle. And it was best for the couple that I work on supporting John before the couple met together again. And from our previous work, my sense was that such work would be too difficult for them to do together as it would have a high risk of triggering Jean, which would likely trigger John.

Later that day I called Jean and apologized to her also, saying that the signs were there that John was off-balance at the start of the session and I was very sorry that I did not pay attention to them and that I did not support her and John well. As with John, this seemed to surprise her and also to relieve her to some extent. I then spent some time listening to her reactions to what had happened earlier, in the session, which were mostly focused on her disappointment and hurt at what John had said and her feeling foolish and dumb that she expected anything else from John. I reiterated several times that I had not noticed or provided the support that each of them needed and had not warned them ahead of time that this kind of shame reaction was a possibility during or after their Thanksgiving trips. This seemed to calm her. At the end of the conversation, I mentioned to her that I had suggested to John that I see him alone the following visit. She concurred saying that she still wasn't sure that she could come back to couple therapy at all, but at the very least she could not return the following week.

While I never want to make mistakes such as the one I made with not anticipating or noticing John's need for support, repairing such mistakes often opens doors with clients, perhaps because it allows them to feel like they are not the only ones who make mistakes, and perhaps because it expresses that I am concerned about their experience.

In the following session with John, I started with again apologizing to him for missing his experience and not supporting him. He seemed moved by this. He also related that he had called Jean and apologized to her for his behavior and she had accepted his apology and agreed to come in for future sessions. I then moved to my other concern. I thought that John needed more support for his inner experience during the rages that he found himself in from time to time. I said to him that it appeared to me that he had learned somewhere that he was not supposed to get support. Because of small references he had occasionally made about his experience of his family of origin, I continued, saying that often happened with people who had been in environments, often families in which they grew up, in which there was some kind of hardship or trauma. It wasn't that these were bad families, just that the people in them, usually the parents, had experienced significant hardship, loss or trauma without sufficient support. As a result family members had formed hardened beliefs that reception and support were impossible and had come to treat each other accordingly. But the sad result of that was that family members then had to bear their inner experience alone, while learning to hide their inner experience using strategies such as rage, blame, withdrawal and so on. And the use of such strategies only further reinforced family members' sense of isolation and shame. I asked him how the picture I was painting resonated with his experience.

He then shared with me in much more detail how his family of origin had been a very chaotic experience, filled with occurrences such as incest and severe verbal abuse in combination with extreme religiosity, and more. He said that family members even to present day had been and were very angry at each other and for the most part did not talk to each other; when they did they could be very hurtful. These were matters he had been focusing on in his individual therapy but had alluded to only very vaguely during the couple sessions. Toward the end of the session I asked John if he would enter into an experiment with me now and in future sessions to explore what support he might need when he felt off-balance. He said that he was not used to such thinking but that he appreciated my bringing it up.

The additional information that I had learned during this session gave me an insight into why John had so much trouble in general in listening to Jean. It appeared that in John's family of origin there was a taboo around listening to other family members' inner experience. People did not want their inner experience to be noticed. That would be potentially too dangerous and/or painful/shameful for them. Instead what people thought they needed was to be deflected from what they were experiencing. And that was what John was so good at. When he would notice that Jean was at all off-balance, the slightest bit hesitant, he would often launch into a story. While his stories were always artful and entertaining, they would frequently leave Jean feeling that she was being abandoned, that John was not interested in her and that he only wanted to talk about himself. But in fact it became clear to me that part of his motivation in launching into stories might be that he was trying to help her in a way that he had learned to help others in his family of origin. Grasping his relational striving in this regard and giving voice to it, was very important in deshaming John. Jean then had the opportunity to affirm how much she valued John's artful ability to "make her feel better" at times. And with a sense that his motivations were being understood and appreciated, he was able to hear from Jean that there were other times when she needed something else, namely for him to listen to her as she tried to give voice to her inner experience. It turned out that this man who had such resistance and difficulty taking in and responding to what others said, was a natural at listening. Of course being so adept at distraction requires being sensitive to when and how distraction is needed, which in essence requires a good listener. With only a little practice John became very good at not only hearing and responding to Jean's stated message but also hearing when Jean might need support to develop her voice further.

This was a time when, as in my bait-casting metaphor, this knot seemed to just fall away. Again the key to its falling away was John's underlying unvoiced relational striving being noticed and given voice. Without this, no amount of trying to motivate or train John was going to transform him into a "good listener." This example under-scores the importance of our relational ethical imperative of hearing relational strivings and providing support. Undoing this knot and continuing the monitoring of support for both of them then allowed Jean to focus on her issues of not believing that reception was possible, which John's behavior had reenforced.

Matt & Nola: More on Birthing Voices

As exemplified by John's inability to recognize his need for support in both of the above vignettes, it is difficult for people to be aware of their needs and yearnings before they perceive that there is at least the potential of reception for them. Thus as emotional safety is built between couple members, they often come to a place where they find themselves forming a voice for a more vulnerable part of themselves in a way that they didn't think was possible.

It is important to help people birth voices in these situations. This of course is not just an individual process. Our relational ethic tells us that in order for an individual to be healthy and thrive in a field, he/she must have other healthy people in the field to connect with. Thus the field, in this case the couple system, must grow to the place where a voice can be heard and received before there is any chance for this birthing process to succeed. Likewise, when the couple system has developed the level of emotional safety for new, more fragile, voices to start to emerge, it is important to support both couple members during the birthing process. Without the success of this dual venture, no amount of negotiation, good intentions, or trying to "be better" will produce a result that will lead to a true sense of connection and satisfaction. As long as people do not have a sense that a relational striving can be received and thus do not develop a voice for, or perhaps even an awareness of, that striving, they are at high risk of experiencing shame, adding further camouflage to their yearning and resorting to shame-maintenance strategies. The effects of this of course are not only experienced in the quality of verbal intimacy between couple members but also extend throughout their relationship in areas such as problem solving, affection, sexuality, compatibility, and interest in one another.

In short, helping people give voice to the desire for a different kind of connection, a kind of connection that has been taboo or dangerous previously in their lives, requires a special delicacy. Consider the following examples involving Matt and Nola.

Matt and Nola, a couple in their early thirties, had been seeing me for about a year and a half when the examples below occurred. They were newly married at the start of therapy, and they had come to see me because they were troubled by the severity of the fights in which they found themselves, in spite of how much they loved each other. They had each been raised in deeply shame-bound families, although loving families, in which there was very little emotional safety. And they were both on guard, in their own styles, hyper-vigilantly focused on the other's possible transgressions. Both had little ability to verbally expose or to some extent even to know their needs for intimate connection. They prided themselves on being self reliant and "strong." In addition to their each being easily triggered by subtle (real or imagined) transgressions or mistakes by the other, there were other signs of how fragile they were in this regard. They would take a long time at the start of sessions discussing current events before beginning to discuss anything relevant to their relationship. And when they did start talking to each other about their relationship their voices would often become very soft, a whisper, and they would have very few words. For example, one might shyly whisper, "What would you like to talk about?" And the other might, equally shyly, whisper back, "I don't know. How about you?" It would be awhile before either of them would risk mentioning something.

I came to understand that this latter kind of interaction between them was one of their strengths as a couple. Creatively, it was a way that they had found to join and to experience and show the vulnerable sides of themselves as well as their love for one another, while at the same time protecting themselves and each other from exposure of the details of their vulnerabilities. Thus supporting the delicacy and specialness of their process (their relational strivings) was important. However, with all these signs, I imagined that we would be going slow with respect to their voicing much about their inner experience.

Now a year and a half into therapy they had become much less sensitive to being triggered when the other was triggered, the first very important task they took on. And as the other ceased becoming triggered when they were triggered, they gradually became less sensitive to the possible negative motivation of the other.

They had now become interested in experimenting with finding ways that they could connect with each other from their vulnerability, exploring the prospect that their vulnerability might be a gift to the other, which of course was a very strange concept for them. The following are two examples of my helping them birth voices as they experimented with being in the world in this new fashion.

To set the scene for the first example, the previous week Matt had spent some time talking about how he had become very angry with me, something which he and I had then resolved in that session. But he had not told Nola of his anger toward me in the week prior to that session. A short time into this meeting, Nola announced that she had something that was bothering her. After Matt said that he would like to listen, she started by saying, "I was completely surprised when you said you were so angry at Dr. Lee last week. I had no idea that you felt that way." She continued with a note of anger in her voice, "It was like you were a stranger." And then contemptuously she added, "I don't know what makes you think you can do that!"

Matt flinched, and I intervened saying to Nola that it was clear from the intensity with which she was talking that what she was saying to Matt was important to her. But I said I was concerned that if she just focused on Matt's behavior there was a risk that he would become defensive and miss her message about her inner experience, and she would not get the connection she desired. I asked her if she could talk more from how what she was saying was important to her, from her inner experience. The anger and contempt on her face seemed to subside and she appeared more vulnerable. She thought for a moment and replied shyly, "I don't know how to say it." Whereupon I asked her if she wanted me to make a guess at what she was experiencing. She nodded yes.

When I make such guesses, my intention is to try to give voice to what the client is experiencing, not what I might want her/him to be experiencing or what I think she/he should be experiencing. At the same time I try to voice only the yearning—that lies under the shame and manifestations of shame management that cover it. To do this I will pay close attention to what the client might be saying "between the lines" as well as to the client's nonverbal signs such as tone of voice, facial expression, gestures and so on. And I will try to imagine myself in the client's posture. I then see what comes inside of me. I also am always aware that this process only produces a guess at the client's experience, not the client's actual experience. So I always present such guesses with plenty of support for the client to say whether what I have guessed is at all close to her/his experience and for her/him to tell me in what ways the guess doesn't fit with her/his experience. With these cautions, I find that this can be a powerful technique in providing support to clients who are struggling to birth a voice for a piece of their experience that is new for them or which has been taboo or dangerous for them in the past. My assisting them in this manner at times is the first sign for them that such a voice is at all possible to exist for them, let alone that it might be possible for this voice to be heard by others.

In this case with Nola, I told her I would speak my guess as if I were she talking to Matt. Then looking at her, not Matt, I started my guess, "having a sense of who you are (again speaking as if I were she talking to Matt) is a major way that I know there is a connection between us. It is like an anchor for me. Without it I start to become lost and feel adrift. With it, I also feel of value. Noticing what is happening with you is an important way that I take care of you. And to find out that something as major as you reported was going on in you without my knowing it scares me greatly." I then asked her if that at all reflected her experience. She said that it did. So I asked her if she could say that to Matt in her own words. She turned to him and said with a smile, a quick wave of her hand and a short laugh, "all of that." So I supported her again by asking her to put it in her own words. She sat a moment and then said to Matt, "I do depend on my sense of knowing you, even when you don't verbalize what is going on inside of you. I think that I'm very good at reading you. There are many times when you can't tell me what is going on inside of you. And I have a great deal of pride that at those times that I have at least a sense of what you are experiencing. So for you to be experiencing something as deeply as you reported that you did and for me not to know that anything was happening, that makes me start to question our connection."

That appeared to soften Matt, but he didn't respond. So I asked Nola if she would like to hear how Matt received what she had said. To which she replied with a smile and a firm but playful voice, "yeh, you ask him." She was a step ahead of me, and I was glad that she could ask me for the support she needed. His reply to my asking him was, "it felt good, a lot better than before." I knew the last part of what he said had a high potential of triggering her. He had not told her much about himself, and what he had said could be read as meaning she had done it wrong the first time. So I asked him to enlarge on his experience if he could, staying with what it had meant to him to hear her say what she did. And he said more fully, "I like how you know me. I often feel inadequate and uncomfortable that I can't tell you all that is going on in me. It is not my style. But I think you are good at the guesses you make, and I do feel it as special that you are with me in that way." They were clearly both moved by what the other had said. They had both taken new risks and had liked what the risks had brought them, which helped them to want to continue to explore this way of being in the world.

The second example between Matt and Nola occurred about a month after the last example and about three weeks after they learned that Nola was pregnant. Nola was saying to Matt that she was very happy with how much he was doing in response to her being pregnant. She said that contrary to what she had expected, she found herself every day feeling grateful for what he had done. Matt's response was to say in an offhand manner, "that's nice to hear, but I don't feel like I have done much." On hearing this, a faint look of concern crossed Nola's face. It didn't last long. Rather quickly she replied to Matt that in fact he had done a lot, and then enumerated the ways that he had extended himself, saying again that she appreciated his actions. Matt said that he heard what she was saying, but again he didn't feel like he had done much. Once more a look of concern crossed Nola's face.

It appeared to me that they were in a subtle couple shame cycle, one that was probably not going to escalate and one that I believed that they were going to rebound from without much difficulty. But I also sensed that with the right support this might be an opportunity for them to connect on a deeper level. There might be some yearnings here that were not being given a voice. I was guessing from Matt's off-handed manner and the look of nonchalance on his face when he replied to Nola that he had been slightly shamed by what Nola had said about liking what he had done—as if he had improved, which could imply that he had wrongly been inattentive in the past. And I was guessing that Nola was interpreting Matt's offhandedly responding that he hadn't done much as meaning he did not care about her. It appeared to me that Nola's looks of concern might hold the key to voicing the yearnings behind this couple shame cycle, if in fact my guessing was at all correct.

I intervened, saying that I had noticed Nola's look and asked her if she had had a reaction to what Matt had said. Nola nodded that she did, but said that she didn't know what to say about it. I asked her to explore her reaction a bit more to see if she could identify the nature of what she had experienced. But again she replied that she did not seem to have words for her reaction. So I asked her if she wanted me to try to give it voice, that of course my attempt would just be a guess. She said that she did, that my guesses were usually right. I replied that if I got close to what she had experienced that was great, but I wanted her to tell me how what I guessed didn't fit also.

I said to Nola that perhaps a voice for her experience would be something of the form that when Matt said that he didn't think that he had done much, that was of concern to her because she thought that his actions were motivated by a sense of caring of her, and in that light she had experienced what he had done as very special gifts. Her eyes moistened with the start of tears and she said that was right. I asked her to say that to Matt, and as she did her tears became fuller. She said to Matt that she knew how much he had worried about their financial condition and how he had wanted to wait to have a child. And that she had always figured that when she got pregnant she would be doing much of it alone. That was just the way it was going to be. Matt was doing as much as he could just consenting to trying to get pregnant. But to find that Matt appeared to be with her and to be thinking about her as exemplified by the things he had been doing, it was so wonderful. Her tears flowed more freely, which she embarrassedly wiped away.

Matt appeared to be moved by what Nola had said and told her that he didn't know that was what she was trying to say. That in fact she was right about what she was sensing. The news that they were going to have a baby brought a sense of happiness and caring inside him that he had not expected either, and in fact he had been more attentive of her. This was clearly a very special moment for them. And again this moment was facilitated through the application of our derived ethics of supporting the whole field by noticing relational strivings and providing support for both couple members. Matt and Nola had experienced the possibility of connection in this manner through this and other experiments. It took several months of supporting them as they experimented with this way of being in the world before they were able to do it on their own.

Wrapping Up

We have been witnessing what practicing the relational ethic in couples therapy can bring. Interpreting conflicts as a need for support by the whole field, following the signs of shame and listening for yearnings, helping to give voice to new or fragile yearnings—facilitating couples' explorations into whether it is possible to interact from a sense of belonging rather than from an adversarial or distance-minded existence—these are the actuations of the ethics of understanding and support for the whole field that we derived from Gestalt theory in chapter one. As we have seen here, the benefits can be immense.

I still have a sense of awe when the knots in a couple's snarl fall away. The main difference between my bait casting metaphor and what I experience in working with couples is that this same experience happens with even the smaller couple's knots. And again, undoing the smaller knots builds the emotional safety needed to tackle larger knots. At the same time, it is all about the same thing. The crux of marital satisfaction, intimacy, problem solving ability, and interest in partner is the degree of emotional safety built up in the couple. And it is the tools we have been discussing—the ability to be interested in the quality of each other's experience, to monitor the support level for both partners, and to repair ruptures that occur—that build and maintain emotional safety.

References

Lee, R. G. (1996). The waif and Mr. Hyde: One couple's struggle with shame. In R. Lee & G. Wheeler, (Eds.), *The Voice of Shame: Silence and Connection in Psychotherapy*. San Francisco: Jossey-Bass.

Lee, R. G. (1994a). Couples' shame: The unaddressed issue. In G. Wheeler & S. Backman (Eds.), *On Intimate Ground - A Gestalt Approach to Working with Couples* (pp.262-290). San Francisco: Jossey-Bass.

Lee, R. G. (1994b). *The Effect of Internalized Shame on Marital Intimacy*. (Unpublished Doctoral dissertation, Fielding Institute, Santa Barbara, CA.)

Editor's Note:
In this chapter, J. Richard White updates his creatively insightful, award winning article (White, 1995) on the ethics of understanding and treating the drug addict. In his original article he used a different language derived from Existentialism and Linguistics to arrive at a very similar perspective on ethics to that presented in Chapter 1 of this volume. Where White uses "emic," I would say "relational." This article makes it clear that a relational perspective, such as we are espousing in this book, does not diminish the individual: it enhances and enriches him/ her as well as our understanding of him/her.

8

• • • • • • • • • • • • •

A Special Case for Gestalt Ethics:

Working With the Addict

An Update

J. Richard White

Therapists working with addictive behaviors often do so from a moralistic or medical perspective that ignores the values and immediate experience of the client. Learning to recognize the character of the addict's world from his or her perspective, viewing addiction to a psychoactive substance in relational terms, and understanding addiction as a search for meaning—all contribute to an ethical approach to therapy for addicts.

An understanding of an ethics of process, as opposed to an ethics of content, can be developed by drawing on three paradigms: (a) the emic perspective, which provides a subjective orientation to the experiences of others; (b) existentialism, which strives to find the fundamental basis for all human experience; and (c) Gestalt field theory, which focuses on how our intersubjective experience is interconnected. Although an argument will be presented, as it must, in terms of metaphor (subjective observation, therapy, and philosophy), the reader will appreciate that one is, in the end, always left with the metaphors the client presents in session. That is, no matter how elegant one's *apologia*, in the instant of the therapeutic experience, one must abandon all arguments and face the client.

That, indeed, is the kernel of the present exploration.

The Emic Perspective

Although the terms *emic* and *etic* are part of the basic vocabulary of anthropologists, they are, despite their utility, rarely employed in other related disciplines. Neither psychologists nor sociologists typically include them in their specialized lexicons; and the science that provided them, linguistics, generally ignores them. Each art or science has its own idiosyncratic terms, of course, but it is difficult to see how any human study survives without concepts represented by these two words, assuming of course that no adequate synonyms exist. The linguist Kenneth Pike (1966) is the creator of these terms, although he applied them to the specific sciences of phonetics and phonemics. He seemed, however, to have intended that they be employed to address such global issues as I do in the present discussion. Human behavior, Pike suggested, can be studied by analogy to two linguistic approaches to human speech, the phon*etic* and the phon*emic*. That is, humans are potentially capable of making certain sounds; they possess the physical vocal apparatus, the associated wiring, and perhaps a universal motivation, to make certain discernible utterances, the study of which is called phonetics. The actual *meaning* of these sounds, which is the science of phonemes, varies across cultures. Theoretically, anyone can perceive the phonetics of a culture by simply listening. However, the meaning of these sounds can only be apprehended by entering the culture and, as it were, experiencing it from the inside out. Furthermore, an emic perspective carries with it an understanding that we can never know in advance what emic units—that is, what structural bits of meaningful sound—make up a culture.

This linguistic analogy illuminates all human experience. We cannot, for instance, fully understand a client in counseling for addictive behaviors if we only know what our etic perspective tells us about drugs and drug users. Unfortunately, addiction counselors usually base their approach on a view of drugs that is totally alien—that is, totally etic—to that of the drug user. The simplest example of an etic value in addiction counseling is, "Drugs are bad" or, the slightly less obvious, "People who use drugs have a problem." These values are so ingrained in the system of the dominant culture that I feel urged to apologize for suggesting that they are not facts, merely ideas that serve secondary human needs. That is, they represent values of convenience rather than values for growth. From the drug culture, these values can only be understood by drug users who have themselves developed an emic perspective about the dominant culture; that is, drug users are pressed to develop an emic perspective about the outsiders' view of the drug users' world. Surely, an ethical issue emerges whenever an oppressed group is charged with the primary responsibility for understanding the motives of the oppressors.

Although I am often accused of it, I am not just presenting a case for a more tolerant view of drug users. Tolerance implies judgment, since we must exercise tolerance only for behaviors that challenge our goodwill. An emic perspective, at least as I am developing it in this discussion, is not so shallow an idea; an emic perspective carries with it the view of ontological relativism. And, more importantly for the present purposes, an emic perspective in counseling engenders a creative ethics, whereas the etic perspective demands conformity. If counselors encourage conformity, according to May (1983), they are responsible for the destruction of the individual (and the impoverishment of the shared field):

> [There is a] tendency to use the social sciences in support of the social ethic of our historical period; thus the process of helping people may actually make them conformist and tend toward the destruction of individuality. This tendency, I believe, increases radically with the spread of behavior modification, a form of psychotherapy based on an outspoken denial of any need for a theory of man at all beyond the therapist's assumption that whatever goals he and his group have chosen are obviously the best for all possible human beings (pp. 15-16).

We know of course that "behavior modification" is but one of several expressions that identify technological psychotherapy, that is, therapeutic approaches that are designed to alter people's individuality through the use of standardized techniques, rather than through an interpersonal therapeutic process.

The principles of an emic perspective are at the base of all understanding. Prejudice is largely a failure to understand another's epistemology, a failure to understand how another person arrives at an apprehension of the universe. Anthropologists as a group and, to a lesser extent, sociologists as a group, are in the business of emic understanding; psychologists as a group have historically been in the business of destroying emic understanding by attempting to conceptualize human experience in terms of common principles. This is not a judgment against psychologists; I am only defining their traditional role in the human services. Counselors, on the other hand, have assumed, it is hoped, a role in understanding the world of the client.

The World of the Addict

An emic view of the addict's world can be encouraged by focusing on the *relationship* the addict forms with the drug. Biological predeterminants, underlying psychopathology, and social dynamics, while providing theoretical details on etiology, are not particularly helpful in terms of understanding how the addict apprehends his or her universe (White, 1993). In fact, the concept of etiology encourages alienation, since it is only deemed necessary to explain behavior that is considered deviant. Acts that are considered saintly by observers are usually promoted as free of developmental features; acts that offend observers are often rationalized by an examination of genetics, personal history, or family dynamics. At any rate, by attending to the person-drug relationship, as it exists in the counseling moment, one avoids much of what falls to the etic view and discovers what is important to the addict.

I must emphasize that the Golden Rule for appreciating the addict-drug relationship is the same as that for appreciating any other relationship. That is, the relationship is dialectic, functional, and beneficial to the client in terms of ultimate survival. Although people may kill themselves directly with poisons, or more slowly with poisonous psychoactive drugs, the addictive relationship itself is also an attempt at survival, specifically, spiritual survival. The counselor who appreciates addiction as a desire for meaningful life will tend to be freed of the rigid restrictions of etic codes. Such a counselor will understand that all the client's efforts to maintain a steady relationship with the bonding substance were made in an attempt to come alive and to stay alive. This knowledge frees the counselor from the content ethics which attempt to govern addiction as disease, deviance, or insanity and the elimination of content ethics always provides a free space for process ethics.

Note that people form relationships with drugs in much the same manner, and for many of the same reasons, that they form human relationships; and the motivation to form such relationships is generated, in large part, by unfinished interpersonal business, just as it is with relationships with other people. Consider, for instance, an interpersonal disappointment, or series of disappointments, in early development that organizes one's ground (underlying belief system combined with innate relational strivings) toward bonding with non-human entities or activities or ineffectively or perilously bonding in risky human relationships or dangerous activities. A specific example could be that of the person who has lost faith in the possibility of finding pleasurable excitement in ordinary interpersonal interactions (perhaps because of the absence or withdrawal of such stimulation by a primary nurturer) and therefore seeks *dependable* excitement from psychostimulants such as cocaine or methamphetamine. Another specific example, considering a drug pharmacologically distinct from psychostimulants, could be that of the person who has lost touch of any hope about human relationships (perhaps because of multiple betrayals) and therefore seeks the *raw optimism* that is produced by exogenous opiates mimicking the body's confidence-supporting endorphins.[1]

---

[1]Such disappointments in interpersonal relations do not of course mandate a significant relationship with psychoactive drugs. Other

Of course there are many addict-worlds. Etic perspectives tend to universalize alien experience, to imagine that the basic features of addiction, for instance, are common to all men and women who form these relationships with drugs. Although the demands of forming such addictive relationships in a hostile environment, such as the dominant sociopolitical culture of the technological world, encourages stereotypical responses (e.g., those needed to avoid detection and to maintain supply), the subtleties of each relationship are as remarkable as those of any other compulsive relationship. A willingness on the part of the counselor to surrender preconceptions and to permit individuality to manifest itself is a key attribute in developing an emic perspective.

The Existential Ground

As stated above, an emic perspective takes us away from a valuing from outside a culture, an etic idea, to questions regarding the process of knowing another. And to explore the ground for these questions of process ethics, we must first complete some basic ontological and epistemological tasks, namely, we must determine what we know, in general, about human values and how we know it. Let us first look at how existential theory can inform us in our quest.

Sartre's Ethics

Sartre (1947) was characteristically emphatic:

> [Man] isn't ready-made at the start. In choosing his ethics, he makes himself, and force of circumstances is such that he can not abstain from choosing one. We define man only in relationship to involvement. It is therefore absurd to charge [existentialists] with arbitrariness of choice. (p. 51)

---

dependencies—on food, work, sports, sex, religion, and so on—may be formed for a variety of reasons that may tend to exclude (or support) the option of drug use.

That is, there is nothing random or arbitrary about any person's ethics; personal ethics are never anything more than an extension of the process by which a person is defined. Although this may sound painfully elementary, the reader, I trust, will note that most people reject this notion categorically. In fact, a pervasive human desire is to find an inviolate source for ethical values; the volatile ethics of Sartre are often devalued into concepts such as "situational ethics," "humanism," and "secular morality." But Sartre was not speaking of content, as the absolutists do; he was speaking of process, just as you, the reader, and I are now exploring.

Sartre continued: "To say that we invent values means nothing else but this: life has no meaning a priori. Before you come alive, life is nothing; it's up to you to give it meaning that you choose. In that way, there is a possibility of creating a human community" (p. 58).

This, of course, is one of Sartre's most explicit clarifications of his famous principle of existence preceding essence. If we begin our exploration of the possibility of an ethics of process, we are strengthened by the fundamental existential observation that nothing exists without us, including a system of ethics. This is the specific axiological case of the general existential principle of ultimate ontological groundlessness. This may lead us not only to an ethics of process but an ethics of figure. That is, what has meaning as a value preference is, simply, that which has emerged as figure.

Sartre's position in history demanded that he overstate his case. His assertion that human nature did not exist provided an orienting point but ultimately conflicted with the existential template underlying all human experience throughout history. The fact is, there do appear to be human conditions, givens that apply to all men and women irrespective of time and location. If, for instance, Yalom's (1981) four ultimate concerns—death, freedom, isolation, and meaninglessness—are universal and eternal for the human condition, then we have a basis for an existential ethics. Whereas Sartre paints himself into a corner with his rejection of human nature, Yalom and others have identified the features of personality that will support a universal basis for ethical practice. Paradoxically, by identifying universal components of human nature, we avoid much of the dilemma of the modern problem of multicultural counseling—that is, the problem of trying to be all things to all people (Vontress, 1988)—and discover an ethics of process, an ethics of emic orientation.

Although an etic perspective suggests a global view of the human condition, its effect is to deny individuality. Only the imaginary modal man is safe from the etic perspective; all others are eliminated by definition. The apparent paradox found in the view that the etic perspective, ultimately the perspective of the individual culture, leads to an unbiased ethics is resolved in the understanding that only the instance can reveal the true nature of the template. That is, the template of an ethic is an abstraction that finds expression in the etic perspective; the manifestation of the ethic is found in the individual case and can only be found through an emic perspective. This is not, of course, an argument for the abandonment of the etic perspective, even if such an accomplishment were possible. The etic perspective is as necessary to the development of an emic perspective as accommodation is to assimilation in the general apprehension of information. The point emphasized here is that in the moment of ethical counseling, the light of the etic perspective must dim in order for the individual to be revealed. Or to be even more blunt, the counselor who bases his ethics solely on the code of his culture denies the existence of the individual client. The client then becomes the template, rather than the instance of existence.

But this is the sophist's argument. The proof of the existential base for process ethics is in the common conditions of life. While recognizing the importance of cultural levels, the ethical counselor keeps as priorities those conditions that both individualize and universalize the client (Vontress, 1988). It is difficult to err against the client when the counselor is grounded in the groundlessness of the existential position. When the primary issues are those that the counselor and client *must* share, due to their shared existence rather than their individual essences, the client (or, for that matter, the counselor) remains in ethical care. For example, the counselor who is keenly aware of the most powerful existential condition, that of personal death, will *naturally* respect the ultimate vulnerability of the client. A counselor who is not bound to a Judeo-Christian ethical system, for instance, is less likely to violate a client's fears, whether or not they are superficially identified as mortal fears. Such a counselor respects the tentativeness of life and therefore is sensitized to the individual client's uncertain existence.

Although the intersubjectivity I am discussing here is closely associated with Sartre, in Camus (1956) we find one of the most gracious, heartfelt expressions of this concept of the interconnectedness of human beings. In acknowledging the rebellious nature of a self-conscious organism thrown into a world of temporary existence, Camus discovers the limits of that rebellion in the imperative to relate to others in a humane manner. Only one who is totally aware of his or her own existential limitations—in the terrible limitations of death, isolation, and meaninglessness—can know the limits of rebellion. To strike out against another is to deny one's own existence. To lie to another is to lie to oneself.

The Tyranny of Models in the Addictions

I will make some distinction, perhaps an artificial distinction, between theory and model for the purpose of present illustration. I will define theory, however inadequately, as an epistemologically tentative but functional system of ideas that is more or less organized for a specific purpose; I will define model as a construction that is explicitly or implicitly designed to describe a phenomenon. Although the synonymous relationship of theory and model may be technically strong, the two are delineated in real life by assuming for theory a more speculative character. Models are the ugly step-children of theories, which tend to take on a life of their own, usually outliving their parents.

That such a distinction is useful, at least in some disciplines, can be supported by a familiar example. Currently, and for over half a century, the phenomenon of drug addiction has fallen under the dominion of the so-called medical model. Although this model has two or three names and several varieties, its essential features are not difficult to identify: addiction to psychoactive drugs is a disease in terms of its etiology, development, and resolution; it generally operates outside of human will, occurring without prompting by the organism, progressing along a predictable path, and ending in either death or cure (i.e., total abstinence). This model is so crystallized in our culture that, as I write the words to describe it, I am amused at its inflexibility. It clearly has been a great solace to the generations of professionals who sought convenience over curiosity.

But what is the effect of this model on ethical treatment of addictive behaviors? This model denies individual will and, ultimately human variability. It is the most severe of the Brickman et. al. (1982) generic models of helping, the one that denies the individual responsibility for either the cause or the solution of his or her own issue. Apart from the hypothesis that this model is weak in terms of treatment effectiveness, it is fundamentally unsound on existential grounds: an approach to treatment that denies personal responsibility reduces the client to an automaton. An existential approach assures the client of responsibility on the grounds that there is no one else available for the job, that each of us is ultimately alone with his or her own needs and desires, and that each of us bears the task of dealing with existence and nonexistence. It's a terrible responsibility, but one that brings freedom from the tyranny of the models of others.

Gestalt Ethics

What does Gestalt theory have that might support or clarify our ethical grounding from existential theory? When I first wrote this chapter, in the form of an article (White, 1995), the Gestalt literature did not contain an appreciation of Gestalt theory's foundation for the ethical stance I was developing. In fact, Gestalt theory had little to say about addiction in general (and, unfortunately, what it did say was often curiously antithetical to itself). However, Gestalt theory has always carried the spirit of process ethics (e.g., Latner, 1992; Perls, Hefferline, & Goodman, 1951) which suggests, in terms of its open, creative character, an ideal approach to the ethical treatment of addictive behavior. Repeatedly in Gestalt Therapy the axiom is offered, "Focus on what and how, not on content" (e.g., Yontef,

1983). The following excerpt underscores Gestalt's spirit of process ethics:

> [I]n this process of creating and experiencing one's world, no legal or moral set of ethics and values can be superimposed on personal experience without doing violence to the one who is experiencing. One may make a choice to live in situations accepting such a set of superimposed values; one chooses, in such a case, to violate personally held standards or values for the sake of something or someone with a higher priority or a stronger demand. The valid ethical stance in Gestalt therapy is based on the situation in which the interaction takes place. All persons are responsible for themselves in that interaction, and for the choices made in the existential moment (Korb, Gorrell, Van De Riet, 1989, p. 19).

But, I repeat, the application of Gestalt therapy ethical principles to addictive behaviors had been disappointing. For instance, while Carlock, Glaus, and Shaw (1992) deserved credit for making a contribution to a topic generally ignored by Gestalt therapy writers, they unfortunately based their approach to working with the alcoholic on the etic assumptions that alcoholism is a disease and that recovering is, basically, delineated by following the somewhat rigid protocol the program of Alcoholics Anonymous. That "disease" and "program" are concepts of stasis and clearly antithetical to the spirit of free and spontaneous functioning in terms of Gestalt theory, seemed to escape these authors. While their understanding of Gestalt theory in general was sharp, they had difficulty applying it to the experience of the addict. This constitutes an ethical issue for them, since it ignores the experience of the addict who will always see his or her relationship with alcohol and other drugs in terms of personal etiologic factors and will see recovery in terms of personal accomplishments (e.g., gestalts), rather than programmatic elements.

An important step in exploring a Gestalt theory foundation for the emic ethics of understanding and treating the drug addict that I had proposed came from Wheeler (1992), which provided us with an initial discussion for escaping this ethical trap. In a remarkable article, Wheeler called for answers to questions concerning a Gestalt ethics. Is there an ethics of process which is derived from Gestalt theory or, at least, compatible with a conceptualization of a cycle of experience that emphasizes the formation of figure against—in Wheeler's terminology—an organized personal ground? Further, is it possible to imagine, indeed, to practice, an ethical preference that is thoroughly syntonic with Gestalt theory and is clearly distinguishable from the theory of content-based psychotherapies? In fact, is not ethics the domain that demands that the Gestalt therapist either put up or shut up on the issue of immediate experience?

The next step came recently from Lee (2002) who shows us that a Gestalt theory derived emic ethics is in fact possible. Lee and other authors remind us that Gestalt recognizes the field (while other theories focus on the individual or his group.) And the field includes you and me; and therefore, what you do and what I do are inextricably linked, not just through our behaviors but more profoundly through how we co-influence our respective sense of who we are in the world. The Gestalt ethical imperative is *whenever we meet we are in it together*, and this does not sound much like the Gestalt Prayer.[2] Our clarity here has been facilitated with the advent of Perlsian notions of figure-bound autonomy giving way to a more developed understanding of the organization of ground, an organization that includes the formation of rigid belief systems that may be thought of as problematic from an emic perspective.

Again, this recognition of the field alerts us to the intersubjective, to how our interactions as interdependent subjects (not objects) creates our individual and collective sense of the world. And it cannot be otherwise: if the field and the organism are conditions of experience, then both are equally "real" (and, of course, there aren't really two components of the field except for the purpose of this

---

[2]This is in reference to the will-known dictum of Gestaltist Fritz Perls: "I'm me and you are you..." (with the suggestion at least that that was the end of our shared story, rather than the beginning).

illustration). What this means is that when "I" encounter "you," the connectivity of our intersubjective experience is limited primarily by the quality of awareness that exists between us, and that awareness is a function of our ability to gain a good-enough view of each other's experience. And this is the emic ethic.

Thus Gestalt theory provides us with a foundation to a emic perspective. And notice that this foundation encompasses significant elements from our existential grounding—from Satre's statement that man is only defined in relationship to involvement and his sense that relevant ethics emerge as figure, to Camus' sense of the limits of rebellion. This then is a guiding ethical beacon which can serve us in how we relate to and treat the addict.

Working with the Addict

Let us look first at how we know or think of addicts. In this respect, the use of diagnostic labels works against an understanding of the client. For example, one often encounters a common set of fixed characteristics in clients, namely, those associated with the label "antisocial personality disorder." This disorder does not, of course, actually exist, it's simply one of innumerable devices for statistically categorizing humans so that they can be tagged, stigmatized, treated, tracked, and controlled. It is a convenience for diagnosticians, cops, and third-party contributors, but provides no benefit to the client and, indeed, has the potential to develop considerable harm. The label, in fact, carries a content value, embedded in hard ground. Nevertheless, people with addictive behaviors are likely to display many characteristics that can be identified as DSM-IV criteria for this so-called developmental disorder, simply because addictive behaviors are supported by certain other behaviors, such as disregard of authority, failure to learn from mistakes, and a tendency to manipulate others. All these characteristics do not necessarily constitute a particular character, certainly not a character disorder; they exist together only because of syntonic affiliation. On the other hand, certain groupings of characteristics may constitute character in the pejorative Gestalt sense; for example, they may constitute a personality that is characterized by a fixed way of behaving. In an oppressive culture, for instance, drug users may develop a fixed way of behaving in order to survive.

In fact, I have noted elsewhere (White, 1993), even the label "addict" is only helpful if the client is the one who selects it. In this culture, "addict" has become both an etic and an emic designation, which does not free it for use in all situations, but does seem to provide a useful term for the exploration of identity. In order for process ethics to function, the counselor, however, must abandon stereotypical identities that set ethical codes.

The treatment of people who display these affiliated behaviors presents several other ethical dilemmas, not the least of which is whether treatment should occur at all. Indeed, addicts are most frequently encountered in coerced treatment, either within the walls of an institution or as a condition of parole. An affiliated characteristic of many of these people, namely, a good-natured interactive style, complicates the matter even further. That is, many addicts are not only pressured into a treatment they do not desire, they are often amiable about the coercement! We should not pass this all off as a personality defect, as is often done, since this ostensibly cooperative attitude has considerable face value as a personality asset, namely, in terms of its survival function. One has only to think of the belligerent attitudes of countless good old business drunks in treatment, men with long track records of laboring at Kohlberg's third and fourth stages of moral development, to appreciate the hard-core addict who, while seldom rising above the first level of morality, is always ready to enthusiastically engage a counselor on any topic.

Of course, we could explain the resistant drug addict's "cooperation" in terms of his or her pathology, but that puts us about the task of assigning values to the client, a topic which, while of ethical importance, is not the subject of this discussion. The fact is, we find ourselves in the counseling rooms with these people to either provide presence or not. From the ethical perspective being developed here, it really does not matter whether the client wants to be in treatment, as long as he or she retains the power of choice on whether to remain (which, of course, he or she seldom does). At least as I see it, I have no mandate to work against the client's wishes, but only a responsibility to find out whether his or her interactions with me result in some growth. As I see it, it is my responsibility to work with the client toward his or her potential to respond, not toward some pet goals I may cherish.

Final Comment

The poet Charles Olson (1950) observed that "Form is never more than an extension of content." A paraphrase of this axiom of projective verse might be: the raw material of one's experience assumes meaning only in its organization, that is, *value* does not reside in things, only in the structure of the relationship of things. Although this principle—the validity of which is the central theme of this paper—is often expressed with a shift in componential emphasis (that is, that content emerges from process), the issues remain essentially the same: Is the genesis of values, particularly those values we call ethical, discovered through dynamic or static search? Is the residence of values firmly planted in personal ground, organized or not, or do we find them only in figure? If values are figural phenomena, does not process determine both valence and intensity?

But in order to pursue the issue of ethics in addiction counseling, one must recognize that the clinical concern exists not in drugs but in the relationships that people develop with them. Given this, ethical issues begin to generate around relational dynamics rather than content. Then the therapist's work involves helping the client identify the nature of the relationship and eventually consider whether that relationship needs to be redefined or, perhaps, just defined. The therapist then is likely to find himself coming to terms with the Jungian concept of *separatio*, the alchemy of "differentiation," of distinguishing the drug from the person (Moore, 1992). What has occurred in addition, I suggest, is a boundary disturbance. The addict has lost identity by permitting the drug's boundaries to serve as the boundaries of the self. Addiction to a substance (or a person, or a thing, or an idea) is wild confluence, total dedication to the other at the expense of the self. Although addiction may always begin as a search for meaning, for a sense of soul through biochemical enhancement, it eventually ends in undifferentiated bonding.

The ethical risks in addiction counseling emerge when the therapist works solely from a content orientation, that is, when the client is seen only as a conglomeration of contributing components. Biopsychosocial factors may serve to soothe the therapist's intellectual exasperation about the client's addictive relationship, but they are virtually meaningless to the client. In my own practice I am not aware of working with any client who viewed himself or herself as "diseased," except of course after introjecting this idea from abstinence-oriented authority. Addicts are usually so enmeshed with their drug—and that is how I am defining addiction—that they are unaware of the relationship, sensing its existence only when the threat of abstinence appears. In other words, abstinence means death to the addict, since elimination of the drug is identical to elimination of the self. The ultimate therapeutic question for the client is, "How do I deal with my own death, the death that will occur if I differentiate myself from the drug?" The ultimate ethical question then becomes, "How do I, as a therapist, deal with the death of this client?"

The answers to this ethical question only appear in the dialectical experience of the therapeutic dyad. The ethical handling of this differentiation—which the client knows only as personal oblivion—can only be known to the therapist as the drama of the relationship unfolds and the therapist gains some emic understanding of the world of the addict, not just any addict, but *this* addict. Only through creative adjustment and a release of pet values can the therapist discover the guiding ethics for working with someone who has found a new existential condition, namely, the relationship with the psychoactive substance. The therapist who enters the counseling experience with the willingness to acquire emic understanding, the skill to respond to the client's spontaneous needs, and an awareness of the existential meaning of addiction, will be ready for the therapeutic differentiation that will lead to increased freedom, responsibility, and awareness for the client.

References

Brickman, P., Rabinowitz, V. C., Karuza, J., Coates, D., Cohn, E., & Kidder, L. (1982). Models of helping and coping. *American Psychologist, 37,* 368-384.

Camus, A. (1956). *The Rebel: An Essay on Man in Revolt.* (A. Bower, Trans.) New York: Vintage Books.

Carloek, C. J., Glaus, K. O., & Shaw, C. A. (1992). The alcoholic: A Gestalt view. In E. C. Nevis (Ed.), *Gestalt Therapy: Perspectives and Applications* (pp. 191-237). New York: Gardner Press, Inc.

Korb, M. P., Gorrell, J., & Van De Riet, V. (1989). *Gestalt Therapy: Practice and Theory (2nd ed.).* New York: Pergamon Press.

Latner, J. (1992). The theory of Gestalt therapy. *Gestalt Therapy: Perspectives and Applications* (pp. 13-56). New York: Gardner Press, Inc.

Lee, R. G. (2002). Ethics: A gestalt of values/The values of Gestalt. *The Gestalt Review,* 6(1), 27-51.

May, R. (1983). *The Discovery of Being: Writings in Existential Psychology.* New York: W. W. Norton & Company.

Moore, T. (1992). *Care of the Soul.* New York: Harper Collins Publishers.

Olson, C. (1950). Projective verse. *Poetry New York 3* (pp. 13-22). New York: Poetry New York Publications.

Perls, F. S., Hefferline, R., & Goodman, P. (1951). *Gestalt Theory: Excitement and Growth in the Human Personality.* New York: Dell Publishing Co.

Pike, K. (1966). *Language in Relation to a Unified Theory of the Structure of Human Behavior.* The Hague: Mouton.

Sartre, J. (1947). *Existentialism.* (B. Frechtman, Trans.). New York: Philosophical Library.

Vontress, C. E. (1988). An existential approach to crosscultural counseling. *Journal of Multicultural Counseling and Development, 16,* 73-83.

Wheeler, G. (1992). Gestalt ethics. In E. C. Nevis (Ed.), *Gestalt Therapy: Perspectives and Applications* (pp. 191-237). New York: Gardner Press.

White, J. R. (1995). A special case for Gestalt ethics: Working with the addict. *The Gestalt Journal, 18* (2), 35-54.

White, J. R. (1993). *An Emic Perspective of Drug Use: Treatment Implications.* Unpublished manuscript.

Yalom, I. (1981). *Existential Psychotherapy.* New York: Basic Books.

Yontef, G. (1983). Theory of Gestalt Therapy. In C. Hatcher & P. Himelstein (Eds.), *The Handbook of Gestalt Therapy* (213-221) Northvale, NJ: Jason Aronson, Inc.

Part III

•••••••••

Widening the Lens

Editor's Note:

Lee Geltman has been facilitating professional development groups and training therapists for over 30 years. He and his colleagues at the Gestalt Institute of New England have conducted over 60 training programs in a number of North American cities, including Boston, Pittsburgh, Phoenix, and Ottawa. I have had the pleasure of visiting his institute, and I have been impressed with the atmosphere he and his fellow trainers set for their participants. Their program embodies and exemplifies the relational ethic that is being explored throughout this book. In the following conversation, I talk with Lee about what he knows about fostering the connective tissue required for exposure and learning in a group situation.

9

•••••••••••••••••••

The Relational Ethic of

Understanding

in Groups:

A Conversation

Lee Geltman & Robert G. Lee

Bob: You have been leading groups and training therapists in a group format for a long time. More than just the nuts and bolts of how to set up groups and group dynamics, you seem to know something about people, how to understand them, and how to support them in a group setting. These qualities are the basic elements of the relational ethic in interacting with people in general. So I am interested in what you know about people and how that helps you facilitate people feeling sufficiently safe to participate in a group setting?

Lee: I have come to expect that when people come to a group experience, a workshop, a personal growth group, training program, or any kind of learning program that focuses on them as a person—they want something, both generally and very specifically. They want to show themselves and to be seen by others and to be appreciated and respected for what they show, to be understood for who they are and why they do what they do. And they want to understand themselves. They want to re-know themselves, re-hear themselves as they evolve. It often takes people awhile, sometimes a great while, to realize this and to consciously move in this direction.

Bob: From my own experience that makes sense to me. Say more.

Lee: I think of the T. S. Elliot quote about going on an extended exploration and arriving back where we started and knowing the place for the first time. Implicit in that quote is that people come to understand and appreciate how they fit—with past connections and the potential for future connections, with how they are valued and how they value others. I think that is what people want. They want to know themselves through a connection with others as they continue to evolve. And this is not a one-time occurrence as my using this quote implies; it is something we return to time and again. It is a foundational element of growth throughout life. Being heard and understood while giving voice to what's inside of us in response to meeting someone else is how we come to know, and how we are supported in the knowing of, ourselves. I think that is what people want when they come to groups, and I expect this to happen. You don't have to do anything to make it happen. You only have to be able to tap into it, tap into people's desire to connect with others and in the process rediscover themselves.

Bob: How do you tap into this resource?

Lee: Well, just knowing that it is there, that this is what people want, can be a guide in everything I do as a leader. Let me give you an example. If you do a lot of groups inevitably there are going to be difficult situations that arise—people don't get along, or can't hear each other, or don't like what they hear. Tension and difficulties are a part of all group experiences. Fortunately, much of the time, over the years, I have had some idea of what might help. But to illustrate the point that I am making here, there have also been many times in when I did not know what to do or not do next, how to respond or even what to highlight. The way I supported myself and the group during these times, what got us through these times, was my having an unshakable belief in the ability of the group to figure out a way to get through a situation. I stayed with the group, stayed with the process, kept bringing process to the foreground. That wasn't the only factor, but it was an important piece. In a very high percentage of these difficult situations, groups have found a way to work it out. Such a belief in the process, which is underpinned by a belief in people's wanting to connect, has buoyed me and the people in the group. It has infused me with a certain confidence. I sometimes say to trainees that one way of handling a situation where you don't know what to do is to say to the group or to the person, "I have no idea what to do about this." That keeps the responsibility for what's next where it belongs—in the group. The secret is to say it with confidence, thereby indicating that it is part of the process and that I'm going to be there figuring it out along with them.

Bob: I catch the paradoxical gift here. I think of how the Gestalt notion of responsibility applies here in a couple of ways. First it means that you don't take on a task that belongs to the people in the group. But in addition, the word responsibility means having the ability to respond. And this message, and the way you say it, appears to provide a holding for people as they experiment with, and further develop their ability to respond in the current situation.

Lee: This message implicitly expresses my confidence in the people in the group, my appreciation of the difficulties being encountered and my willingness to travel with them. In particular, it supports both my creativity and their creativity, because they "know" and I "know" there is a solution to whatever it is that we are struggling with. When people believe there's a solution, they are much more likely to find it.

Bob: It would seem that this faith of yours fits well with Gestalt theory.

Lee: Well, from a Gestalt perspective, it is the act of contact, of meeting another that is the crucible for living, evolving, and thriving. And the moment is not predictable. We don't know what will happen, what we and others will do, until it happens. This, in itself, holds a sense of the possible, of what can come from contact. My faith that people in groups will find a way to "figure it out" as well as what I have come to understand about what people want when they come to a group are supported by Gestalt theory. However, these beliefs of mine are mostly born out of the many experiences I have had as a group leader in which I have had the opportunity to discover/witness these qualities in people and groups.

Bob: Do you have examples of how you have witnessed this in groups?

Lee: I remember a series of workshops that I did many years ago with teenagers, who, as you know, are often reluctant to talk with adults about their lives or anything of a personal nature. We did an exercise in which everybody had five minutes, measured with an egg timer, to tell their life story, followed by a minute to tell the happiest experience in their life. I co-lead these groups with a colleague, and one or the other of us would always go first to model the experience, and to make it an activity that the kids did not have to do alone. Some of the kids would then take a turn, then the other leader would do it, and finally the rest of the kids would go. People who were listening in the group, when it was not their turn, were not allowed to comment on what was being shared. With this level of support, the kids wanted to participate. They wanted to be heard! In fact, once they started, they couldn't stop talking. They would start talking as soon as their time came, they would share very intimate details, and they wouldn't stop talking until their time was finished.
    Another thing that impressed me was that out of any group of fifteen or so kids, about three of them would *not* have a happiest experience! That really caught my attention, since these were relatively affluent teenagers who were youth group members and therefore were social, not isolated, and appeared to have support.

However, in spite of not having a happiest experience, they wanted to tell their story just as much as the others.

Bob: That sounds like a powerful experience.

Lee: Yes, it was. And there have been many other group experiences that have contributed to my sense of what people want when they come to groups. However, I think that the roots of this belief predate my experiences as a group leader and come in relation to how I listen.

Bob: What you say sparks my curiosity. Usually when people develop a skill it is because they have had the experience that the skill is valued. Is that true for you? Was there a time that you learned that your listening was valued?

Lee: Well, over the years people have consistently told me that I was a good listener, so it has continually been reinforced in me. But, if I think back, my initial experience with listening came as a child. I was forced to listen, in a way, to my family, and to my aunts in particular, who would talk about the most inconsequential things or would tell the same stories over and over again.

Bob: How was that for you? The way you say it, it doesn't sound like it was something that you enjoyed, but it certainly must have been a large ongoing statement that your listening was needed and thus valued.

Lee: Yes. I knew that I was valued, and in particular I knew that my being able to be a good boy and listen was valued. I didn't have to do anything except listen. At the time it depressed me. I was a captive audience. But I didn't have words to describe my plight, and no one was listening to me who would want to hear my experience in this way. However, the power of listening to others was deeply impressed upon me.

Bob: What you say is an excellent example of what I have said about self-confidence, namely that self-confidence is a misnomer. Self-confidence is not just about a knowing of the self. Instead it is a sense that we will be responded to, a sense that we will be valued by others for something that we do. Thus it is a confidence in others' interest in us and their ability to respond. And is what you're saying that your aunts' valuing of you in this way, needing you to listen to them, has translated into your developing a confidence in your ability to listen which has served you well in groups?

Lee: Yes. That's right. And correspondingly there are other things that I don't have confidence in because I didn't get support around those things growing up. For example, I still don't have confidence about putting clothes together, or what looks good on me. I don't have confidence about that because growing up that was always decided for me.

To bring this back to what we are talking about here, my family growing up was the group that had the biggest impact on my sense of self. I believe that is true for most people. And when people come to a group, it is patterns of experience and concomitant belief that often extend back to early learnings such as these that people are revisiting and exploring. These patterns (this template) are recreated both to support an old sense of how we can be known and how we can know others and to explore new possibilities where the old patterns are no longer satisfying, are limiting, or are the result of trauma. However, we do not make these changes easily; our habits are extremely powerful fixed gestalts.

Bob: So how does this play out in a group situation? Maybe a better question, from a relational ethic perspective, is what allows these patterns to be explored within the dimensions of group interaction?

Lee: Well, that's a complex question. Almost anything that happens in a group can be used to explore these patterns. The real ongoing experiments constantly being conducted by the people in the group revolve around whether it is possible to be known and to know others, to connect with others in some fashion, to provide relief, acceptance, perspective and hope that stems from a sense of additional possibilities and choices.

Bob: Can you give some further examples of how you came to discover, develop this core understanding you have of what people want, are about, when they come to a group?

Lee: Play is an area where many or most of us as adults have yearnings that we might not think are appropriate, will not be well received, are silly, or dumb. Our society tells us that when we grow up we are supposed to be serious, and in fact as adults there is much in modern life about which we have to be serious. So in addition, we can tell ourselves that we are not supposed to play or that play has very specific boundaries, rules, and occasions. I once ran a group titled "Play Therapy for Adults" in which I filled the room with toys, drawing materials, and various paraphernalia of childhood. When the group started I asked people to spend the first 30 minutes nonverbally. They could make sounds but no words. That half hour generated more than enough material for us to attend to for the rest of the weekend workshop.

Bob: What kind of themes emerged in this workshop?

Lee: What was both surprising and reassuring to me was the similarity in the themes. People were less inhibited, less practiced in how they connected with others and in how they presented themselves. They were literally and figuratively projecting themselves into and onto a set of interactions that most were years removed from. At the same time the creativity, comradery and fun of playful interaction was something they yearned for or they would not have signed up for this workshop.

Bob: This seems like a very valuable experience for people. You said you once ran a group like this. Do you not run groups like this now?

Lee: I ran a few groups like this, but now I prefer to run groups where material emerges more organically from where people are in a particular moment. However, I learned a lot from these groups. I now notice and pay attention when people are embarrassed by exposing their desire to play. Play can also be used to help us through a particular situation. Also from these experiences, I have learned to use humor in groups to lighten, lubricate, and counterpoint the seriousness, highlighting that this type of learning and exploration can be enjoyable as well as "heavy." Using humor is a two-edged sword, however, since people can be shamed if they think they are being laughed at rather than joined, appreciated, or understood.

Bob: Do you have other examples of themes that help people clarify their on-going experiments with how it is possible or safe to make connection with others?

Lee: People's relationship with time is a gold mine of material about how they organize their sense of themselves and how they fit in their world. Like play, I originally explored this domain when I did a whole weekend on people's relationship with time. This occurred in a professional program in which people had been arriving for group meetings at very different times, which was often a source of contention between participants. Some came a little early, or a lot early; others got there on time, a little late or a lot late. I asked people how their preferred choice of arrival time for the group was representative of how they lived their life. I invited them to think about where they learned their style, how it fit into the environment in which they learned it, and how it worked and didn't work now in their life and in this group.

Bob: This is obviously a topic that could engender a great deal of shame and/or humiliation. Approaching this material in the non-judgmental, inviting manner that you describe must be important in enabling people to open the door and expose and explore their connection to the world in this area. I imagine part of the secret of the extent to which this approach is successful is looking at this material from a field perspective rather than an individualist perspective, helping people appreciate and be proud of how their styles served them in a particular contextual setting—usually their family of origin—and how it is serving and not serving them in this group, and by extension, in their life today. It is how we have learned to fit into a particular context that holds the key for us understanding our behavior.

Lee: Often in exploring this kind of material we learn how developing our style has been necessary for our survival or how it has been our way of shaping the context to discover and create our identity in relation to our environment.

Bob: Can you give me some examples?

Lee: Well, I remember one of the women in that group recalling her experience as a young child. She and her sister used to spend every night looking out the window for their father's car, unsure when he would arrive. They longed for him to come home as their mother was often unavailable. The woman's memories of the waiting shared by her and her sister were painful to her, and she realized it made her uneasy when anyone that she cared about or was involved with was late. In an attempt to keep these feelings in the background, she became the one who was late.

Another story that I remember involves a businessman who carried tremendous shame. He hated confronting people as he knew what it is like to be shamed. He said, "if I'm late, I feel like I'm disrespectful to the person or persons that I am meeting. If I am early, and others are not there when I arrive, I don't like it. Thus I try to make sure that I am on time." When this man was a child his father would call to say he was on his way home from work, but he would never be home on time. Yet when he and his father, or all the family, went some place they were always on time. His father would leave at the last minute, he would drive very relaxed, but they would glide up to the arrival point exactly on time. That left this man with a sense that his father didn't like or enjoy coming home, which helped shape his own feelings of worthlessness. Thus, everything about moving through space and time to any meeting with others was bound with anxiety and potential shame.

Bob: As you say, hearing people's individual stories gives their behavior new meaning. So how do you tap into people's relationship with time in the context of a group setting?

Lee: This often comes up when there is some disorganization in a group. If people coming in late becomes an issue, it offers a way for everyone to explore their relationship with time. Having a person or couple of people or the entire group explore this allows people to understand other possible relationships to time and as such offers them a more flexible connection with others. It also allows for a more balanced negotiation between people of differing styles since it cuts through the assumptions that people can make, when they are faced with not knowing, as to the meaning behind styles that differ from their own.

Bob: As our theory predicts[1], when people get to know one another, developing a deeper awareness of the larger field and a sense of belonging, it changes how they relate to one another.

Lee: Taking advantage of the opportunities that occur in groups, because of what people want when they come to groups, to help people to explore and re-know themselves through their contact with others, in an environment that is more responsive to them and allows them to be more responsive to others, does engender a different, more humane, caring set of internal ethics.

Bob: I imagine that this is particularly important in training groups because an important part of becoming a therapist is developing an ethical sense of relating to clients. Such an ethical sense must be best secured by being in an environment where you can experience from the inside out that you are valued and that it is possible to value

---

[1]See Chapter One of this volume.

others—where you can explore the map that you carry about the possibilities of connecting with others. The ethical lessons that come from this kind of immersion experience must be so much more profound than those acquired from any didactic presentation.

Lee: Yes, people learn directly about their assumptions and style of relating to others, which of course is their basis for relating to clients.

Bob: And this process must start with how you understand and relate to them. You were talking about people's relationship with time. Did you have more to say about that?

Lee: Yes, it's also how people say hello and goodbye. We devote a great deal of attention to this issue in our training program. It is an indication of how people move into and away from relationships. Because it starts and ends the process of meeting another in every relational episode, saying hello and goodbye raises questions about belonging—Do I belong? In what way? At what price? Beginnings and endings are one area in which this material is always present and therefore reachable. It is only necessary to ensure sufficient safety, direct participants' attention to them and organize your attention and interventions in terms of them.

Bob: Do you have examples of how you "organize your attention" in this regard?

Lee: Well, some people hang on at the end of a group, meeting or party. You want to go home or go to sleep and they're standing at the door; they want a little bit more; they don't want to let go of the experience quite yet. Leaving might make them anxious about saying "hello" to what is next. And there are people who are out the door a hour before everyone else. They might not want to be left; they might want the illusion of controlling how they will feel when they leave and/or how others will feel. So "organize my attention" means putting that "transparency," that "template," that "filter" on my experience of people's behavior and then being open to the myriad ways people and groups in relationship "come" and "go."

Bob: Do you have examples of other areas that offer a possibility to understand people on a deeper level?

Lee: Well, I think of prejudice. In some ways it is no more than an extension of what we have been talking about. People can get shamed, feel like they don't belong, have to hide all the ways they are different from others. However, with prejudice comes exclusion.

Bob: Thus it is experienced more profoundly.

Lee: Yes. The experience of exclusion is the total opposite of belonging, and offers us no opportunity to tell our story, be known, or to know others. The topic is not only extremely important in itself, but it also offers us a way to explore our sense of belonging from a different perspective.

Bob: With the other areas that you have identified you have given stories of how you came to understand their importance and potential. Could you share a similar story for this area?

Lee: Years ago, I had a chance to be a participant in a group that dealt with difference and prejudice. It was a workshop in which people of various racial, ethnic, religious, and other backgrounds were brought together. It was a week-long workshop with about 15 people. Each day they started the workshop with what they called a "clarification session" in which, over the course of the week, each person had an opportunity to tell how they first learned or became aware of prejudice in their life. This resulted in placing people in the context of who they were and where they came from, very personally and directly. One woman's parents were missionaries. She grew up in China and we heard what it was like for a Caucasian minister's daughter to grow up in a culture where she was identified as the one who was different. It always turned out to be about difference. At the same time there was a sense of universality in what the experience of prejudice was like and what it did to people regardless of the form it came in. In later years, on a couple of different occasions, I did that exercise with training groups with which I was working. As it had been for me, it was an extremely potent experience for the people in those groups. These were people who had already shared a lot. They had revealed intimate aspects about their families, their relationship with their parents and issues in their childhood. But, when we did this, we got to see a whole different view of people. The universality of it and the commonality of feelings brought people together in a new and multi-layered way.

Bob: What was your story?

Lee: I grew up in what was called the Golden Ghetto in Baltimore. It was referred to as a ghetto because it was Jewish and golden because it was reasonably affluent and middle-class. I went to a neighborhood school that was built to take care of the expansion of the area. From the third grade through the sixth grade my classes were composed essentially of Jewish kids. When the Jewish holidays arrived, the school remained open, unlike what happened on Christian holidays; school officials, however, didn't ask who would be out for the holidays, instead they asked who would be in school. Two or three kids, who were not Jewish, would raise their hands in the whole class of 30 or so students. Hence, there was a way in which I knew about prejudice against Jews, which was reinforced by the wider culture in books and TV. But I didn't directly experience much prejudice while I was growing up, insulated by living in that neighborhood. My first significant experience of prejudice came in an unexpected way, when I left my neighborhood to attend a junior high school that drew from all over the city. There were kids from every race, color and creed in the classes. I didn't think of myself as prejudiced, but what I learned in attending this new school was that I, in fact, was prejudiced—because my family was. They were xenophobic, being afraid of anyone who was not of their culture. Non-Jews were "Goys," and blacks in particular were "Schwartzahs." I didn't hear the word "Nigger;" I heard "Schwartzahs." But the attribution was the same because my family was afraid of them. My family was fearful of anybody they did not know, who wasn't family. I thought I had escaped that because I didn't consider myself prejudiced, but when I went to this new school I was confronted with my feelings of uneasiness and especially an awareness of "difference" when I saw people of different color and background.

Bob: I notice the link you make between your family being scared of non-Jews and their being prejudiced. That fits with the ethic of understanding, that we have been talking about, as an example of what can happen when there is a sense of danger or lack of support in a given situation rather than a sense of being received and belonging. I am curious further about what enabled you, what supported you in breaking this family tradition of using prejudice as a way of dealing with fear of difference.

Lee: It is an ongoing evolutionary process that is by no means over. Attending junior high, high school and college while still living at home was the first real step. I was no longer insulated from the experience of difference. However, I still had my family's attitudes and reactions to my encountering that world on a daily basis. I also had their tremendous support and caring for me on a daily basis. Leaving Baltimore and studying psychology was the second step. Practicing my craft in diverse ways with diverse populations in diverse settings is the third step, which continuously brings me into contact with my prejudices. Living with my wife and raising a family is the ongoing fourth step. This sharpens my awareness and fear of difference while giving me the support to constantly approach and withdraw from it.

Bob: Listening to you gets me thinking about my own struggle of knowing and dealing with my prejudices. As with you, it as an ongoing learning for me. And it broadens the sense that I am getting of the basis of the relational ethic I believe you work from in a group situation.

Let me summarize my sense of what you say. The ethic of

understanding means that you have a sense of people's yearning to connect with others and in the process discover themselves anew, when they come to a group. You have given several examples of your understanding of the possible dimensions of people's underlying yearnings to connect, and of the template that people carry from their past experience, often their family of origin, that funnels or shapes how their relational strivings get expressed or even known to themselves. And you have shared examples of areas which hold potential for providing a window into people's template, allowing them the opportunity to rediscover themselves and to add to their sense of possibility, areas such as play, their relationship with time, and the overarching experience of prejudice. I am interested more in how this ethic of understanding, this sense you have of who people are and what they want, guides you in a group situation.

Lee: When I see behavior that seems to me to have more intensity than the situation calls for, in terms of the relationships that exist in the group, I think about the Gestalt concept of unfinished business. I become interested in the question of how this inflated intensity, that is being displayed, is reflective of incomplete relational strivings, that the group (through two or more people) is recreating in an attempt at resolution.

Bob: You mean as opposed to just an interpersonal difference or conflict between two or more group members that needs to get resolved?

Lee: Yes. I use the interpersonal as a generative episode to focus on the intrapsychic or group level.

On the intrapsychic level, I want to find out what is impacting you about him, and I want to find out what in the relational field is stirring him about you. It might be as small as you raising your eyebrow like his brother does. This minor similarity is used by him, without awareness, to make you, in the moment, his brother. He can then experience and attempt to resolve, with you, what is unfinished for him with his brother. Then I might inquire how you are similar to his brother. This is an attempt to bring into "figure" his unaware projections, so he can begin to recognize to whom, in addition to you, he is reacting. I might then ask how you are different from his brother. He can then begin to dissolve his projections and re-see you both separate from and connected to his brother.

A group intervention might be, "this is the third fight we have had this morning." Again, this an attempt to reconfigure the group focus: from the interactional episodes to the unfolding thematic process represented by the episodes.

Bob: Let me see if I understand what you are saying from the perspective of the ethic of understanding that we have been talking about here. Are you saying that even though issues often arise in the interpersonal domain, what drives them is something on the group level or in people's internal map/screen of experience that isn't in their awareness, that is perceived of as perhaps too unsafe to know? And thus, supporting an attempt at resolving the glitch interpersonally is tantamount to continuing to support the person's or persons' sense of unsafety or lack of possible support? That is, it continues to keep people in a situation in which they don't perceive sufficient support to risk developing a voice and exposing, or even becoming aware of, a vulnerability. Thus they must continue to hide even from themselves.

Lee: I hadn't thought of it in those terms. More than an understanding you bring an important additional perspective and support for what I am trying to express. To add to what you are saying, let me talk about politics for a moment. People joke that politics exists whenever there is more than one person in the room. In this regard, people's "politics" are what we in the therapeutic professions often refer to as personality, behavior, neuroses, and style. This often gets an individualist label when it is in reality the result of an interpersonal process. People learn their politics—meaning how to get what they want, how to organize and obtain support, how to attempt to manipulate, overtly or covertly, to achieve their ends— initially and powerfully in their family, growing up.

Bob: It sounds like you are using people's "politics" to mean both how people learn to approach one another when they need something and in particular how to go about getting a need met when they don't perceive, with or without awareness, sufficient support for that need to approach it directly.

Lee: Yes, and the training ground for our politics, which becomes our map for how the world functions, is our family of origin.

Bob: Your use of the word, "politics," appears to reflect people's sense of the availability or scarcity of support for what they need, and what they have learned to do in such cases. These in turn are their internal values or ethics around interpersonal interaction. That is, these are the values that reside in their muscles, what they actually do, as opposed to what they would think or say they might do if they were asked.

Also I would add that the family itself resides in a larger context—its own history of support and loss, and its culture's history of support and loss, and the realities of the family's ongoing support or lack of support economically, socially, educationally, and so on.

Lee: I agree on both counts. When I see behavior that stands out in the group, interpersonal behavior particularly, I think intrapsychic and group in terms of attending to it and getting people to identify what's happening, rather than attempting as we used to do in the '70s to have people work it out interpersonally.[2] However, sometimes it's useful to help people work something through because that shows the group that it is possible.

Bob: Again, from an ethical perspective, I would say that you want to help people's voices, that come from their own personal struggle, become clearer. This is similar to how I think about working with

---

[2]Lee is referring here to the Encounter Group movement of the 1970's in which emphasis was put on interpersonal engagement.

couples.[3] A couple's stuck conflict is envisioned by the couple as an entrenched struggle between them. But I think of these conflicts as two separate struggles that don't have sufficient safety to fully emerge. Thus, attempting to help the couple negotiate interpersonally, I believe, is keeping them in a sense of lack of support and is therefore not an ethical solution. Instead I listen for signs of unreceived pieces of self/other, that haven't had sufficient support to emerge and develop. These appear in the guise of some form of shame, or strategy to cope with and camouflage shame and/or nonverbal or verbal indications of yearnings. I then help couple members explore and develop sufficient safety to allow a voice for such unreceived pieces of self/other to emerge. And to use your words, I believe that couple member's map for their politics, their internal ethics, around dealing with being unreceived stems from the learnings of previous experience, often from their family of origin.

Lee: That adds considerable depth, color and an additional perspective to what I am saying.

Bob: Do you have examples of what people do in a group situation when they organize their experience from a sense of unsafety, when people are acting out of their learned politics?

Lee: All of us act from our "learned politics" and it requires mindfulness and intention to do otherwise. But to answer your question, my experience is that people are endlessly creative in how they deal with this. The possibilities are multitudinous, everything that you can think of—being aggressive, withdrawn, surly, flirtatious, manipulative, deceitful, helpful, kind, polite, smart, stupid, irrational, very rational—you name it, I've seen it... done to perfection. Behaviors... any port in a storm, usually the port that people have learned and learned to do well. So for example, in groups, when we talk about scapegoating, blaming, or even any consistent personality

---

[3]See Chapter Seven of this volume for a fuller description of this perspective on working with couples, with examples.

trait—this one is really sweet or a pain in the butt or very macho or very sensitive. I don't think of them in those terms. I think of every one of them as this is the way that this person has found, successfully, to organize in and with the environment they know, using the behavior(s) they have learned to protect themselves and to advance their longings, goals, desires, needs, urges and appetites, and to survive. Everyone has their own style. I do it by becoming five years old, and being very winning and becoming helpless. "I am a cute 5-year-old; come help me."

Bob: So you start by receiving a person's style—as their sense of the world, as what they learned to do, as an expression of the ethics of interaction that were possible in their culture or family.

As to your own strategy of gaining support, using your set of skills around being a "cute 5-year old," as I have experienced you, this is clearly a choice for you. I can imagine, as you are implying, that even this strategy could be employed to circumnavigate a lack of support in other areas, potentially avoiding responsibility and taking unfair advantage of others. So it sounds like being able to act/respond/ engage from a sense of safety/belonging as opposed to a sense of isolation, danger, potential lack of support, makes a huge difference in one's politics, internal ethics.

Do you have an example of what can happen at a group level when people relate from a sense of unsafety?

Lee: The act of scapegoating. When I see people in a group focusing blame, dislike or prejudice on a particular member, this alerts me to the fact that there is someone they are, figuratively, trying to send out into the desert with their sins. The word scapegoat comes out of the Hebrew tradition of early biblical times in which a sacrifice was used to absolve the community of its sins. The sins were put on the back of a goat which was sent into the wilderness. When I see this starting to happen with group members, I look for ways to support the side of the scapegoat and/or bring the process to the awareness of the group.

Bob: Do you have the group members that are participating in the scapegoating look at how the group might be unsafe for them to risk exposing a part of themselves in the group?

Lee: Yes. The question is what are the "sins" that the group believes it needs to cast out? How has the evolution of the group, the interaction of people's politics, their unspoken, usually unaware, sense of themselves that is not acceptable—how has that led to a situation of perceived unsafety in the group, such that people need a scapegoat to purge themselves?

Bob: So developing group safety is an important goal of yours with regard to helping people explore their politics, their internal ethics.

Lee: Developing and monitoring group safety is a crucial focus. We do many things in our programs to promote this, including setting an atmosphere in which people know that we will continually attempt to understand and respond to them. However, safety is an illusive commodity, and one that must be approached to a large degree indirectly. In general, when I am working in a group, I don't think in terms of "is the group as safe as we can make it?" I think about educating people as to the nature of safety. The group is neither a safe nor an unsafe place. It is a somewhat organized and a somewhat chaotic place, especially as people are getting to know one another. As with quantum mechanics, you cannot specify with any certainty what will happen or how much safety there will be. What you can do, as with quantum mechanics, is assert some probabilities. An important element is the extent to which members are able to assess the degree of support that exists in the group for connection in general and for themselves in particular.

Bob: I imagine that people's templates and politics, their internal ethics, have a lot to do with how they assess the support level in a group situation.

Lee: Their models, if too rigid or too loose or just not in sync with the culture of the group, can misjudge the nature of support. For example there are a number of people in training programs who have had significant trauma in their lives. That may be because people with a background of trauma are attracted to the helping professions, or it may be that is simply representative of the number of people that have had trauma in the larger population, or it may be an artifact of what participants project onto Gestalt therapy training or groups in particular. In any case, many people have had experiences that have been scarring, to such a degree that they organize their experience and their perception in terms of those previous experiences. So I have people coming into the group who are extremely cautious and who don't want to work on their own personal blocks to professional effectiveness. And I have people who are very open, sometimes too open.

From a Gestalt perspective, it is important to help people test out their beliefs and experience about safety and trust against the real-time experience of what is transpiring in this particular group at this particular time. They then can decide, *with support*, how much they want to reveal, how much they want to risk, how much they want to try out. And I support them in not risking when they don't feel safe, and in risking when they do, and sometimes I support the opposite. For example, I might say, "You're putting yourself way out on a limb here. I don't know if you have enough information about (this person) or (this group) to support (where you are heading) (what you want). How did you get the idea that..." It is not so much trying to create a safe environment as it is helping people learn to assess the degree of safety, for them, in this environment, in this moment, and how to take care of themselves based on that assessment and how to continually monitor and respond when fresh experience alters their assessment.

Bob: I would guess that the stance you suggest helps develop trust in itself. There is no judgment of right or wrong about people's style in what you say. In addition you are with them as they experiment. It gives information to the whole group about people's intentions, while protecting others from having to respond when they are not ready. I find that something that can shame people most is not having their intentions understood. When people are shamed, they are more likely to enlist the side of their "politics" that is geared toward a lack of support and therefore oriented with less concern for others.

Lee: A major interest I have in assisting people in this manner is in helping people to develop the tools they will need for all interactions in their lives, not just in this group.

Bob: Do you do something similar with people's "political" styles (e.g. being aggressive, withdrawn, surly, flirtatious, and so on) as you have been describing with safety?

Lee: Yes, in the sense that I am attempting to show them and importantly the group (since it also is a teaching/training situation) how there are both benefits and costs to any particular fixed personality trait. This is something that many Gestalt therapists pay attention to. What I am focusing on in particular is illuminating this process for the other members of the training program. As we bring into figure over the course of the training every person's "intrapsychic" "political" approach, the group gets to experience over and over again how this was learned in a communal context, and how the behaviors that stimulate the rest of the group to anger or excitement or repugnance are attempts to solve the current "political" situation as that individual experiences it.

Bob: This would seem to bring us full circle with regard to what you have been saying about how your way of understanding guides you in a group situation. You understand people's desire to connect with others and to re-experience themselves when they come to a group. You are attuned to helping them in this process, to explore their map for connecting with others, their learned "politics" from previous experience. This map reflects what people have learned to do in times of perceived lack of reception or unsafety. It also contains or implies their ethical system, which will be based on their felt beliefs about the real possibilities for connection, support, and belonging in the shared human field. This also contributes to their map for understanding and engaging clients. Thus you endeavor to provide an atmosphere of sufficient support that people may explore their style and their sense of safety. And in being with them in this process, as you describe, you offer them a sense of belonging from which to craft alterations to their "politics," their internal sense of ethics. And you have graciously shared examples from your own life that model this process.

Lee: As I have shown in relating my own experiences, this process is an ongoing exploration for all of us in the helping professions. It is often painful, sometimes poignant, occasionally exhilarating and almost always challenging and deeply satisfying.

Editor's Note:
Philip Lichtenberg has been writing on relational topics, from a Gestalt perspective, for nearly three decades. Over the last decade and a half he has focused on the subject of oppression. In the following pages he takes up a natural extension of his work, namely the ethics of treating people who oppress. Lichtenberg's conclusions here parallel and give detail to the ethics that we derived from Gestalt field theory in Chapter 1 of this volume. He reminds us that we all have the potential to oppress, and that oppression is a field phenomenon. He finds that in working with oppressors we not only need limits, but we also need empathy and an ability to become interested in the experience of oppressors. And to do this work we need sufficient internal and external support.

10

••••••••••

On Treating

Agents of Oppression

Philip Lichtenberg

As we learn to nurture both by being nurtured and by nurturing others, so too, we learn to oppress both by being dominated and by dominating others. Nurturing and oppressing, the issues in *treating oppressors*, are alike in that they are characteristics of relationships. To nurture, it is necessary to have someone needing care; to oppress depends upon someone or some group being available to become the oppressed. Furthermore, because nurturing and oppressing are relational, persons learn the principles of nurturing and oppressing whether they are predominantly the agents in such relationships or the objects of nurturing behaviors or oppressing acts. Whether one renders nurturing behaviors, is the recipient of them, or is a bystander to nurturing events, one learns what nurturing is about. Watching a four-year-old tend his turtle may suggest how his father talks to him on a Saturday morning. Another possibility would be the little boy watches how his father talks to his mother or his sister. If done well, nurturing contains one set of characteristics. If done poorly, it possesses a different set. Either set can be acquired no matter which position the person holds in the relationship. So also with oppression.

Because oppression is a relational phenomenon, it is likely that all persons are sometimes oppressors and sometimes oppressed. No one is always underneath, though it may seem so when one is being oppressed. When one is being dominated, the feeling is all encompassing and it is difficult to believe at that moment that one can also be in a position of power. Thus, a battered spouse is usually unaware that she is on top sometimes with her husband and often with her children. This means that we must be careful in treating persons that we not fall into the habit of believing "they" are oppressors and "we" are the oppressed. When we do believe that this is true, we tend to deny our own propensity to dominate in certain relations and alienate our dominating behavior by projecting it onto those we have designated as "oppressors." Accordingly, when I refer to the ethics of treating persons acting as oppressors, I am directing attention to what is involved in our nurturing those persons who are *now* acting as an oppressor in order that they become more prone to engage in more humane, respectful relationships. Our aim must not be to dominate the oppressor and hope to eliminate the tendency to exploit others, but rather to create a transforming relationship that will foster mutually rich encounters.

Since my topic is how to treat an oppressor, I am inviting the reader to enter into the perspective of someone who is other than an oppressor at the time of engagement. Care must be taken, therefore, not to overlook the contribution of the oppressed to an oppressive relation since such relationships are mutually created. Indeed, part of transforming these relations of dominance and submission depends upon those slated to be the oppressed not colluding in establishing the disrespectful nature of the relation. Care must be taken as well to have empathy or concern for the oppressor as well as the oppressed. I think it is probably the case that the oppressed may appear to have a leadership function in undoing oppression, not because they suffer more, or the persons on top are satisfied with their lot. Rather, the influence of the oppressed is more hidden in oppression and becomes more figural in its transformation. I believe that in undoing the clinch of oppression, sometimes the oppressed and sometimes the oppressor takes the lead. In the discussion that follows, obviously, the person who is not the oppressor takes the leadership position.

When we think of oppression, we tend to imagine Hitler, Stalin or others who have held such powerful positions. But we can better see that they "represent" vividly persons who oppress, that they are primarily extreme examples of what occurs regularly in everyday life. Such political figures build on the everyday instances of oppression as when a teacher intimidates in the classroom, an employer threatens and exploits workers, or a man or woman acts to control his/her spouse. I believe we can learn from the mundane how to deal with the larger social scene if we study the local in deep fashion.

The Challenge is Great

There is good reason to expect that persons who are most often acting oppressively, who are committed to such behaviors in some way, are more difficult to treat than are persons who are less often in this position or less committed to it. An individual may be seen as committed to being an oppressor from a personal base, from being in a social role in an exploitative system, or from both. That is, a person may *need* to be dominant and may *need* to avoid being vulnerable, or even an equal, to satisfy personal integrity. Such a man or woman may feel threatened, frightened, or unstable if he or she is not in command of the relationship, and so may insist upon being dominant. These individuals learn well the methods for manipulating relationships, whether overtly or covertly, to achieve the position of oppressor in the relationship. We are familiar with the resistance to psychotherapy that is typical of batterers as well as the assaults on the field of mental health by right-wing politicians and religious leaders. These are individuals who must cover their basic vulnerability with personal needs for power over others, and psychotherapy would challenge these needs. Striving for power that diminishes the other (power *over* rather than *with* others) signifies intolerance of felt weakness without that power.

On the other hand, a person in a superior position in an authoritarian system may carry forward oppression by implementing the organizational principles of that institution. These individuals can be oppressive because they have social support, even requirement, for acting in this fashion. One is not simply free in an autocratic organization to act in a democratic way, though there may be some possibility to act more democratically if creativity is used (Lichtenberg, 1988). It is often the case, however, that persons with an authoritarian personality (Adorno, Frenkel-Brunswik, Levinson and Sanford, 1950) rise up to positions of power in authoritarian institutions so that both personality demands and social requirements promote being an oppressor.

I am convinced that we are not restricted to psychotherapy when applying the psychological insights concerning oppression. As I have proposed in two works (Lichtenberg, 1990/1994; and Lichtenberg, van Beusekom and Gibbons, 1997/2002), one can try to undo the clinch of oppression and make possible a change of orientation in oppressors in social action efforts and also in relations among family and friends. When we understand both the social and psychological dynamics of oppression, we can enter relationships in potentially transforming ways. I am suggesting here that the principles I will enunciate are guides not only to therapists but also to citizens more broadly. Although these principles derive from therapeutic work, they can be applied outside the therapeutic context as well as inside the consulting room. Productive citizenship embodies the best of what transpires in a therapeutic endeavor. While the average citizen has not been educated to know all that a therapist is presumed to know, good living in everyday life parallels good connecting within therapy. We should not keep these as separate as they are usually made to be. Thus, the ethics of treating oppressors generalizes to the ethics of social life when oppressive behaviors are active. I think that this is coherent with the position Lee (2002, Chapter One of this volume) takes in this book concerning the ethics that emerges from Gestalt field theory.

Attending to both personality dynamics and properties of large and small social systems brings me to the two central reasons that oppressors are hard to treat successfully. Insofar as persons acting as oppressors hold positions of power in social institutions, the therapist or person doing the treating is vying with the countervailing pressures emanating from the authoritarian institution. (I would include auto-cratically run families and schools in this category.) Years ago, in therapy with children, we found that helping the child while ignoring the parents meant that every gain in the therapy was likely to be challenged by the needs of the parents to have the child as he or she was previously. This was the origin of family therapy. Similarly, when we had therapeutic communities for the mentally ill (Jones, 1968), the patients did well in hospital but reverted to their problematic functioning when they returned home to dysfunctional families. Transforming an oppressor into one who is not an oppressor raises the ethical concern that one may bring that person into grave trouble in work or social life if the environment in which he or she functions is not taken into account. In any case, the social circumstance in which the oppressor exists often militates against a treatment that would bring the person to function in an equalitarian, humanistic style.

Social institutions vary along a continuum ranging from democratic to authoritarian. Insofar as they are democratic, institutions encourage individual members to discover and invent their truths within the social relationships defining the institution. Finding and sharing one's truth means that one must accept and experience all kinds of desires, those that are conventionally recognized and will be received by others, and those that are private or will likely be misunderstood by others and are thus best kept hidden. We are all like one another and have the full range of needs, from the most benign to the most malevolent. Sharing these needs involves trust that the community will support us not only in owning what is true for us but also that the community will help us to engage in social relationships that are mutually fulfilling. Our emotions are vitally important in democratic institutions. We can fear, be angry, know jealousy, love, and so forth in the best manner when we are embedded in democratic settings.

The same does not hold for authoritarian institutions, those that promote and sustain oppression. Indeed, oppression can be defined by the methods guaranteed to authorities in these institutions to *coerce* persons in managing their desires and feelings. In the social structures that facilitate these coercive methods, personal wants and emotions are strictly regulated, as I intend to argue more particularly, and such regulation leads to personal distortion and problematic group functioning. Because authoritarian institutions promote oppressive relations, they create problems for those treating oppressors. Oppressors are protected by the mores of the system from challenges within these institutions when they assert autocratic control over others.

Similarly, the personality characteristics that promote being an oppressor at a given time and in a given context make for challenges in the treatment process. In any action a person is simultaneously attending to the shaping of the social relationship in which he or she is embedded and also to the organization of his or her interior life (Freud, 1895; Lichtenberg, 1969). When we who are Gestalt therapists say that experience is at the contact boundary of the organism/environment field (Perls, Hefferline, and Goodman, 1951), we are referring to this double-sided moment: the creation of a figure by mobilizing components of the organism while simultaneously meeting and bringing forward aspects of the environment. A person is not an empty vessel in engaging the world, but someone who is organizing the complex interior of his or her being. Likewise, a person is not a simple object of social forces but is an actor in co-creating relationship. Accordingly, to be fully aware means to account to both organizing one's inner life in the relationship and at the same time shaping the social relation being developed.

Why the Project is So Difficult

An important aspect of limited awareness, one that is relevant to the unfolding and maintenance of oppression, is the obscuring of one or the other of these two elements of all experience. Either attention to the shaping of the relationship is maximized and interior life is hidden; or the reverse is true, the internal features of experience are highlighted and the management of social relations is vague or unclear. This is the background, I believe, for Jung's (1923) conception of introversion and extroversion, which has had a prominent place in the history of psychology. Often overlooked is Jung's assertion that the healthy person is *both* introverted and extraverted while the neurotic person emphasizes one or the other.

Similarly, Freud provided us with analyses of the two tendencies in two remarkable papers. In *Mourning and Melancholia* (1917/1957), Freud referred to the woman who talked at great length about how worthless and futile she felt. He noted for us two strange parts to her complaints: 1) She was telling him how worthless she felt, yet she was actively taking up his time and effort, which demonstrated in behavior that she believed she was at least worth listening to. And 2) many of the complaints that she related to him about herself fit more perfectly to her dissatisfactions with her husband. Thus, while she emphasized her interior life in her narcissistic ruminations, she kept obscure that which belonged to social relationships, that with Freud and that with her husband. In a later paper in which he addressed the problem of paranoia, Freud (1922/1955) proposed that the paranoid individual, by means of projecting, puts in the other that which belongs to his or her internal life. The paranoid process, as a mirror image of depression, focuses on problematic social relations while hiding through projecting what is internal and is threatening to come into awareness. From early in his career, Freud (1895) suggested that consciousness involved the integration of what was coming from instinctual impulses—the equivalent of what I am considering internal matters—and perceptions. If either representations of the desires or perceptions of the external world are limited, consciousness is diminished.

Whereas serious depression and clear paranoid processes both show diminished consciousness, experience in more normal existence may not reveal the problem quite as unambiguously. When my friend tells me she is angry with me, she may do this either pushing me away or pulling me into a bonding with her. If she believes that in telling me simply that she is angry at something I have done, she is *fully* revealing her inner life, she is mistaken. She is, in fact, effectively blaming me, which causes me to distance myself from her. She has failed to include those aspects of her inner world that I have offended. Her anger touches our social relation, but it does not illuminate sufficiently her inner life. When she adds to her irritation about my behavior a more complete account of her desire that is being frustrated, a desire I might otherwise wish to satisfy, she makes it more likely that I will approach her. I may or may not choose to meet her want, but I am now privy to as much about her as I am to what she sees about me. So: "I'm mad that you are late for our dinner date" is different from "I'm mad that you are late for our dinner date because I was afraid you had forgotten me and I felt lonely." Or, "I'm mad that you are late for our dinner date because I imagined I had come to the wrong place and I felt foolish." Or, "I'm mad that you are late for our dinner date because I was excited by my expectation for the evening and I became very disappointed." When my friend includes herself in greater detail, she puts herself on a level with me rather than in a superior position.

I take only a short step, then, when I propose that awareness in oppressors is limited and distorted. By keeping obscure their inner life, and by directing excessive attention to the conditions of the social relations around them, persons acting oppressively possess a narrow awareness. They are "anti-intraceptive" (Adorno, Frenkel-Brunswik, Levinson and Sanford, 1950). These authors point to the meaning of anti-intraception: "...impatience with and opposition to the subjective and tender-minded...." "The extremely anti-intraceptive individual is ... afraid of genuine feeling because his [sic] emotions might get out of control" (p.235). Oppressors, thus, not only avoid emotions, especially the more tender feelings, but they are positively antagonistic to the appearance of such emotions in social relationships *unless they are expressed by those who are oppressed*. It is all right from the standpoint of oppressors for the oppressed to demonstrate these emotions—though often contempt is shown for their appearance—but it is not perceived to be permissible for oppressors themselves to be seen in the light of possessing such feelings. Furthermore, I believe that persons who often act as oppressors become expert at evoking in the primed vulnerable others these feelings which they can then try to control socially by criticizing, blaming, ridiculing, and so forth.

The direct consequence of being anti-intraceptive is the readiness to project onto others what is not accepted as something of one's own. When a person cannot integrate in awareness the internally rising feeling with perception of the other, the desire or emotion does not disappear simply because it is not integrated. Instead, it is attributed to the other and enters awareness as a characteristic of the other. A representation of something of oneself is now organized as a representation or perception of an external influence and enters awareness in this distorted form.

A General Theory of the Psychology of Oppression

I have argued at length that oppression involves projection upon a primed vulnerable other by the oppressor (Lichtenberg, 1990/1994). Similarly, oppression involves identification with the aggressor on the part of the oppressed. Persons are prepared to be oppressors in the degree to which they emphasize social relations while making interior happenings obscure in their awareness, the precondition for projecting to take place. And persons are primed to be oppressed in the degree to which they take on as their personal, inner concern what is occurring in relationship while making vague all that is involved in shaping that relationship, the precondition for faulty introjecting.

In my analysis of oppression, I have said that the oppressor and the oppressed collude in creating and maintaining oppression. I have referred to "the clinch of oppression" to indicate that the interlocking of projecting and introjecting leads to confluence between the oppressor and the oppressed. The oppressor projects; the oppressed introjects these attributions; and the boundary delineating these actors is made unclear. They become fused in living out their psychological lives and become dependent upon each other in unwholesome ways.

In a description of psychoanalytic treatment that enables a patient to grow, Jay B. Frankel (1993) describes in a way parallel to my own assessment the movement from collusion between analyst and patient to intimacy as analysis proceeds. His description is heavily indebted to Jessica Benjamin's *The Bonds of Love* (1988) in which the focus is on domination in the sense I am calling oppression. In collusion between the patient and analyst, Frankel notes: "...each may sense in the other a frightening possibility and may position her-or himself in a way that gives the illusion of control over the frightening other. Misunderstanding and coercing the other are intrinsic to collusion." He goes on to say: "I propose that intimacy is the opposite of collusion. The word 'intimate' refers to what is innermost in oneself and to an interpersonal relationship in which one can make this known to another. Writers on intimacy from the interpersonal school… have talked about how the personal and interpersonal aspects of intimacy are interrelated." "Unlike the pretense in collusion, intimacy implies the desire to know and the capacity to accept all one may find in oneself and in the other." He labels attention to the innermost in oneself "subjectivity," and he remarks that subjectivity is lost in collusion, which leads to misunderstanding and coercion. This parallel between his thoughts within the psychoanalytic tradition of inter-subjectivity and mine within the domain of Gestalt therapy is striking.

Critical to the unfolding of this confluence or collusion in oppression is the division of labor in handling emotions. I have described a series of feelings that accompany the creation of oppression. Early on in the development of new oppressive rela-tionships, both the oppressor and the oppressed attend to the anxiety of the weaker one and hide more or less the anxiety of the stronger or superior person. The stronger person in the relationship may be solicitous of the weaker around anxiety, all the while shielding his or her own feelings from exposure. When anxiety is too great to be sustained by the participants, anger becomes prominent in the relationship. That is, anger replaces anxiety as the dominant emotion in the relation. On the one side, helpless rage is promoted in the oppressed. On the other side, both controlled rage and projected anger appear in the oppressor. When anger grows too threatening to be contained by the participants without violence erupting, it is retroflected, turned back upon the self, and, consequently, guilt and self-hatred are the major feelings that surface. Direct guilt and self-hatred are common afflictions of the oppressed, while a seeming shamelessness and projected guilt and self-hatred in the guise of moral condemnation and blaming the victim describe the oppressor.

Finally, when the confluence is entirely realized, the oppressed allow into action in the presence of the oppressor only those desires that are acceptable to the oppressor. These desires are precisely those that the oppressor refuses to own, but they are wants that are aroused and handled by being projected onto the weak. The oppressor and the oppressed enter into the "delusion of fusion" described by Hellmuth Kaiser (1965). The tyrant demands obedience without the decision to obey. The submissive individual obeys by not thinking his or her own thoughts, by not making decisions, by making fuzzy his or her individuality.

From the perspective of this understanding, the challenge in treating an oppressor is as follows. *The goal is to nurture an oppressor by "meeting" him or her through undoing faulty projecting and avoiding submission to premature demands for confluence.* Given the anti-intraceptive bias of the oppressor, this is no easy task. Yet I believe it is possible. We cannot force an oppressor to become non-oppressive, but in meeting such a person committed to oppressing, we can increase the probability that this person will choose to live and behave differently. Many such meetings will be required for change to become likely. He or she will come to prefer humanistic, equalitarian social life because it is intrinsically more satisfying personally and more effective as a principle of social organization.

We cannot force upon an individual a democratic orientation because we would be undemocratic in doing so. This is a major problem in totalitarian societies because it means that coercion would be met by counter-coercion, the very issue that causes democratic revolutions to fail. When groups intend to promote a democratic society and yet act undemocratically by coercing allegiance, their means prevent the achievement of their ends. To demand that oppressors become democratic is to demand that they become confluent with their opposition without *choosing* to do so. It would be a faulty "meeting" or collusion. We who are opposing oppression would be attempting to have the oppressor submit to our perspective, not by seeing its value and deciding to pursue it, but by introjecting our demand and submitting to us.

Understanding the Basis for Projection

If the key to being an oppressor is the tendency to project upon primed vulnerable others, then the linchpin in undoing oppression must be based on our understanding of the basis for projecting in the first place, more particularly unhealthy projecting. As with all other ego functions, a Gestalt term for patterns of organization of contact, there is healthy projection that enables us to have empathy with others and to recognize the value and validity of their subjectivity; and there is unhealthy projection which involves the diminution of one's own subjectivity and accompanying distortion of the other's.

An individual tends toward the healthy or unhealthy pole of projection depending both upon his or her developmental history and upon the nature of the social scene in which he or she is embedded. Projection is a necessary element in growth in that the infant and child is fascinated with the other—picture the infant's first smile or the small child's interest in the bathroom habits of its parents and older siblings as he or she learns to toilet train. In learning to cooperatively regulate its social relations, the child imagines the inner life of the other and fills that inner life with what he or she experiences inside. When the small child imitates and is imitated, and delights in the process, projection as well as introjection is taking place. When the teething child bites her mother's breast, she can fill in the interior behind the mother's reaction when the mother reacts with pain. Throughout infancy and childhood and into adult functioning, the individual will project in healthy ways if he or she is "met" sufficiently by the other, if his or her interior life is recognized and the other's is acknowledged openly, and together they co-create experiences that please them both.

Insofar as infants and children are either subjugated by their caretakers or, conversely, are made into kings and queens who dominate their elders, they are prepared for projecting in an unhealthy manner. The adage that children are to be seen and not heard leads to limitations of the child's subjectivity in social life. The child is exposed to unwholesome demands for confluence by means of introjecting parental authority. Such children learn to retroflect and subdue themselves from these introjects and develop severe guilt and self-hatred as a consequence of these internalization processes. Self control, it must be remembered, is the self controlled. Even when they are made into the dominant players in relationship, they hold the introjects associated with self-hatred and guilt by way of confluence with their self-negating caretakers.

In short, developmental history prepares one to be democratic or authoritarian as can be seen on any playground where there are mediators and bullies.

In the same way that developmental history predisposes one to be an oppressor or oppressed, so social circumstances can promote faulty projecting and introjecting. Any community or society that creates solidarity through constructing in a major way an enemy or denigrated out-group will foster premature demands for in-group confluence via introjecting and projecting. Such a community makes an in-group by inducing or exaggerating similarities among its members, which means that the identifications of the individuals within the in-group come from beliefs established by authority rather than achieved meetings of persons registering their particular present concerns and convictions. Tight in-groups that depend upon a common enemy limit differences within the group and then must place that which is inhibited within the group onto the out-group. These groups are typically anti-democratic. Freud described this process in *Group Psychology and the Analysis of the Ego* (1921/1955) as if it were normal group process, which it is not. And Volkan (1979), among others, elaborated the theme in his discerning account of the relations of Greeks and Turks on the island of Cyprus. Fundamentalist religions indoctrinate children, demand the wholesale introjection of dogma, and invariably project upon out-groups or simply on the nature of God. Freire's *Pedagogy of the Oppressed* (1970) is based on undoing faulty introjects and tendencies to project upon landowners and other exploiting actors. And Memmi (1984) describes pathological and healthy dependence in much the same way. There is by now a vast literature describing how social circumstances support these basic losses of ego function (again, patterns of contact process) although there is less attention to this in recent, conservatively dominated years.

Toward Meeting One Who is Presently an Oppressor

Oddly, while there are many descriptions of these faulty ways of building community, there are relatively few analyses of how to undo them. Freire's educational approach, referred to above, is one attempt and it has proven to be quite fruitful. Fanon's (1968) argument is provocative, yet its advocacy of violence, its introduction of coercion, its requirement for in-group solidarity against a common enemy, and its intolerance of deviation within the in-group, all promote the losses of ego function, ability to navigate creatively between the demands of one's internal and external fields, which I am suggesting must be overcome. Bulhan (1985) has brilliantly assessed the strengths and limitations of Fanon's perspective. He shows the validity of Fanon's analysis of oppressed and oppressor, including the pathology of the oppressor—to which I am much indebted—and also the problem entailed by his reliance on violence. We in Gestalt therapy, using our clinical experience in undoing losses of ego function, restoring the ability to navigate between the demands of one's internal and external fields, and promoting healthy social relationships, can try to contribute to a strong and firm opposition to the dynamics of oppression without the resort to riots, violence, and war. One modest attempt follows.

The person who is polar to anyone and any group now acting as oppressor is called upon to direct concern to the two-sided nature of human experience. That is, the person who is treating an oppressor or who is socially opposing an oppressor must be aware simultaneously of his or her inner life and of the social relation that is being engaged. One must keep an eye on what is happening within oneself when being subject to the demands for confluence via the introjections demanded by the projecting agent. There are common reactions to faulty confluences (e.g., resentment of the other), typical responses to efforts aimed at forcing introjections (e.g., anger—I don't want that), and to being a container of projections (e.g., What is this strange feeling of distrust I experience?). Each of these must be managed during the course of meeting someone acting as oppressor. I propose some thoughts on handling one's innermost reactions in these contexts. Similarly, there are common do's and don'ts in dealing with the social relationship involved in encountering oppressors. I will offer some ideas in this regard as well.

I address first the issue of the inner life of the person treating an oppressor, not because it is necessarily the first thing to be done in creating a meeting. I have to start someplace and I think this domain is a particularly obscured area in thinking about oppressor-oppressed relations. I conceive of three different matters calling for awareness in the person treating an oppressor in order that he/she not fall into the trap of becoming either oppressed or an oppressor him/herself: 1) What is happening inside when one is internalizing projections that come from the oppressor? 2) How is the person experiencing the demand for confluence from the oppressor? 3) How is the person treating an oppressor gathering and utilizing support from peers?

As we well know, to introject in a healthy manner, with the full use of ego function, with full awareness of the implications for ourselves and others, is to destructure what is coming in. One identifies with what is congenial to one's orientation and alienates or discards that which is not. Every projection is grounded in some perception, whether what is perceived concerns the individual who is the object of the projection (e.g., something the therapist has done) or whether it is connected to an out-group (e.g., negatives which are emphasized in discriminating against a hated other). A person operating with full ego function, which is to say, fully flexible use of various potential ways of organizing the contact process, will thus be called upon to acknowledge some validity to attributions that are usually negative or unpleasant but are the reality that serves as the basis for the projection. The receiving person may subsequently interpret differently from the projecting person what has been perceived and used as the ground of the projection. Recognition of the basis for the projection by the receiver will be accompanied by awareness and representation that the truth underlying the projection is not the whole story, or even the best interpretation, but that truth must be adequately and honestly accommodated if the projection is to be destructured in a satisfactory fashion. On some occasions, the projecting person's attribution will be accepted as a common if incomplete understanding. At other times, the individual will differ with the projecting person while not attempting to deny the person's experience. Each party is given space for what each has experienced in the past while the current destructuring process is taking place. When a racist remarks that Latinos do more poorly than Caucasian-Americans on college entrance examinations, one can accept the reality of that perception, not of an individual Latino but of an average of a group known as Latinos. To be added, then, is the conclusion that is reached from such an observation. If the racist points to lesser intelligence, a respondent can offer that there are other possibilities: the nature of the test, the educational background of the examinee, or the greater poverty level known by Latinos in general.

When a client comes into my office and greets me with "How's Freud today?" I may ask what I have done recently that gave him the impression that I could be such an exalted figure. He will have noticed something and I will have to review my experience of what he saw so that we can compare our differences on an equal plane. Thus, "You seem to think I was being smart, while I was struggling to understand what was going on. Let us see how we might resolve our difference here." Or, alternatively, "I like the warmth with which you say that. Did I do something special the last time we met that I have not remembered? May we compare our sense of the last session?"

To destructure what is being presented, one must first internalize what is being given. A person cannot identify with something or alienate it until that person has some experience with it. An idea or orientation cannot be dealt with until it is somehow known. Thus, in healthy introjections as well as unsavory ones, the individual engaged with an oppressor internalizes in the first instance what is being projected. Accordingly, a person becomes a "container" (Bion, 1970; Sandler, 1987) of another person's projections when that other is acting now as an oppressor. Being a container of another's projections means that internal awareness is confounded. Internalizing that which the other has projected, one becomes, at least temporarily, confluent with the oppressor. Until the person has sorted out what is his or her own, independent contribution to awareness of the here and now and what has been stimulated by the projecting other, the feelings and thoughts that are activated are complex and confusing. Whose feelings are these anyway—how much are they mine and how much the other's? This means the person acting as a container must stay with the confusion, not project, and then come to a new clarification.

If the person dealing with an oppressor adopts, by introjecting, the anti-intraceptive mode of the oppressor, the task of defining whose feelings are whose becomes even more taxing. Each party to the transaction is likely to speed up the encounter so as to avoid the challenging feelings. This is probably why escalations take place between batterers and those who are battered, or between couples who are known to fight with each other. Right-wing activists often interrupt their opponents, use loaded terms, and lead to confrontations and violence possibly as a way to avoid attending to their inner lives which might be uncomfortable for them.

If, on the other hand, the person can tolerate discomfort as a container for the projecting person, that individual is likely to experience two classes of affect. One kind of affect is the sense of vulnerability, helplessness, or powerlessness that is threatening the person acting as an oppressor and is presently being projected. To be an oppressor one must present oneself as invulnerable, steel-hardened, powerful, immune to attack. Whenever any indication of weakness, tenderness, or softness begins to arise in the context of oppression, the oppressor must somehow divest self of awareness of that feeling. Some persons can simply stop the feeling from developing, but most will rearrange matters by producing or vigilantly noticing the affect in the weaker party. They can then act to control it by managing the social relation, as, for example, in becoming overly solicitous or protective of the other. The person who is a container of the oppressor's projection must then contend with an inner life that is confusing in its felt powerlessness or helplessness.

The other kind of affect that is experienced by the person who is the object of the projection is the particular affect that has come to permeate the social relationship. I refer here to anxiety, anger, guilt and self-hatred, the projections of which are basic to the installation and maintenance of oppressive relations. Because I have described these in brief above, and at greater length elsewhere (Lichtenberg, 1990/1994), I need only to point to them now as a challenge to the person who is a container of a projection.

As a container of another person's projected affect, the individual who is engaged in modifying the oppression faces several problems.

Experiencing the Complex Feeling

First, the individual must "own" the feeling, must experience it fully in all its complexity. Being aware of powerlessness, rage, or guilt, for instance, is no simple matter; and, when the feeling is further confused by seeming to be inappropriate to the situation, staying with the emotion is doubly difficult. A feeling may appear to be inappropriate when it is stronger than the circumstance merits—"I feel angrier than I usually do in situations like this." Or, although appropriate, it may be inapt in its intensity—"I feel very guilty for being raped. I may have taken less precaution about drinking than was safe for me, but my guilt seems to be greater than that." A precondition for destructuring a feeling is experiencing it vividly. In addition to a tolerance for ambiguity, thus, a person acting as a container for a projection must have a tolerance for intense affect or must have social support for allowing the affect to unfold.

Discriminating Self and Other

When the feeling is allowed into awareness and kept aware, the next challenge is the discrimination of who has contributed to that feeling and in what way. The psychoanalytic attention to projective identification (e.g., the several authors in Sandler, 1987) develops this theme. Is the affect purely sent forth by the projecting person? Does it represent something from the past of the containing individual which surfaces in the connection between the projecting person and the individual who is the container of the projection? Is it a typical feeling tied to a given circumstance such that anyone in that situation would know the feeling, whatever his or her past? How much of each of these possibilities is present this time; that is, how much is mine, how much the other's and how much a function of the situation? Destructuring this complex feeling may be too much to do alone and may call for another kind of social support. So it is that psychotherapists working with clients who project often and in subtle ways rely upon consultants. Similarly, individuals dealing with bigots in social settings may need support from others as they try to meet the bigots (Lichtenberg, van Beusekom and Gibbons, 1997).

Meeting the Oppressor Anew

A third demand faced by a person who is becoming a container for a projection is to ready oneself to meet the oppressor on an equal plane. The most common reactions when one is being induced to introject another's disowned feeling are defensive reactions. They represent attempts either to avoid the other or to dominate the other. Having internalized something that has been considered to be unacceptable, and having temporarily become confluent with the other, the person carrying the projection may defensively withdraw from connection to the projecting person. While such withdrawal may enable the individual to try to assimilate what has been taken in, drain away the awful feeling, mobilize social support and reassurance, or simply get out of the way of further projections, it leaves the projecting person unsettled in his or her arousal, an arousal that provoked the projection in the first place. Like persons who are paranoid, oppressors often find themselves isolated and alone because others have moved away from them, when their intention has been to join with others safely.

The alternative to withdrawal is the effort to make the projecting person stop projecting, which is also a defensive reaction. People try to reason with oppressors, though it is common knowledge that projections do not give way to rational argument. People also contest with projecting persons, demanding that they change their attitudes or stop doing what they are doing. Persons acting as containers become impatient, use their anger to combat the other, or attempt to make the projecting person feel shame or guilt. All of these strategies are the mirror image of oppression; they are aimed at dominating the dominator. They seldom result in the meetings required for the undoing of oppression.

I have been analyzing what is happening inside when one is internalizing projections. I want now to shift the angle of vision slightly and look at how the person who is treating an oppressor experiences and reacts to the demand for confluence that is part of the projecting process. Some of this I have already done, but there is more to be noted.

As I have asserted above, by internalizing the emotion that has been projected, the person acting as a container has become confluent with the projecting individual. In addition to the feelings that have been internalized, the person who is acting as a container has another set of reactions to contend with. These are the common responses to being subjected to demands for premature confluence. Oppressors require that the other in the relationship should forfeit his or her autonomy, his or her registration of a separate will. The demand for premature fusion is the call for in-group homogeneity.

Polster and Polster (1973) have described the effects of faulty confluence as follows:

> Two clues to disturbed confluent relationships are frequent feelings of guilt or resentment. When one of the parties to a confluent contract senses he has violated the confluence, he feels obliged to apologize or to make restitution for his breach of contract. He may not know why, but he feels he has transgressed and believes that atonement, punishment or expiation is in order. He may seek this by asking for or meekly submitting to harsh treatment, scolding or alienation. He may also try to provide the punitive treatment himself by retroflective behavior wherein he deals cruelly with himself by self-degradation, abasement, or feeling worthless and bad.

Accordingly, the person dealing with an oppressor has to master this other set of attitudes and behavioral tendencies without falling into the trap of overdoing things by aggressively defining self as separate and unwilling to merge under any circumstance.

If withdrawal, physical or emotional, and attempts to dominate the oppressor are defensive reactions to the demand for premature confluence, what is the alternative that will promote a meeting with an oppressor that might lead to the undoing of oppressive actions? While managing well the internalization of an oppressor concerns the inner life of the person dealing with that oppressor, presenting oneself to the other in a non-defensive and, also, non-threatening way, is critical to the social relational process. On the non-defensive side, the person aims to become a distinct "You" to the oppressor; on the non-threatening side, he or she helps the oppressor to become a distinct "I" to himself or herself (Lichtenberg, 2000).

An individual becomes a vivid figure in the eyes of another through openly expressing his or her experience in all its complexity. Since experience is composed of elements stimulated by the other, by one's involvement in the present situation, and by one's past, there are many avenues for revealing one's awareness. I refer here to what Perls et al. (1951) called a person's "Id function": "...the Id is the given background dissolving into its possibilities, including organic excitations and past unfinished situations becoming aware, and the environment vaguely perceived, and the inchoate feelings connecting organism and environment" (p. 156). For example, "I am feeling anxious now because I am remembering hearing something akin to what you have said and that memory is loaded for me." Or, "I want to tell you how I am receiving what you have said to me." Or, yet again, "I am suddenly aware that I am cautious because I feel eerily vulnerable." Because the experience is confounded, as I have indicated above, merely revealing one's experience can be a challenge because it leaves one somewhat unguarded. Yet a person can be both strong (firm, of oneself) while at the same time owning his or her vulnerability. The main goal is to become a clear, open, present figure in the relationship. As a therapist, this means one will know how to modulate self-disclosure. At the end of his life, for instance, Ferenczi (Dupont, 1988) was experimenting with this very matter in psychoanalysis when he developed what he called "mutual analysis." By revealing one's inner life, a person lays the groundwork for a healthy confluence, a merging of individuals each of whom is possessed of will and agency.

When the person connecting with an oppressor does so in a non-threatening manner, he or she is asking about the oppressor's experience and is doing so forthrightly and respectfully. If an oppressor is targeting an out-group with a projection (e.g., Arabs are untrustworthy), that person may be asked about his or her prior experiences with members of that out-group. If an oppressor is projecting upon a therapist, then the therapist is ready to explore what has happened that serves as the basis for the projection. The aim is to enable the projecting person to own and tolerate a complex awareness so that a meeting of differentiated persons is made possible.

In helping an oppressor become a distinct "I" in the relationship, persons can act in a non-threatening way and yet they can be perceived by the projecting person as somewhat dangerous. Such perceptions are not entirely inaccurate, since the undoing of projections involves the projecting person experiencing a troubling inner life. There would be no projecting going on if the individual felt comfortable with what was coming up inside, whether that which is bubbling up is guilt, shame, self-hatred, anger or anxiety. That is to say, the projection stands in the place of these social emotions which are felt to be too difficult to master alone. Thus, the person who is in fact nurturing an oppressor will probably be met with suspicion and mistrust. These are the emotions that surface within an individual when projections are being re-owned. A therapist who expresses admiration for a client after a moment of intimacy is often faced with disbelief. "You only say that because you think it is therapeutic." This is a mild form of suspicion, which we meet regularly in psychotherapy. Anyone treating a person committed to the role of oppressor will need to manage being seen as a threatening other even when he or she is acting in a non-threatening manner.

To be non-threatening and to be perceived as dangerous is central to correcting the confluence demanded by the oppressor as well as undoing the projecting. The nurturing person observes and promotes the differentiation of participants through this contrast in behavior and experience. Rather than nurturing by becoming obscure, like the old butler, valet or house slave, the therapist or active citizen is a vivid figure, self-contained and open to the other, neither dominating nor submissive. Such a nurturer can define self clearly and allow the oppressor his or her uniqueness, even in the throes of mutual discomfort and intense feelings. No easy task. Thus, not only the social emotions connected with undoing projections must be faced, but also renewed demands for confluence from the oppressor will appear. The nurturer will be pushed to feel guilt, to reinstate the prior condition of faulty confluence, to become dependent rather than independent. Awareness of the basis for these reactions will help the person working to undo oppression stay inside him or herself without crumbling.

Many years ago, the Norwegian psychoanalyst, Nick Waal, lectured on her experience in a Nazi concentration camp. She had access to drugs since she was a physician and rendered service to other prisoners in the camp. She related that at first she gave drugs that would dampen the prisoner who was to be interrogated by the Gestapo—an equivalent of promoting withdrawal. This did not work well. She learned to provide drugs that enabled the prisoners to be vividly present during interrogation in order that they could humanize themselves without withdrawing and, obviously, without dominating the Gestapo representative. She suggested that this was a more successful strategy in preventing the worst treatment during and after the interrogation. The prisoners were helped to deal with the demand for confluence in a self-preserving and self-defining way without submitting to the demand and without setting off an escalation by threatening the Gestapo representative. The prisoners, while not independent nurturers, became active citizens in the concentration camp. They preserved their personal integrity and often "met" with those who questioned them.

We say that the person is acting toward enriched contact by exploring his or her own experience and equally fostering the other in exploring his or hers, including what accompanies the undoing of projection. When contact is rich and full, persons meet as equals and oppression is likely to be laid aside. The cure for unhealthy confluence consists of first an unfolding of the individuality of each participant, which is then followed organically by a merging on the common ground that comes forward. We know this in Gestalt therapy as the contacting and withdrawing process (Perls et al, 1951).

Healthy forms of projecting, introjecting and of confluence replace distorted forms in the ethics of meeting oppressors. Because oppression is a characteristic of social systems, the countering of oppression relies importantly upon social support. Rarely can exploitation and domination be undone well by an individual, even within the context of psychotherapy. The therapist needs support in metabolizing projections and struggling to reach a helpful confluence. The client needs support, not only from the therapist, but also in the larger social setting, when the lessons of therapy are taken elsewhere. And persons outside of the therapy room, where there is no contract for personal and social change, depend upon the support of each other in transforming oppression into democratic and fraternal relations.

When I refer to the necessity of support in dealing with an oppressor, I become aware that "support" is an ambiguous term. Sometimes persons think they are supporting others by giving them encouragement, rallying them to overcome that which they are facing. At other times, persons want to make the others feel better, to rid themselves of the discomfort or unhappiness they feel, as when mourners are humored rather than met in their grief. Or persons may join in the discomfort, not from their own direct experience but rather from an attempt to mirror what they imagine the suffering one knows. Whether acting as booster, comforter, or mirror, such supporters more often than not fail to provide what is necessary for successfully mastering the challenges of oppression. When an individual is depressed, for example, he is not helped too much by being told there are better times ahead, that there are positive things in his life, that he should focus on happier matters, or that the other "knows how he feels." So, too, with the experiences of vulnerability, powerlessness, rage, guilt and other manifestations of being in an oppressive relationship. These forms of support represent efforts to minimize or overcome the intense and confounding experiences that have been brought to the surface, and, in this respect, they foster an anti-intraceptive mode of functioning. Since the oppressor is similarly promoting an anti-psychological stance in obscuring inner life, these kinds of support simply don't do what is needed. They do not enable the person treating an oppressor to nurture well that oppressor while also taking good care of self. *That is, these means of intended support fail the test of being both practical and ethical.*

The support I am pointing to pertains exactly to what is most stressful in meeting an oppressor. It is support directed to the person's inner life that is confusing, scary, filled with a sense of weakness and vulnerability, all the feelings that are projected by the oppressor and are aroused by the demand for premature confluence. This support is aimed at making possible a "staying with" one's confounded experience such that the individual will be able to disentangle that experience into its component parts. It relies on the belief that the individual, through self-regulation, will do the creative work that will transform both self and the social relation into a humanistic, equalitarian encounter. Only the person affected directly by an oppressor can know his or her own contribution to both the relationship and the confusing inner experience that is coming into awareness. How much of my anger now comes from the projected anger of the oppressor, how much from my avoidance of felt weakness, and how much is a residual of my retroflected anger during childhood when my parents were rough with me? I feel quite vulnerable now. How much of that is exaggerated? And if my vulnerability is excessive relative to the real situation, how much is a function of my disposition to be vulnerable and how much a result of what the other is raising up in me? Am I a "primed vulnerable other" or a person open to experiencing vulnerability and, thus, a container of another's sense of weakness? Only by staying with the experience can I sort out—however incompletely—my part and the oppressor's part in the emotions of the relationship.

While this form of support will often take place apart from the oppressive relationship itself, it must not serve as a means for avoiding the relationship. Rather, its purpose is to help the person to devise new ways of being in the relationship such that the needed nurturing of the oppressor works to transform oppression. The weakness that is experienced will be accompanied by a sense of also being competent and effective. The anger that is aroused or noticed will be shepherded into directed anger rather than helpless rage. Regrets over errors or defeats will be paired with intentions to proceed further, not as moral commands, which become odious, but as organic components of staying with intense experience and creating new resolutions from this process.

This kind of support cannot be expected from an oppressor until late in the undoing of an oppressive relationship. Thus, a nurturer cannot tell of his or her experience of vulnerability with the hope of obtaining support on an equal plane from the person who is dominating. If this were possible, the dominating individual would no longer be projecting his or her vulnerability. Asking for such support would be placing oneself as a supplicant, thereby carrying forward the superior-subordinate exploitative relation. Therefore, this kind of support depends upon others who are dedicated to the undoing of oppression; and these others are likely to be in a similar psychological state, themselves needing support around the same or similar issues. The required social support is that which is rendered by equals.

The ethics of treating persons who are prone to being oppressors can be summed up as follows:

♦ Promote fuller ego functioning among all persons engaged in oppressive relations. By promoting fuller ego functioning in the oppressor, I refer to the undoing of faulty projecting and demanding confluence endeavors. In the nurturer, fuller ego functioning entails healthy introjecting patterns and finding ways to avoid premature confluence while enabling healthy merging at the culmination of contacting, at the time of consummation of a meeting.

♦ Promote full democratic group processes. By promoting full democratic processes I refer to the development of group practices that support all members in *finding* and *expressing* what they want and what they mean such that these enter into the final determination of what the group engages and accomplishes. Democracy fosters self-discovery and self-assertion by all members of the group while the group proceeds to accomplish practical purposes.

In countering faulty projecting processes and faulty demands for confluence, and in practicing and fostering healthy introjecting processes, the nurturer is promoting enriched ego functioning in these senses. In developing group processes that replace authoritarian propensities with democratic qualities, the nurturer is socially progressive and humane. These are not different activities. They are the same seen from different vantage points, the personal and the political. They are challenging activities. Of this there can be no doubt. They are, indeed, what describes living one's life well.

References

Adorno, T. W., Frenkel-Brunswik, E., Levinson, D. J., & Sanford, R. N. (1950). *The Authoritarian Personality*. New York: Harper & Brothers.

Benjamin, J. (1988). *The Bonds of Love: Psychoanalysis, Feminism and the Problem of Domination*. New York: Pantheon Books.

Bion, W. R. (1970). *Attention and Interpretation: A Scientific Approach to Insight in Psycho-Analysis and Groups*. New York: Basic Books.

Bulhan, H. A. (1985). *Frantz Fanon and the Psychology of Oppression*. New York: Plenum Press.

Dupont, J. (Ed.). (1988). *The Clinical Diary of Sandor Ferenczi*. Trans. by Michael Balint and Nicola Z. Jackson. Cambridge, MA: Harvard University Press.

Fanon, F. (1968). *The Wretched of the Earth*. New York: Grove Press.

Frankel, J. B. (1993) Collusion and intimacy in the analytic relationship. In L. Aron & A Harris (eds.). *The Legacy of Sandor Ferenczi*. Hillsdale, NJ: The Analytic Press.

Freire, P. (1970). *Pedagogy of the Oppressed*. New York: Herder and Herder.

Freud, S. (1895). *Project for a Scientific Psychology*. In: *The Standard Edition of the Complete Psychological Works of Sigmund Freud, Volume I*. James Strachey, (ed.). (1966). London: the Hogarth Press.

Freud, S. (1917). Mourning and melancholia. In: *The Standard Edition of the Complete Psychological Works of Sigmund Freud, Volume XIV*. James Strachey, (ed.). (1957). London: The Hogarth Press.

Freud, S. (1921). Group psychology and the analysis of the ego. In: *The Standard*

Edition of the complete psychological works of Sigmund Freud, Volume XVIII. James Strachey, (ed.). (1955). London: The Hogarth Press.

Freud, S. (1922). Some neurotic mechanisms in jealousy, paranoia and homosexuality. In: *The Standard Edition of the Complete Psychological Works of Sigmund Freud, Volume XVIII.* James Strachey, (ed.). (1955). London: The Hogarth Press.

Jones, M. (1968). *Social Psychiatry in Practice: The Idea of the Therapeutic Community.* Baltimore, MD: Penguin Books.

Jung, C. G. (1923). *Psychological Types.* Trans. by H. G. Baynes. London: Routledge and Kegan Paul.

Kaiser, H. (1965). *Effective Psychotherapy: The Contribution of Hellmuth Kaiser.* L. B. Fierman, editor. New York: Free Press.

Lee, R. G. (2002). Ethics: A gestalt of values/ The values of Gestalt. *Gestalt Review,* 6(1), 27-51.

Lichtenberg, P. (1969). *Psychoanalysis: Radical and Conservative.* New York: Springer.

Lichtenberg, P. (1988) *Getting Even: The Equalizing Law of Relationship.* Lanham, MD: University Press of America.

Lichtenberg, P. (1990). *Undoing the Clinch of Oppression.* New York: Peter Lang. Re-issued as: *Community and Confluence: Undoing the Clinch of Oppression.* (1994). Cleveland, OH: GIC Press.

Lichtenberg, P. (2000). Creating a distinct "I" and a distinct "You" in contacting. *The Gestalt Journal,* 23 (2): 41-50.

Lichtenberg, P., van Beusekom, J., and Gibbons, D. (1997). *Encountering Bigotry: Befriending Projecting Persons in Everyday Life.* Northvale NJ: Jason Aronson. Republ.: GestaltPress, 2002.

Memmi, A. (1984). *Dependence: A Sketch for a Portrait of the Dependent.* Boston, MA: Beacon Press.

Perls, F., Hefferline, R. F., and Goodman, P. (1951). *Gestalt Therapy: Excitement and Growth in the Human Personality.* New York: Julian Press.

Polster, E. & Polster, M. (1973). *Gestalt Therapy Integrated.* New York: Bunner/Mazel.

Sandler, J. (Ed.). (1987). *Projection, Identification, Projective Identification.* Madison, CT: International Universities Press.

Volkan, V. (1979). *Cyprus—War and Adaptation: A Psychoanalytic History of Two Ethnic Groups in Conflict.* Charlottesville, VA: University Press of Virginia.

Editor's Note:

In the following chapter, Jeffery Parks shares with us troubling stories of trauma experienced by men during the process of divorce. That the experience of trauma is a possibility for men during divorce, let alone a somewhat common occurrence, is a relatively new and surprising phenomenon. Historically we know that divorce practices and laws favored men: the idea that women would get the children, or any significant property share, is quite a recent thing, really a post-war trend in the US. Many wrongs have been righted by this general trend, and in many cases the interests of children were better served.

However, the law is a blunt instrument, and at times needlessly, destructively blunt. And, as frequently occurs with trauma, the resulting current incidence of trauma in men in the divorce process has profound broader ramifications—for the families of these men and for society as a whole.

Parks' approach in helping these men and their families recover from trauma is another excellent example of an approach based on understanding people from the perspective of their relational strivings and of supporting the larger field. He insightfully understands these men from the viewpoint of the trauma they are experiencing, which is such a severe, forced rupture in their connections with their families and their way of life, as opposed to the individualist oriented understanding from solely a position of power and control. The curative solution that he brings is based on helping these men recover a deeper sense of and be able to respond to their relational needs—something that women often say they want more of from men. Parks also gives us some structural suggestions of how divorcing families might be better served in this difficult process of uncoupling and forming new identities in the world.

11

•••••••••••••••••••

Men's Relational Needs
Through the Trauma & Recovery
from Adversarial Divorce:
A Conversation
Jeffrey Parks & Robert G. Lee

Bob: Your work primarily focuses on men. Still the title you have given our conversation here brings up for me how the process of divorce, which so many of us have been through, can become a nightmare for both men and women, filled with escalating cycles of misery, which are so far from the hopes, dreams and good will that started the relationship.

Jeff: Yes, all too often this is the case. Our society still has not developed an adequate structure to hold men and women and their families as they make their way through the difficult, vulnerable process of uncoupling and establishing new identifications in the world. Mostly, resolution of "unresolvable marital differences" falls to the jurisdiction of the courts and the legal system. However, this is an adversarial system in which accusations, blame, identifying the "guilty" or "incompetent," and power can too often rule. This does not leave much room for supporting or even understanding people's vulnerability. Also by defining the problem as resolvable only by lawyers and the courts we create a population that believes this is true.

Bob: How have we arrived at this state? Has it always been like this?

Jeff: Well, as awful as it is, in some ways, legal and other family conflict and change interventions are in the process of evolving. We don't have to go back very far in history to a time in which it was not possible to get a divorce at all unless you could prove adultery or extreme physical or mental cruelty. Nor do we have to go back far to find a time when women primarily bore the brunt of trauma in divorce—a time when it was unheard of for women to get the children or any significant property share. Even more egregious, during an era when otherwise unobtainable divorce was sought through surreptitious means, a time when legal practices in general favored men, it was not unheard of that a man could go to court and have his wife judged insane and put in an asylum simply for the purpose of getting her out of his life.

Bob: So while there is still much to do, many wrongs have been righted.

Jeff: Yes, ironically, the current level of possible trauma caused by the divorce process, for men and their families, started in the early '70s when divorce rates suddenly soared as new "no fault" divorce laws were passed. Until that time, not only was "unresolvable marital difficulties" not a legally acceptable reason for divorce, but in addition it was culturally shameful to expose that you had "problems" as a couple and it was even more shameful to get a divorce. So people most often stayed together when they had "unresolvable marital difficulties."

When my parents, in 1962, separated in my middle class New York suburb, at age 13 it felt like a bad secret that I had to carry alone. So people, in the main, hid their marital problems. And of course that also meant that instances of physical abuse, extreme verbal abuse, and other forms of domestic violence were also hidden.

Bob: So the loosening of the taboo around divorce followed the free speech movement of the '60s in which traditional relational structures were questioned and replaced with experimentation with new and different ways of relating.

Jeff: Yes, and it was this age group, that experimented relationally in the '60s, that also started to experiment with divorce in the '70s. Older generations, to a high degree, still did not see divorce as an option. But the new surge in the number of divorces created a market in the legal system, which again was oriented around competition and adversarial resolution, in which the side with the most power tends to win. Ironically, when new divorce laws were written in this state in the early '70s, reflecting the loosening of taboos connected with divorce, the intent was to establish a venue in which people could be granted a divorce through a no fault process.

Bob: Why do you think that this has not worked out as intended?

Jeff: Well, it is partially cultural. There still exists a taboo around exposing one's vulnerability in our culture, unless you can justify your vulnerability because it is someone else's fault. So instead of being able to own some of the problems that underlie marital difficulties, couple members are left with having to blame one another. Again we do not have adequate social structures that support couples when they experience marital difficulties, especially when they get to the point one or both want to end the relationship. And shame/blame cycles, usually without awareness, are too often unavoidable as defensive posturing cloaks the pain of the failed dream from being acknowledged. Without sufficient support this leads to escalating conflict and dysfunctional behavior as the sense of failure and suspicions of future threat mount.

We do have an ever expanding network of marriage and family therapists, but there is still a taboo in many sectors of our culture on seeking out this network. This network is even less utilized during the process of divorce. We have a developing network of divorce mediators, but in many states, like in our state, mediation is still a choice and not mandatory. When the courts take a "formulaic" approach, rather than assessing and attending to what is best for all in the family, those who may benefit most from mediation are deprived of this resource.

Bob: What you are saying about our cultural taboos around ending a relationship reminds me of a research study that was done some years ago on the process of uncoupling (Vaughn, 1986). The researcher interviewed couples who had split up and discovered that there was a consistent pattern to the uncoupling process. She found that most often the ending of the relationship was not a joint decision. Further, the people who left, the initiators, very often decided to leave six months or so before they mentioned anything to their partner. After deciding or during the process of deciding, but before telling their partner, the initiators would build up a support system for leaving, intentionally or unintentionally. Initiators would find new friends, become involved in new activities, perhaps even change jobs, locating people and places where they could tell their story and get support that their partner was "bad," inadequate, or just not worthy of them. And this would be happening in the main with people who didn't know the partner, and would serve as a way for the initiators to undo their sense of belonging with their partner and form a new identity that didn't include their partner. Usually when the partner was told of the initiator's decision to leave, he/she was caught off guard, did not know what was coming. The person being left would usually then go through a period of trying to jump through hoops, attempting to hold the relationship together and feeling like it was all his/her fault. However, it would be too late; the initiator had long ago made up his/her mind and had formed a new identity. The person being left would eventually go through the same assessment of blame process, as the initiator had done before telling the partner of his/her decision to leave—finding something wrong with the person who left—so that he/she too could form a new identity.

Jeff: Well, variations on that theme are what often happens in the divorce process. However, they are greatly exacerbated by an adversarial legal system that attempts to deal with conflictual marital situations by finding fault. Finding flaws and weaknesses in your adversary enhances your negotiating position. Under these conditions it is difficult to establish a strength-based and cooperative approach to conflict resolution.

Bob: I can understand where if this common cultural uncoupling pattern of needing to find something wrong with your partner and locate blame in order to leave him/her is reinforced by an adversarial legal system, it can become a very dangerous enterprise.

Jeff: Yes, it frequently is. And the saddest thing is that it is not only dangerous for the men and women struggling with ending their relationship, but it is also dangerous for their children. It often means that children are used as pawns in these wars and they too often lose emotional access to both parents and physical access to at least one parent. And kids internalize conflict and loss as their fault. So the stakes are high.

Bob: The findings of the research study that I mentioned also underline the holding that is needed in uncoupling from old identities and forming new identities that is often not recognized or is poorly addressed in our culture.

Jeff: Yes, support and education structures are very important and much neglected elements in the divorce process in general. And I have found them to be crucial in my work with men.

Bob: You have been assisting men caught in the miseries of the divorce process for many years now, and you have forged a unique style of working with them. I have a number of quotes here that come from the men that you work with.

Jeff: Yes, and in some cases from the women that have asked me to work with their current or ex-husbands.

Bob: These are startling stories, often about trauma.

Jeff: Yes, and they should be heard in the context of the overall condition of our culture, which we have been discussing.

Bob: What stands out to me first, in looking at the quotes is that I'm impressed that you've been able to provide an atmosphere for these men in which they feel safe enough to tell these stories.

Jeff: Well, it's often helped that I am seen as a normal guy who has been "through it" and that I am able to tell my own story. From the start when I introduce myself to the men with whom I work, and share my experience, they are able to see that I have been there and that I can understand what they are going through. The understanding and connection are both personal and professional. Thus I can authentically present myself as an ally. This is particularly important. Because of what these guys have been through, they are very suspicious. Their experience has been that people are out to exploit them, take advantage of them and betray them. I first identify myself as an advocate for children, and tell them of my strong belief that children are best served by having both parents available to them. And I tell them of the admiration I have of the courage and commitment they must have to be there, in caring for their children. Considering their situation, it's often the hardest thing in the world to face their feelings, and yet that is what they are doing.

Bob: So from the start you make a relational connection with these men. And from your own experience, you have the background to understand them from their perspective and to understand their relational strivings. You often work with men in a group setting. I imagine the atmosphere that is possible in a group must help as well.

Jeff: Yes. Most of the quotes that you have come from stories told by members of the group. Of course, when guys first come to the group, they are cautious and hesitant. When a guy first starts to share his story, he doesn't show much vulnerability or affect as he talks about his problems. However, what he says resonates in the other guys because they have similar stories. All of them have been through the disorientation induced by how the state can respond to marital conflict and have experienced their own version of what can occur around separation, divorce, custody, and visitation decisions. So a new person's story connects with the others, even if it is presented hesitantly. And because they are touched, the other guys in the group respond according to their natural tendency in our society to be helpers, fixers, problem-solvers. Thus someone new quickly learns that he is not alone, that his experience is not unique. And the men wind up helping one another. This in itself is validating to them, and gives them a sense of safety. And it sparks in them a great deal of interest in the group. Often participants do not arrive on time; their apprehension about the group is evident. Just as frequently, when the group is over, everyone hangs around for over an hour, sharing stories and nodding enthusiastically while discussing their problems and possibilities. You can hear the relief and joy that these guys experience in finding out that they are not alone.

Bob: It sounds like, from what you say, that this experience is rare for them. Actually, the quotes that you have given me here, bear that out. Let me read some of the quotes that you have accumulated from the men you have worked with, and then ask you some questions about them. Here is the first one:

> I can't believe this has happened to me. I was doing everything the right way. Not even a speeding ticket. Then the bomb drops. Suddenly I'm a criminal. In jail for just going to my house. All I did was work my ass off. Took care of the bills, the kids, the house; and what did it get me but a restraining order?

This quote is dramatic and shocking. Are stories like this common?

Jeff: Unfortunately, yes. Ninety percent or more of the guys I see are not the stereotypical wife-batterer, abuser. But that's how they have been treated. They come into my office after having received a restraining order or an order to vacate, barring them from returning to their home and limiting their access to their kids. They don't know what has hit them. Often they are totally shocked. And similarly to the research study on uncoupling, that you mentioned, sometimes they don't even know that there were serious troubles between them and their wives. They feel their survival is at stake. And they are caught in an obsessive spiral of trying to understand; it is all they can think about.

As I alluded to earlier, the law is an instrument that at times can be blind to the destruction it might cause. Particularly egregious, in our present context, is the way that men can be quite arbitrarily barred from their home and from being with and parenting their children, at least temporarily, and be thrown into a situation by a restraining order or order to vacate, where they would have to get a lawyer to get into their own house—after no hearing at which they were present. This is questionable due process—even if it's intended to be an emergency intervention in violent situations. There are far too many abuses that occur needlessly and destructively as a result of these policies as currently employed.

Bob: Can you say a little more about the number of men that have experiences such as this? You are well connected in this field, active in parenting groups, in touch with lawyers and judges. Do you have an estimate of how many men you are talking about?

Jeff: The numbers are much, much larger than you might imagine if you are not in this field. I am constantly surprised by how often I encounter cases such as this directly or hear about them from other professionals. Unfortunately, they are not uncommon occurrences.

But let me continue with what I was saying. Most often what has happened is that the men have just experienced the first step in a divorce process. They are the victim of a power move that the other side, helped and even guided by the legal system, has employed simply to get the men out of their lives.

Not that it doesn't happen the other way around, in which men use the legal system abusively against women in divorce struggles.

And not that, in these cases, the women are always solely responsible for invoking this kind of power move against their husbands.

There are many lawyers who think of this as an acceptable tool in solving conflictual marital problems—making the other side experience so much pain that they will settle in a manner favorable to the offending lawyer's client. In addition, often an attorney or a paralegal or a victim-witness advocate will grill the wives so intensively around any possibility that their husbands may be abusive, that the wives are talked into the frame that their husbands are abusive.

Our society is currently keenly attuned to the possibility that men might abuse women. Not that that shouldn't be a concern. It definitely should be. But it seems there is very little awareness at present of the damage that is being done to fathers, and the children involved, by the misuse of legal actions prior to, as well as during, divorce and custody proceedings. In addition, these practices leave the women involved locked into a position in which they lose the potential future support of a parenting partner in raising the children, which leads to long term problems and consequences for the family in general.

Bob: What about the issue of women and children needing to be protected in violent situations? How do you distinguish between guys who are potentially violent and those who aren't.

Jeff: As you suggest, this is very important, and there are a number of factors to consider. I pay attention to men's histories and look at their capacity to accept responsibility as they allow themselves to be vulnerable. I look at whether they can accept the loss of the dream and embrace their contribution to the failed relationship. I look at how bitter they are. And I look at their relationship with their children. When I see men that don't have the capacity to be vulnerable, or who blame, or who vilify others or the system without taking any responsibility, or who have any history of violence then I think there needs to be more structured limits.

But even in these cases of men who are more at risk at displaying violence, the men are often identified as being driven by control and power. However, what I find is that they are most frequently driven by their relational needs. Thus, to deal with them solely through power and control very often just makes the situation worse.

Bob: I hear implicitly in what you say how there is no room in this process for vulnerability. Tell me more about what you know about how the bulk of the men that you work with, who are not abusive, find themselves in this kind of spot.

Jeff: Well, very often the guys who get involved with me are guys who have grown up in families where there has been an absent, alcoholic, or abusive parent, often a father. And they learned to be caregivers early on in their lives, with their mothers and siblings. They wind up learning that they are valued for being a rescuer. They are often compared to their irresponsible fathers, when they let their mothers down. Once established, the rescuer role becomes a model for adolescence and early adult life. At the same time the systems they have grown up in often have an impaired ability to respond to loss or distress, which these men internalize. So they learn to ignore their own distress by turning off their needs and to cope where they receive gratification and identity—as a bread winner or "good boy."

Bob: In many ways you are not just describing men who have a history of childhood loss or trauma. If men are not lucky enough to come from a family that knows how to deal with loss and distress, there are not many constructive models in our culture to assist men in handling such feelings.

Jeff: That is so true. The model that many or most of these men carry to deal with their distress is the fantasy of rescuing the proverbial "damsel in distress," a model which of course permeates our culture. Unfortunately, this doesn't get them very far in understanding or dealing with their own relational needs. But, in line with their training, when these men become adults they often get involved with women who, because of the women's own trauma and loss, look to be rescued. In some cases the women, because of their own inability to deal with loss and distress, have issues around addictions or emotional instability or psychological or personality problems. And the men, without an ability to deal with loss or distress, become stuck in co-dependent relationships, with only denial and the immediate gratification of seeing their "job" through as crutches.

Bob: This process must set the women up as well since there is little chance that the men can actually rescue them, particularly if the men are not able to respond to their own feelings of distress.

Jeff: Yes. The problems tend to just get worse. Because of the guys' training in their family of origins, as fixers and caregivers, they are as often as not the real rock, in terms of doing, in the family, working their behinds off, trying to hold things together in their way. Often these guys are the primary parent. Sometimes they're working two jobs. And they believe in the American dream! As that quote demonstrates, this process takes them by surprise. They are too busy to see, and are limited in being able to grasp, their fragile hold and the bigger picture of family disintegration.

Bob: Of course, we are not forgetting here all the cases in which women get involved with men who are emotionally damaged, because of the women's training in their family of origin and in our culture to take care of, rescue, men.

Jeff: Yes, that is true. And in both cases we need to appreciate, as you often say, the relational strivings of both parties. However, by and large the latter is not the population of men that find me. At the same time, with regard to the latter population, I have had success in "reaching out" to fathers, at the request of the ex-wife, who is concerned about the impact of the conflictual relationship on the children. The secret is appreciating and working with how these men yearn to connect with, and the relational experience they want for their kids.

Bob: So tell me, what transpires that changes the balance in these men's relationships? How do they wind up with the stories they are telling?

Jeff: Well, the problems in the family, individually and systemically, get worse if they're not attended to. So what happens in these cases is that behavior starts to appear and get noticed in the community, with the children at school, or on the job, or by neighbors, and then outside parties or agencies step in with an examining eye. Ironically, the problems often escalate at this point because the underlying issues are still not being addressed.

Bob: How do you mean?

Jeff: Well, often the fighting that goes on in these unstable families...

Bob: between husband and wife?

Jeff: Yes. Or the resentments and frustrations that build up get expressed in the form of parents yelling at children, or the alcoholism or drug dependency getting worse, or the psychological problems worsening...

Bob: Of the husband?

Jeff: Of both! The family's dysfunction gets heightened. But it is just as commonly the men who have acted in a protective nature to keep their wife's secret from coming out as the reverse. In the former case, they have been over-functioning in their role as the father and caregiver. I know this is a different image from the stereotypic one of guys just abandoning the scene, but this is what I see frequently.

Bob: You are describing a situation in which it seems that both members of the couple are victims. There is a build up of worsening problems that neither person knows how to deal with directly, and one or both have to keep hidden to the extent that they are in touch with them.

Jeff: Yes, and often the crucial point in this ongoing alliance to deal with underlying vulnerability, for which neither partner has the resources, comes in the step when behavior from the family's dysfunction (frequently reflected in the children's behavior) gets sufficiently noticed by outside parties. When the secret of the underlying problems is about to come out, it is too much for the couple to handle, particularly for the couple member that exhibits the bulk of behaviors that are considered shameful in our culture, emanating from addictions or other dysfunctional attempts of dealing with deeper problems. The power of the impending shame is a force that is too difficult to manage and desperate unilateral decisions get made and actions taken, with the aid of denial, that are unimaginable under other circumstances. Again, there is not an adequate structure in our culture to hold men and women during this process.

With many of the men I see, who have been in the rescuer role in their relationships, when the women in their lives reach this point of imminent exposure, the women too often find a serendipitous, but troubling, solution that is currently available in the legal system. With the validation, permission, and education of the community, they convert and externalize their shame to blaming the guy whom they have been with and who has been committed to them and their family. Remember the legal system is geared to solving problems by finding fault. The result is a huge crisis as the problems become redefined, increasingly complex, and costly.

Bob: I am just struck by how different the latter story is from the one you usually hear. And I know there are many women who have struggled and/or been injured by men who have the kind of problems and shame that you attribute to these wives.

Jeff: Again, that is certainly true. And these stories don't diminish the severity of what happens in those situations in any way. At the same time violence is often an escalating dynamic.

In our culture, it is also true that there is little awareness that these men's stories exist. Men in general are so often thought of in terms of power and control instead of in terms of their relational needs. And if you are going to work with these guys, you must be able to understand and validate their stories, particularly from the perspective of the relational connections that drive them. That is the ethic here.

Bob: So tell me further of what happens in the typical crisis, that you mentioned occurs with these men.

Jeff: Well, as I mentioned earlier the guys wind up with an order to vacate, and/or a restraining order, being presented to them. These orders appear out of the blue, and are so incongruous to them because all their lives they have been brought up with the idea that if they do "the right thing" and are "good boys" their goals and ambitions will be rewarded in life. And that quote you read brings out the surprise, frustration, horror that they experience as a result of what happens.

And the harsh reality they must face is that once they are put in the role of the identified perpetrator they are often in a defenseless position. After leaving the house, because of an order to vacate or a restraining order, the burden of proof is on the man to prove that he is *not* a danger to his wife, which is very difficult to prove if his wife continues with her story. So very often within a short period of time, guys just give up and feel crushed. From that point they often get into a very defensive posture around their losses. So they can't fight very easily or effectively. If they become angry at what has happened to them, or naturally defensive, they are further identified as the perpetrator.

Bob: Acting otherwise is certainly counter to most men's sense of what they should do in times of conflict or attack. But that feeds into the next quote that you have here:

> I go from being a zombie to wanting to kill somebody. I can't get up in the morning anymore. All I can do is think about my kids and how much I miss them. I had to quit my

job; just couldn't concentrate anymore. I think about what
I can do to get even with those bastards who took my life
from me. I need a drink.

Like the first quote, this quote is extremely intense and difficult
to take in. What is going on here? Is this just a man whose innate
instability and tendency toward violence have finally been exposed?
Again, is this normal? How do we understand this kind of quote?

Jeff: Unfortunately, this experience and reaction is fairly common in
the guys that I work with. It is normal to experience loss in profound
ways. Under such circumstances, people most often cannot function
as usual. People need time to grieve losses, especially unexpected
ones.

The fact that many of these men have experienced huge losses is
problematic enough in itself. However, remember that frequently
these guys have grown up in families with unacknowledged losses
and/or an impaired ability to deal with loss and distress. This is
compounded by our cultural expectations that teach men to deal
with loss and distress by numbing yourself and denying your
experience. Thus, these men have no models and little awareness of
how to deal with loss and distress in a healthy manner. In addition,
the old instances of loss/abuse that remain unresolved (e.g., death of
a parent or having an abusive, absent or alcoholic parent) often
become triggered with the new experience of trauma. The result is
that a huge number of these men have tremendous difficulty
functioning in their normal daily life activities.

This kind of complicated loss, combined with little information
about resources, leads to an intense sense of helplessness and
victimization—which are the ingredients of trauma. *These guys are
dealing with being traumatized.* The resulting symptoms that we see are
the symptoms of Post Traumatic Stress Disorder (PTSD).

Further, these father's main strategy for dealing with their old
loss/abuse was to form an identity as a caregiver and provider, and
that identity is now being attacked and threatened—they are now
being characterized as the cause of the problem rather than the solver
of the problem. In some instances, these guys have not only been

accused of being violent, but they have been falsely accused of molesting their children. When falsely made, these charges have a particularly destructive impact, as not only are they so far from the men's self image, but in addition, they cast the men in a similar light to their abusive/absent fathers, who they vowed they would never become.

And add to that the humiliation of having all this occur in such a public manner in the courts, newspapers, and/or neighborhood gossip. Increasingly they feel a sense of aloneness and despair, which may develop into suicidal thoughts. The impulse to escape is often strong, hence the rageful feelings and the temptation to self medicate with drink or drugs or to relocate.

All of this contradicts their commonly held cultural/social belief that the American justice system will be used in a truthful, beneficial manner.

Bob: So a major part of the ethic of relational understanding here is to understand people and their behavior from the perspective of the trauma they are experiencing.

Jeff: Yes. PTSD as a diagnostic category is very useful here. It gives us a lens that allows us to understand what is happening with these men. And it gives us a direction with regard to treatment. It also helps in de-shaming these men. It describes their experience, giving them answers to why they feel so off balance, a condition which in itself is extremely shaming to most men. It changes the script they learned in their childhood, that when something bad happens to them it is because they are "bad boys." It also takes these men out of the role of the perpetrator, thus providing some of the safety they need to start the healing process. Then, particularly in conjunction with the group process, they can begin the task of establishing an identity that is more in sync with who they really are and who they want to be.

Bob: That is starting to sound a little more hopeful. Perhaps this next quote reflects a man at the stage you are describing:

I go to the woods where I took my son and daughter for walks. I've become an expert on the different trees there. I think about what I've lost and what we would be doing now. My heart is broken. I had it all; now I have nothing.

This man is obviously experiencing great heartache and despair. But in some way this feels a little more hopeful. While you can feel his fragility, he is organizing himself solely from the part of himself that loves and cares. How do you help men stay with and come from the loving, caring part of themselves rather than acting out from the part that society reinforces—the latter being the image of a macho man who denies his experience, employs aggressive ideation and resorts to drink or drugs to numb himself?

Jeff: What you mention is an important task. This man was in the early stages of his grieving, the transformative healing process that we all need to experience following loss. However, it is difficult for these men to embrace their mourning as they are usually engaged in a 24/7 battle around their legal defense. They maintain a sense of the system as "the enemy"—so they can defend themselves from the allegations that are made against them in this adversarial legal system that is currently in place in which someone has to win and someone has to lose. They don't receive the validation that typically comes following other losses such as the death of a significant partner or child, in which people are most often looked to supportively while they grieve and start the process of establishing a new identity. *So these men need support as they find hope.* It is difficult to work through mourning in a productive manner in isolation. So many men, who do not receive support, become stuck in their depression or the surface responses to it.

Bob: So how do you provide support and hope for these guys?

Jeff: It's important to give them the sense that they are not alone. It's also important to address their sense of shame in seeking help. Thus, I understand and acknowledge their discomfort in seeing a therapist and requesting help (they usually call it information). We often agree that it takes a stronger, more courageous person to face his problems head on. There is also an explicit understanding that they are there because of their desire to be connected with and care for their children.

Bob: I imagine that these men need different kinds of support as they progress though the process.

Jeff: Yes, at first it is important to just receive these men and hold them emotionally as they struggle with the trauma they are experiencing. In time the process of the group helps men focus on their relational strengths. For example, the group helped the guy in the quote that we discussed to realize his competence in fathering his children. His knowing every tree in the woods, and the warmth and caring with which he spoke of including his children in this endeavor had a spiritual quality. This activity with his kids started after his marital troubles broke open and was a new way for him and his children to interact, a way which was really not available to them previously because they defined themselves and their activities in material terms. This new form of interaction was a major source of growth in this guy and his children, something that would not have occurred unless he went through his trauma and subsequent healing.

Similarly, many people emerge from their divorce trauma with an increased awareness that they have been transformed in a positive manner. The challenge for us as therapists in helping professions is to engage with people around validating their experiences, holding them emotionally, and enabling them in their pain and fear to be transformed through new experience and awareness. This man was able to achieve that through his walks in the woods and his connections with his children, leading ultimately to a new under-standing of himself.

The good news is that loss can be transforming in a positive way. The identities that these men have been given often have not included a place for them to exist emotionally—to be valued for who they are as opposed to solely what they can produce and provide. They are often caught up in being those tigers out there to achieve material goals for themselves and their families—having a bigger house, a prettier wife, or the right job title. As they move through the loss experience they come to realize that there are other ways of identifying themselves. They frequently come through the experience with a new spiritual and emotional sense of themselves—through experiencing the pain. If you stop yourself from feeling pain, then you also stop yourself from feeling joy. When guys allow themselves to feel pain and can go into a different emotional domain, they are frequently happier in the long run. However, again, this requires support in the form of understanding and appreciation of who they are.

They also come to recognize what dysfunctional relationships are all about. And for many people that I see, they in time develop far healthier relationships with the opposite sex. They are more able to realize that they have a choice—the rescuer role leading to co-dependent relationships or a new path to healthy relations based on interdependence rather than co-dependence.

Bob: What you say about the experience of trauma ironically offering the possibility of a transformative experience reminds me of what Gordon Wheeler said to me a number of years ago in reflection of the men with whom he worked. He said that in order to lead a full, emotionally rich life as a man, you first need to fail the "program," into which most men are indoctrinated, and then you have to survive the failure.

Jeff: It sure seems that way! That is similar to what I have experienced, personally and professionally.

Bob: Are there other ways that you support these men?

Jeff: Yes, as men start to form new identities it is important to be with them as they find opportunities to experiment with and integrate new ways of being in the world. For example, in the last two years, as program director for Fathers and Families, a self help and advocacy organization supporting noncustodial fathers, I organized, with the help of others, a conference called "Helping Fathers Healing Children," which brought together noncustodial fathers, their partners, and their children. Participants attended various workshops, related to their situation, which facilitated their sharing their experience and their learning new strategies around de-escalating their conflict, coping with their losses, healing their trauma, and reaffirming and strengthening their connections (between fathers, partners, and children). We had speakers who shared how various kinds of support (for example, physical activities, counseling, and religious connection) enabled them to deal with their pain, learn about themselves, and find new solutions.

Bob: Yes, I had the honor of leading workshops at each of the conferences. I must say that it was an educational experience for me. I was touched by meeting the men and hearing their stories. They were often stories of trauma. I was also impressed by their commitment and connection to their children. In general their chief concerns revolved around their relationships with their children and their children's welfare. There were men in all the stages that you have described—from men who had recently been served with restraining orders and orders to vacate and were in shock and deep despair to men who had been through the process and talked about the pain they had endured, the mistakes they had made, the support they had received, what they had learned about themselves, and the new resolutions they had found and forged in their lives.

Jeff: I wish more people could hear these guys' stories. Not to blame anybody else, but to understand their experience and to get a sense of how widespread and complex these stories are.

Bob: That's a nice segue to the next quote:

> Staying at my mother's house is OK, but I feel like a kid who screwed up. I've got no money left, just a lot to pay back on my credit card. The lawyers are killing me: hers, mine, they're all the same – just bottom feeders. It is hard for me to imagine how I could ever get out of the hole I am in,

and Im not just talking about the red ink.

In many ways this quote is like the others that we have read. What strikes me about this quote and about the information you present in general, is that our culture doesn't have adequate mechanisms in place to support men and women when they are going through these very tough separation and re-identity periods. Do you have any sense of what our culture needs to be addressing/providing for people going through these situations?

Jeff: I have found that almost all people have the capacity to adapt to changes in family configurations. However, being able to uncouple from old attachments and beliefs is often not possible in the present atmosphere in which blame, aggression, and one side winning at the expense of the other is not only tolerated but reinforced and rewarded.

Let me summarize the negative forces that impede couples' ability to be in the present reality that their situation presents, and to find solutions that support both of them and their children. First, our culture still maintains the puritanical values that attach failure to a marriage ending and that then assess blame. This in itself impedes the processes of grieving and of developing new identities. Second, because we have an adversarial system in which someone has to win and someone has to lose, there is a strong incentive to gain an upper hand despite the cost to the other party. This also provides a strong incentive to act out any resentments acquired during the marriage or from the relationship ending. In addition, as I mentioned earlier, Massachusetts unlike some states doesn't have mandatory mediation. So, again, we don't have a conciliatory process.

These conditions lead to, and are in turn reinforced by, the result that most often the two parties are encouraged not to speak to one another. Further, in many cases, including those in which restraining orders have been issued, this is not just an encouragement but a prohibition since if the parties speak to each other they will go to jail. When it is solely lawyers that speak to each other, the chances of a conciliatory process are extremely low.

Additionally, the cost to families caught in this adversarial process is often overwhelming. I see so many $100,000 plus legal bills. It is reprehensible that our capitalistic ethic extends to this process, enabling people to make money in other people's time of misery and suffering. This causes so much more pain and trauma. Most unfortunately, it puts the children more at risk to be emotionally neglected during this extended period of legal warfare. And kids feel their parents pain; they are emotional Geiger counters. I see many cases that are still unresolved after five years, and the norm is something of the order of 2½ years. Lawyers also are caught in the same adversarial trap, which even in the best of situations can tend to blunt their impulses toward mediation and more humanistic solutions.

Bob: Where do we start in trying to address all of this?

Jeff: Hopefully, with more research all the time pointing to the benefits of shared parenting, there will be increasing demands for changing the laws, and implementing them in a manner that recognizes the fragility of this transitional process and better supports people's strengths. Interestingly, I believe that the needs of all members of the family are best served if we start with supporting the kids. Again, they are the ones that are most at risk. Parents need to be supported in attending to the needs of their children, while at the same time they need to be supported in being able to own their feelings and deal with them in an active engaged way. Jointly attending to the needs of the children can facilitate both, and it leaves the whole family in a better position from which to rebuild their lives once the transitional process of divorce has been transcended.

The state of Massachusetts now requires that all parents going through a divorce take a five hour parent education program that emphasizes putting the kids needs first. This should be augmented with requiring a Shared Parenting Plan to be filed and implemented as soon as possible, before other aspects of the divorce are considered. Shared Parenting Plans that I help construct are individually tailored with input from both parents and the children. They include a declaration of the couple's commitment, with built-in accountability, to continuing to co-parent their children, as they are reminded both of how temporary and fleeting this period of transition is and the need during this off-balancing time to place their children's needs first. I reinforce how the children need both parents, particularly during this difficult time. The Shared Parenting Plan spells out where children will live and parenting times for both parents. It delineates clear avenues (including proposed times) for communication between the parents on logistical and parenting issues and between children and both parents. And it provides standards of conduct.

A well written Shared Parenting Plan can engage a couple's sense of purpose in life and help hold them through this very difficult, emotional period in their lives. In particular the standards of conduct for the plans that I assist in constructing are comprised of a number of items that help guide parents in jointly providing a nurturant atmosphere for their children, which in turn can hold the parents. For example, the first item in the standards of conduct is: each parent shall refrain from discussing the conduct of the other parent in the presence of the child, except in a laudatory or complementary way. There are a number of books that provide formats and philosophy to achieve effective shared parenting during and after the process of divorce.[1]

Bob: I can see where such a document could be extremely helpful in holding a couple during this process. But is it sufficient in itself? People are in a very off-balanced position even in the best of divorces.

Jeff: You're right. Other supports are needed as well, particularly with high conflict couples. Next the court should appoint a Parenting Coordinator who will oversee the Shared Parenting Plan, helping to undo glitches that arise and to make adjustments in the plan as needed. It should be recognized that many couples cannot negotiate this task on their own, without support. Support should be allocated

---

[1]For example, see Lyster, 1999 and Ricci, 1997.

before serious problems arise. In the long run such a plan would be cost effective for everyone. There should be regular scheduled meetings between the parents, the children, and the Parenting Coordinator. And Parenting Coordinators should be drawn from professionals who know how to support people in this process, not just impose limits, or serve as a communication vehicle. Empowering and educating the parents to creatively solve problems themselves is the achievable objective.

In short, we need to create structures which minimize the kind of contact between parents that can lead to escalation, while maximizing the consistency and capacity they have in parenting their children. In the process we want to facilitate building an atmosphere where the children can thrive in being able to become emotionally articulate in responding to the losses they have experienced and the changes they're negotiating. The kids need to find their own voice through this process too. What I have learned in talking to kids of divorcing parents is that what they "hate," as they often say, most of all, is being in the middle and not being able to speak up about it. I remind parents that children cannot suppress their own feelings without paying a price some time in the future.

Bob: What about the parents themselves? I imagine that it would be great if every couple member could have the opportunity that you provide for the men in your group—to be held while they mourn the loss of the dream, examine their own behavior and needs, and experiment with new ways of being in the world as they construct a new identity.

Jeff: Exactly, there would be much less need to blame the other if everyone had that kind of support. People going through this process would be much more able to recognize their own judgmental responses to their and others' behavior and let go of past resentments and regrets while gaining increasing awareness of new possibilities in the present.

Bob: You mentioned our legal system. What needs to be done there?

Jeff: We have to change the perspective that one side must win at the expense of the other. Because if one side really loses (or gives up), then everyone loses, especially the children. Thus we need to find incentives that encourage lawyers to consider the needs of the entire family, not just their clients' needs as seen from an adversarial perspective.

Bob: Are there ways to do that?

Jeff: The legal system evolves slowly. There is an alternative to the regular process that has recently become available in this state. But the couple has to choose it, which of course excludes high-conflict couples. It's called collaborative law, in which an outcome must be reached that is satisfactory to both sides or the lawyers cannot collect for their services.

However, we need more structures of this kind. We need education/training of judges, family service administrators, and lawyers in creative approaches in assisting families in attending to the needs of all individuals in the family as they establish new family configurations. And there needs to be legislation around shared parenting. Many states are already considering this possibility.

Bob: I catch how what you are suggesting is that we need to change the system such that the solutions that are needed will start to be naturally generated from within the system, because of the information base, incentives, and underlying ethic, rather than naturally impeded by the system because of the current adversarial set of beliefs, ethics and incentives.

At the same time how do you propose that the risk of violence be adequately dealt with? Will the directions you have proposed adequately deal with that?

Jeff: Violence can not be tolerated. Providing safety and protection must always be of paramount concern. There will still be times when restraining orders and the like will be needed. We must couple that with true mediation and reconciliation services. However, to really control violence we need to better understand its causes. The divorce process is a highly emotional time for anyone. Too often at present, what are considered to be higher risk situations of potential violence are situations in which the relational needs of the people involved are not being recognized or responded to effectively.

Prevention through relationship education, helping couples learn about healthy relationships, must become a part of our overall approach. Problems often escalate as couples fail to negotiate situations in which they have insufficient awareness and support. Too often others do not recognize or call attention to the couple's or children's distress, which if done would offer the opportunity for earlier and more effective interventions. Our community and family ethic does not presently support sufficient relational holding when others are hurting.

I believe that there are solutions presently available that will de-escalate conflict that leads ultimately to destructive outcomes, including violence. Establishing a Shared Parenting Plan as quickly as possible, affirming children's needs being a priority, providing conduct guidelines, appointing a Parenting Coordinator who teaches, mediates, and empowers, will serve to help change the adversarial nature of the legal process into a relational approach.

Bob: On reflecting on what you have shared with us here today, I realize that you have really given us two stories. One about the trauma that can happen in the divorce process when underlying patterns of vulnerability are not recognized and needed support is not sought or provided. And another about how through recovery from that trauma men can become aware of their relational needs and be transformed, gaining the ability to lead a fuller, more emotionally rich, connected life.

Jeff: Yes, one is a story of horror for too many. The other is a story of hope and healing. All to often the former could have been pre-vented. If properly supported, the latter is a possibility for everyone going through the divorce process.

Bob: I have one final quote here from a man who has gone through the process and come out the other side:

> This process has not been easy. My losses were huge. I still have occasional nightmares. The time that I was drinking, when things were lowest, that was the hardest. But with the support that I found and what I have learned about myself and relationships in general, I now have a quality in my life that I didn't think was possible. I have reconnected, and have good relationships, with two of my three children, and I am remarried to someone who appreciates and loves me as I appreciate and love her.

That quote seems to speak for itself.

Jeff: When people get sufficient holding and support, they can manage the enormity of their feelings and in time can live in the present, face their problems, learn about themselves and their needs, and find new solutions. As people develop increasing awareness and appreciation of their own and other's vulnerability, as well as their relational strengths, they often develop forgiveness for themselves and others. As they let go of old resentments and regrets they experience increased gratitude and a recognition that life is about moving forward. They realize they have a positive choice that can be acted on. At the same time healing is an ongoing liberating process. This is the promise that could be reached much more easily if we can convert the present system from a win-lose adversarial system to a collaborative process.

References

Lyster, M. (1999). *Child Custody: Building Parenting Agreements That Work.* Berkeley, CA: Nolo, Inc.

Ricci, I. (1997). *Mom's House, Dad's House.* New York: Fireside Books, Simon and Schuster.

Vaughn, D. (1986). *Uncoupling: Turning Points in Intimate Relationships.* New York: Oxford University Press.

Part IV

·········

Cultural Reflections

Editor's Note:

Gordon Wheeler is one of the foremost Gestalt theorists of our time. Here he shares with us an illuminating examination of the cultural roots of masculinity and the suppression of the feminine through a new reading of Homer's Iliad. In the process he explores two paradigms of ethical existence, one grounded in the shame-rage, separation of person from relationship orientation of the ancient Greeks and one grounded in the holistic, belonging oriented culture of Troy. As he concludes, we face much the same choice of which paradigm of ethics we embrace in present times.

•••••••••••••••

12

Shame and Belonging:

Homer's *Iliad* and the

Western Ethical Tradition

Gordon Wheeler

Rage—Goddess, sing the rage of Peleus' son Achilles,
murderous, doomed, that cost the Achaeans countless losses,
hurling down to the House of Death so many sturdy souls,
great fighters' souls, but made their bodies carrion,
feasts for the dogs and birds,
and the will of Zeus was moving toward its end.
Begin, Muse, when the first two broke and clashed,
Agamemnon lord of men and brilliant Achilles...[1]

Rage. The first word of the first line of the founding text of Western civilization, older and in some ways even more influential in our history than the Hebrew Bible, is rage. But why? What is rage, and what does it mean to have this troubling term appear so prominently at the earliest beginnings of our cultural

---

[1] All citations from the *Iliad* are taken from the Robert Fagles translation, NY: Viking Press, 1990.

tradition? Why is Achilles in such a state anyway, which we all recognize, in ourselves and others, as unstable and potentially violent? What is the situation that gives rise to this breakdown between allies (the Achaeans are the *Greeks*); and then what are the consequences, for the rest of the story and for the story of our culture, which is the ground of our identity and self-definition? Finally, what is the relationship between all this and the ethical tradition of our Western civilization? Is there a connection? Are ethics and the study of emotion, or moral philosophy and natural psychology, related, or not? If they are meaningfully related, then how—and how is it that these two domains, *values* and *natural science*, have come to be held so separately in our Western culture—a separateness that must somehow contribute to many other deep divisions and conflicts in the world today, as that world comes to be more and more dominated by the West?

To explore all this, we will first take up a Gestalt view of affect and emotion, as enhanced and extended by current findings in evolutionary theory, cognitive psychology and brain research. From there we will look at the story itself: why is the situation of the Greeks so desperate, as the *Iliad* opens, and then what is the war itself really about? This will lead us into a consideration of the deep values and organizing assumptions of Greek civilization, as described and laid down, really, by Homer—both in contrast with the quite different value system of the Trojans they oppose and ultimately conquer, and also in terms of the legacy of those values and those assumptions, down to our own times. When we reach our own times, we will be ready to consider the way our own society has undergone a split in its thinking, between scientific *knowledge* and ethical *opinion*, two domains which are held rigidly apart in our culture, with deep consequences for our world today. With the insights of new thinking in the light of Gestalt psychology, we will then consider some principles and proposals for healing this destructive split, which paralyzes needed action and blocks a *critical shift of vision* in our desperately troubled world.

Affect and Emotion—a Gestalt Model

In 1873 Charles Darwin, having revolutionized our understanding of ourselves and our human story, continued this project with another groundbreaking book, *The Expression of the Emotions in Man and Animals*, which is still the foundation and source of the field we know today as affect psychology (Tomkins, 1963; Kaufman, 1980). The principles of the field, as outlined by Darwin and still basically used today, were revolutionary at the time, and of course grounded in evolutionary theory. Basic emotional states, Darwin argued, are universal to the species, and cross-culturally recognizable: joy, anger, fear, disgust, grief, shame, and so on each have essentially the same facial and body language from one culture to another. This being the case, Darwin reasoned, it must all serve some evolutionary purpose. He found that purpose in social bonding and communication—the need, roughly, of human tribes and societies to be able to attune to each other emotionally, and also to communicate broad affect states (fear, anger, delight, etc.) instantly, across distance, for social regulation and, at times, group preservation in emergencies, before or without the delay of language. Generations of research since, both human and primatological, have generally confirmed (and extended) this basic picture (see e.g., de Waal, 1985, 1999).

Emotional states are grouped, Darwin further posited, into basic affect clusters such as the chief categories mentioned above, each with its characteristic facial expression and body posture—again, for rapid social "reading" at a distance. As such, these states are "contagious"—as every therapist, actor, politician, teacher, or parent knows (even just imitating the body and facial posture of grief, say, or anger, or hilarity will immediately bring up in each of us some echoes and associations, at least, to the particular emotions in question). Lack of facial hair, upright posture, good distance vision—all this Darwin saw as contributing to this essential cooperative capacity in the human tribe, then further supported by calls and cries, eventually evolving into language (but note how in intense emotion we tend to "choke" or abandon words, reverting to an earlier set of expressive vocalizations, universally understood). With all this, Darwin was quite intentionally attempting to counter the extreme Social

Darwinism (the political doctrine that "survival of the fittest" justifies every social inequity, from rapacious capitalism to imperialist conquest) already springing up in his name, just fourteen years after the firestorm of his first book. Certainly we compete for survival, Darwin held, both individually and as societies; but this competition is balanced and checked by our deep social instincts for cooperation and interdependency, which are also survival characteristics of our evolved nature, in common with all social species, but to a deeper extent than any of the others.

The Gestalt model understands this "balance" in terms of a dynamic relation of figure-ground, or integrated focus or characteristic which is supported and made meaningful by an organized, living context. Neither of them, figure or ground, focus or context, makes any sense or adds up to a usable whole without the other; meaning and viability lie in their dynamic relationship, which also is the key to our flexible, adaptable, problem-solving nature as a species. Thus individuality and self-awareness are also species adaptations, necessary for organizing a point of view out of our shared social field, for creative problem-solving, prediction, and *evaluation and choice* (these last two being the same, in our human process). This is why we insist, in the Gestalt model, on the fundamental inseparability of cognition and affect, as Goldstein demonstrated three quarters of a century ago (e.g., 1935) and cognitive models are confirming today (e.g., Damasio, 1994): because our thinking is driven by *evaluative preference*, and our preferences are organized and communicated in our bodymind, to self as well as to others, *by and as emotional state* (for further discussion and explication, see Wheeler, 2000). The ability to know and read feelings, our own and others', is thus not some modern luxury or leisure society "frill:" *it is key to our self-organization and social functioning, which in the end, again, are one and the same thing.*

Emotions "organize" our experience, and thus our behavior (Wheeler, 1994). They tend naturally to lead to focused, directed action, toward or away from some desired state or perceived danger—or, in the case of "activating" or regulating emotions like joy, grief, and shame, toward or away from energy and action themselves. Shame in particular, as both Darwin and Tomkins perceived, has a modulating or governing effect on the other affects, because of the way it takes us toward or away from the social field itself, which is where our human lives are played out. This is a point that was long difficult for Western models of self and psychotherapy to appreciate, because of their bias toward seeing shame in purely individualistic terms, as an emotion of performance failure or inferiority. A Gestalt perspective helps us understand shame more deeply, as the *basic regulator of contact in the social field* (see Lee & Wheeler, 1996). The opposite of shame, in this sense, is not just pride but *belonging* (Wheeler, 2000). Social extrusion or shunning, which would of course be death to the human child or tribe member in the evolutionary period, remains the deepest psychological threat in human society today, and among our deepest fears.

But if emotions organize experience and action, each of the affect "clusters" posited by Darwin, Tomkins, and others has an extreme form, a level of intensity and activation at which it *disorganizes*, rather than organizes our behavior. That is, when arousal is greater than we can "hold" and process, we may enter states in which our actions are no longer grounded in purpose and prediction, and no longer serve either ourselves or our social group. Every society recognizes these states as well, times when we instinctively "move in" to surround and contain a person who has become unpredictable and thus possibly destructive to self or others—or else move to get out of their way. For joy there may be hilarity (which is harmless but incapac-itating)—or mania, which is more problematic; for interest there is obsession; for grief, paralyzing depression; for fear, panic; and for anger, of course rage, often characterized as "blind" rage, because of the way we may lash out at such moments, hurting those around us who mean most to us, or provoking retaliation we would never court when we were in our "right mind."

In each case, it is *extreme shame* that shifts the emotional state *from its functional organizing range, to its dysfunctional, disorganizing extreme.* It is important to note that this insight, which derives from a dynamic, developmental Gestalt field model of self-process as well as from observed experience, violates a number of assumptions of the Western individualist self model, which has tended to emphasize self-structure and self-process apart from social context and relationship. Thus contemporary models tend to treat "self-organization" or "autopoesis" as if these ongoing processes were largely "internal," and unfolded without reference to a dynamic social context. In Gestalt terms, based in field theory, this is trying to understand "figure" (in this case, the cognitive/emotional organization of experience) without a ground. That ground, that dynamic context, is the social field in which our emotional states arise and are co-constructed and resolved (or not), in the ongoing processes of living. There is no "ideal" development or self-process which can be understood apart from these living relational contexts; rather, ground does not just "hold" or locate figure or self, but interpenetrates with it, informs it, and shapes and constrains self-process and felt self-experience (see discussion in Lee & Wheeler, 1996; Wheeler, 2000).

States of extreme shame represent a severe rupture in that self/social field; as such, they are not just one more dynamic factor in resolution of wholes of experience and meaning: they amount to a breakdown of that process. This is because of the way shame cuts us off from that ground of belonging which is an integral part of our evolved self-nature and process, an equal dynamic pole, along with individuation, of our being. If the goal of self-experience, ongoingly, is to integrate liveable, usable wholes of the self/ social field, extreme shame states tell us that that integration is at least momentarily impossible, or only achievable in an isolated, self-contained way (ironically, the way the individualist self-model celebrated as the ideal, here seen as stunted or pathological). Our emotional arousal—anger, excitement/desire, loneliness/grief, and so on—is left to "stew in too small a pot," the container of the "individual self-boundary," now rigidified by the repulsion or withdrawal of social context. The result is a distortion of self-process, which in the healthy case unfolds in some felt (present or imagined) field of belonging, where the figure of our individuated experience makes sense, moves toward some kind of resolution, serves our living self-experience and growth (see Wheeler & Jones, 1996).

Again, such states of social breakdown, which shift the coherent directionality of emotional function toward random or self-destructive (and often other-destructive) acts, are the dynamic result of *intense emotional arousal, held too-alone, in an experiential field of intense shame.*

But why is Achilles in such a state, and in such a field? What is the situation that he and all the Greeks find themselves in, which has everybody on a "hair trigger," where conflict so easily and immediately flares into blind, murderous rage? To understand that, and its implications for our culture even today, let's get back to our story.

The Rage of Achilles

What god drove them to fight with such fury?
Apollo, the son of Zeus and Leto. Incensed at the king
he swept a fatal plague through the army—men were dying
and all because Agamemnon spurned Apollo's priest.
Yes, Chryses approached the Achaeans' fast ships
to win his daughter back, bringing a priceless ransom
and bearing high in hand, wound on a golden staff,
the wreaths of the god, the distant deadly Archer...

What is actually going on here? To see that, first we need to understand the situation of the Greeks at the opening of the poem, quite a different picture from most of our popular retellings, which usually only gloss over both the psychological depth and the cultural implications of Homer's narrative. We need this background in order to make sense of the mood of desperation in the Greek camp, the mind set of the High King, and the actions and reactions of the heroes, especially Achilles, the protagonist and linchpin of the tale.

Our story opens sometime in the tenth year of the war, the long campaign to conquer Troy—nominally to avenge the cuckolded Menelaus, brother of the High King, and "free" Helen, Queen of Sparta, officially said to have been "abducted," or "raped" by Prince Paris of Troy, second son of the old king Priam (this is of course a face-saving spin on what happened—saving face being almost the chief activity of the Greeks. In fact, as everybody knows, Helen simply ran off with the exotic stranger, who must have cut quite the figure in the rude country court of a minor Greek chieftain). All that was twenty years ago now. Of course, what motivates Agamemnon after all these years, as everybody also knows, is not the blemished honor of the Greeks but the fabled wealth of Troy, which Menelaus and Odysseus actually glimpsed some years ago on their failed diplomatic mission to the city, to sue for Helen's return (Helen, who was not a prisoner in the first place, simply declined to leave, and the Trojans refused to force her, a decision the Trojan elders, whom we meet in a scene on the city ramparts, take a decidedly mixed view of now).

Not that the Greeks have been camped here on the marshy beach for the past ten years, some miles before those legendary walls. On the contrary, everything in the story makes it plain that they just arrived at Troy as the story begins, have no plan for how to proceed from here, and aren't even decided about whether to stay or go. So what is it they've been doing exactly, for the past nine years? Why, what Greeks do best, in every myth and legend, from Theseus and Heracles to Jason and the Argonauts, which is raping and pillaging and generally sacking the cities and towns of all the more advanced cultures around the eastern Mediterranean. They have no real land army, know little of civilization and cities themselves, and make terrible sailors (knowing nothing of navigation, they're afraid to go out of sight of land; that's one reason it will take Odysseus ten years to go home, a distance of perhaps 500 miles by water). But they make dandy pirates, plundering up and down the Trojan coast from the safety of their home base out on the island of Patmos—most of the raids being led by Achilles, youngest of the Greek chiefs but already renowned for his battle rages, states of blind possession which make him all but invincible, fiercest of all the Greek terrors. (Agamemnon, the High King, being a generation older and drunk most of the time, generally hangs in the rear of these actions or else stays home, waiting to preside over the division of the spoils. Everybody knows this too: it's one of the things Achilles will throw up at him in their famous spat). The Trojans, who are a commercial power, not maritime and not even particularly military, have done what they can to respond to these predations, but they can't be everywhere, and you never know where the raiders will pop up next. Direct engagements have been few, with few losses on either side, militarily (not counting, of course, the "collateral damage" to civilians), any captured officers or nobles are always ransomed back, some of them more than once by this time.

Nor is there any "siege of Troy," properly speaking. Clearly the Greeks don't have anything like the numbers required to seal off the town; trade, troops, and other traffic flow freely in and out of the city gates all through the story. At most the pirates number a few thousands, maybe less, in any case no more than can be addressed at one time by a single speaker, unamplified, in an open field. (Homer's famous "Catalogue of Ships," which would add up to some 50,000 or more men, is plainly a later inflation, probably added piecemeal to flatter each local tribe or tradition where the tale was performed, at market fairs and rough baronial halls down through the succeeding centuries).

The only trouble is, they've run out of targets to ravage. After ten years of easy plunder most of the towns and farmlands within reach of a coastal raid have already been picked over, villages devastated, temples sacked; anything of value that's still left has long since been transferred to the safety of Troy, which is crowded now with refugees but awash with treasure, still easily able to procure the allies and mercenaries required to mount a force to sweep the invaders from the beach once and for all. There's nothing left the Greeks now but the city itself, or else turn tail and sail for home. But the city is impregnable, both by sheer numbers and because of those walls (a precaution taken since the last sacking by Greek raiders a couple of generations ago, back in the youth of the old Trojan King Priam, now in his dotage). And going home now, sans Helen or the gold of Troy either one, would be humiliating, after making her such an issue in the propaganda campaign to raise the force in the first place (national honor being always a main feature of wars, in the recruitment phase). Even the plunder is mostly gone now, what with careless living and the inflated prices of supplies that war always brings.

Most of all, Agamemnon in particular can't go home, at least not in anything less than complete triumph, because of the political situation he left behind him: a rival cousin done out of the throne by his own father's murder at the hands of a brother, Agamemnon's father, plus a wife embittered by the little matter of Agamemnon's murder of her children from her first marriage, plus their mutual daughter Iphegenia. For his own sake he needs either to come back a conqueror, or not come back at all. (What he doesn't know, but we and the audience all do, is that his wife and cousin are now in cahoots; the High King will be murdered, or more properly executed, in his bath at their joint hands on his first night home).

And it gets worse. If an army travels, as Napoleon says, on its stomach, it settles down, frankly on its bowels. The first task of any civilization, always and everywhere, is how to maintain a large number of people in one place over time without completely fouling the water supply. Unfortunately for them, the Greeks know little of such things. And they don't dare stray far from their ships, because the Trojans would burn them. Their camp is pitched on the swampy lowlands near the shore; the latrines are smack in the water table. In no time at all illness and then plague have struck the camp—typhoid doubtless, and possibly typhus as well, since one of their afflictions starts with the animals. Men are dying like the flies Homer likens us to (with the gods in the role of "small boys, pulling off their wings"). What the Trojans haven't accomplished in ten years by force, pollution and disease will now take care of in as many weeks or even days. It's in this mood that we meet the Greeks in the opening scene of the story.

Since plagues are sent by Apollo (in his role as "distant, deadly Archer"), it seems likely that the problem here, like many another grievance in camp, goes back to the arrogance of the High King, who rashly insisted on plundering one of the Sun God's temples, carrying off a High Priest's daughter as a concubine (a temple which must have long been off limits in wiser days, when there were more targets to choose from, or else it wouldn't have still been available now). Chryses, the Priest, even came to petition for his daughter's return, bearing ransom, but Agamemnon only mocked and insulted him—an additional offense to the god. A seer confirms the High King's responsibility; now all the men are grumbling about the King's greed and ill-judgment, only nobody dares confront Agamemnon, who is dangerous to provoke, like most of the Greeks, and if anything even quicker than the others to flash into violence. Nobody except Achilles. Foolishly enough, the young hero chooses to do this in front of the whole army, where the King will be at his most defensive, the most concerned with saving face, but then Achilles is no politician, and has all the rashness of youth on top of the hotheadedness of all his compatriots. Agamemnon, perceiving dimly that he's facing a mutiny here, grudgingly agrees to return the girl—but only once he receives fair compensation from his lieutenants. That's impossible at the moment, with most of the plunder already gone, and those unscalable walls. Meantime, he'll make do by taking Achilles's own favorite concubine, Briseis, as punishment for the younger man's general insubordination.

Achilles flies into his famous rage. Insults and threats fill the air; swords are reached for. The Greek campaign might have ended right there in a mass internecine bloodletting, but Zeus has vowed to Hera that in the end Troy *will* fall, one way or another—and Achilles himself is under the (temporary) protection of not one but two lineages of gods. The goddess Athena appears (but to him only), staying his hand, murmuring in his ear something that's a whole new thought to this most unreflective, unstrategic of youths:

> *Don't get mad*, she whispers,—*get even. Humiliate the High King, don't kill him—killing's too good for him. Go out on strike. Make them all feel what they've lost, letting you be insulted like this. How long has it been now since the old sot had to suit up and go out on a raid without you in the forefront, bearing the brunt of the battle? How long will it be till he comes groveling to you on the beach, whining, desperate with losses, begging you to return to the fray?*

To everyone's amazement, including no doubt his own, Achilles turns and strides out of camp.

Which brings us to a deeper level of the story, the reason why the tale has *lasted* all these ages, and still matters for us today—and on a narrative level, the real reason for the war itself, behind the cover spin about national honor and the "abducted princess," behind the obvious mercenary level, beyond even the sweep and clang of arms, the blood and guts pouring out on the sand in living color and full cinematic detail (as a popular performance piece, the *Iliad* was the original Rambo movie, graphic and gory, as it had to be to hold its own for centuries at boisterous market fairs and bawdy banquet halls of the Greek Dark Ages, before writing and classic times. The full wide-screen feel and dynamic pulse of the original are surely captured again at last, in our more visual age, in Robert Fagle's new translation, which restores the rollicking energy lost in the literary versions of recent centuries).

At this deeper level, the poem tells us of a great clash of *world views*, a conflict of ethos and values, the point at which one way of life, one organized system of ethics and fundamental assumptions about life and culture gives way to another. In other words, as the Greeks would have put it, a clash of *gods*. On the one side (the Greek side) we have the Olympian skygods, Zeus and his siblings and children, principally Hera, Poseidon, Hades, Athena, and Ares (though Ares can be pulled to the other side by the power of Aphrodite, aggression and sex being easily conflated). What we need to know is that these lot are relatively recent arrivals on the scene, having wrested Olympus from an earlier branch of the god-family, the Titans, and after liberation from their long childhood captivity in hiding from their patricidal, infanticidal father, whom Zeus finally grew up and dispatched. In the earliest days of their reign they used to hobnob familiarly with mortals, in the way of the older deities they displaced, dining for example with Tantalus, who tested their new power by serving up his own son Pelops on the menu, just to see if they were really everything they claimed to be. The gods restored Pelops to life (minus the one bite they'd taken, but still), and punished Tantalus with a powerful curse: in each generation of his house, family blood would be spilled by a family member—a curse that Agamemnon, Pelops's grandson, has already done his part to fulfill, and to which he will fall in his turn. Zeus for his part understands this kind of thing from the inside, being descended from two generations of child-murderers, and having killed his own father and warred with all his siblings and cousins (in one of these battles Zeus is saved from his own brothers by one of those cousins, Thetis the ocean nymph; this too is important, because Thetis is Achilles's mother). Thus the skygods are born in murder and conquest, and pass these traits and values on to the civilization they embody.

Zeus is fond of the Trojans (Ganymede, his kept boy, is a captured Trojan prince), but he's sworn an oath to Hera that the Greeks will win. Hera is implacably anti-Trojan because of the slight to her and her stepdaughter Athena (whom she otherwise loathes) at the hands of Prince Paris, when as a lad he was called to award the judgment of the golden apple ("to the fairest")—at Thetis's wedding to a mortal, Achilles's own father, an early devotee of Zeus (Zeus is forcing the wedding, a social comedown for Thetis, because the goddess is fated to bear a son greater than his father—the kind of prophecy no Olympian wants any part of). Paris, as we know, gives the apple to Aphrodite—rejecting the values of strategy and cunning (Athena) or power and dominion (Hera), in favor of the charms of erotic love. In other words, Paris is no Greek—and Troy will fall for that slight to the new Greek gods.

The Trojans, on the other hand, are long and deeply allied with the other, older lineage of gods—the nature gods and spirits lately defeated and subjugated by the Olympians. As an example, Poseidon, Zeus's brother, *rules over* the sea, which fell to him by lot when the three brothers were dividing the three realms, sky, sea, and underworld (earth, being less important, they gave to their sister Demeter, who was a sort of throwback to their mother's side of the family anyway). Nereus, Thetis's father, by contrast, *is* the sea; he doesn't rule it, he personifies it, and his fifty daughters the Nereids, including Thetis, *are* the frothy wave tops; you may see them playing on the waters, any breezy day. The Olympians, that is, represent conquest and *power over*; the older gods and goddesses, the spirit of—and nature herself.

The same contrast can then be found in every aspect of the two societies. Troy, a center of commercial wealth, lives for music and dance, harmony with nature (the Trojan royal family, including Paris, have long interbred with the local nature deities), a deep respect for the position and nature of women (it would be shameful, Paris reminds the elders, to "hand over" Helen against her will), and the cultivation of all the peaceable arts (Paris, for example, devotes himself to a life of pleasure, although he is captain of the archers and the only leader on either side of the war ever to demonstrate clear, self-sacrificing courage, going *mano a mano* against Menelaus, a far stronger warrior, on Menelaus's terms and weapons, solely in hopes of negotiating a settlement to the war). Apollo, a protector of Troy, is technically an Olympian, but he too is born of both lineages of gods, and as the god of prophecy (as well as the sun, and plagues, and medicine) counts the Trojan princess Cassandra among his chiefest acolytes. Aphrodite too, sex itself, is part of this older pantheon, likewise a force of nature with power over gods and men alike, and also intimately entwined with the royal house of Troy (her son Aeneas, later founder of Rome, is a cousin of Paris and Hector). Because sex is ever-young, Zeus addresses her as "child;" but technically she is his aunt, and rules him too at times, as sex sometimes rules us all: when Hera wants to lure Zeus to sleep so she can meddle in the war against his command, she borrows Aphrodite's powers (using a cover story, since Aphrodite won't knowingly help the Greeks).

In heaven, the skygods have already vanquished their older foes—or more exactly, established a kind of uneasy dominion over them (like all warlords turned monarchs, Zeus finds that conquest is one thing, administration quite another; his life is not an easy one, beset on every side by the residue of the old rivalries, the eruption of new ones among the victors, and the constant threat of palace rebellion). On earth Troy—and especially Paris—still hold to the old ways, obedient enough in their rituals and temple practices (which would satisfy Zeus, who has become a realist), but disloyal in their hearts and dreams. For this, Hera and Athena have resolved, they must be destroyed.

Thus the *Iliad*, viewed at this level, represents the closest thing we have to a historical record of the existence of a legendary "Gaia culture," a civilization based on the unity of nature and the primacy of feminine, "earth" energy (captured here at the very moment of its destruction). Troy is certainly not a matriarchy, but it seems at least to be a culture where masculine and feminine principles, male and female "energies" are well balanced, and one deeply imbued with all those mysteries and values we conventionally call "feminine." The Greeks, as should be clear by now, are "masculine" in that savage, murderous sense that makes men cringe (or identify with the aggressor, or both)—the energy of rape and conquest which has organized so much of Western culture over the succeeding three millennia, and continues to lay down our dominant cultural thrust today. In this mythology, the founding act of the culture, ever-repeated and ever-denied, is *infanticide*—the common hallmark of the House of Zeus and the House of Atreus, Agamemnon's father. Atreus, acting out the curse of his grandfather Tantalus, murdered his little brother Chrysippus (with the help of their other brother Thyestes, whom Atreus also murders later on; thus Agamemnon's cousin-troubles now at home)—but only after Chrysippus's recovery from being kidnaped and raped by King Laius of Thebes, none other than Oedipus's father. Laius is punished by Zeus (hypocritically—remember Ganymede?) with the fate that he will be killed by his own son. To forestall this, Laius determines to murder the infant Oedipus first—who however survives, through the usual kindly woodsman. Oedipus of course then does grow up to kill his father—but unknowingly, in a brawl provoked by the older man, at the very moment Oedipus is fleeing from the same prophecy so as to spare his beloved *adoptive* father, whom he supposes to be the one the prophecy refers to. Freud, in a monumental psychic reversal which remains unnamed in the lexicon of ego defenses, interprets this as a basic instinct for *patricide*. But the story, like all the Greek stories, tells the opposite tale (and isn't that true of every war, really—"wars dreamed up," in the words of the late American peace candidate George McGovern, "by old men, for young men to die in.") Thus the legacy of the Greeks is carried forward, into our politics and psychological models today.

And now here's where the plot gets really interesting, rising from issues of cultural ideology and archetype (and bloody family melodrama) to the level of high art. Because Achilles, the central figure of the poem, *partakes of both these god-natures.* His lineage is dual: the war taking place between the two civilizations—and the two sets of gods—is also going to go on within his own breast. On his father's side, he is a darling of the skygods. King Peleus was a great favorite of Zeus's in earlier days, a defender of the skygod ethic who was rewarded with a kingdom, the land of the Myrmidons (so-called because Zeus created the race for the purpose, out of ants). This is the same Peleus who was further honored by marriage to a goddess (albeit an unwilling bride who seemingly never lived with her husband. Thus Achilles was raised entirely by men, principally his old tutor Phoenix, who is with him now, and then ushered into manhood by his mentor/lover Patroclus, whom Zeus will sacrifice when the time comes, to draw Achilles back into battle).

And on his mother's side, of course, lie the whole race and lineage of nature spirits and deities. Thetis, being immortal, lives under the sea in the palace of her father Nereus—but under the dominion of Poseidon, which probably explains why she helps Zeus when the skygod's brothers join forces and chain him up. Thus Thetis forestalls an Olympian palace coup—the good deed for which Zeus will now grant her a boon, though not as large as the one she will soon ask, on behalf of her aggrieved son. Wretched and alone on the beach (his own men are afraid to approach him, so black is his mood), he calls out to his long-absent mother, imploring her to go to Father Zeus, who he knows holds her in special favor, and persuade him to grant the revenge his heart craves (of course he'd be throwing in his lot with the weaker party here. Zeus may be a god, but first and foremost he's a politician, and in politics yesterday's obligation is always discounted by today's threat, and tomorrow's strategic consideration).

And Thetis comes to him, pitying her son in his wretchedness—not so much because he's been royally "dissed" (in the lingo of street gangs, which is completely apt here) as because she knows well *his* prophecy, as he does too, which makes this disgrace all the more bitter: he is born to have a short life of great glory, remembered through all the ages, *or* a long life and a happy one, finally to die in old age surrounded by children, grandchildren, friends around him—but in obscurity, ultimately unsung. In other words, the conflict of civilizations and values here, the clash of gods, is likewise a fork in Achilles's own destiny. He must choose between the two ways of life, the two kinds of ethics: the Greek way, or the Trojan.

Alas, he made his choice long ago—or rather it was made for him, perhaps from the moment his mother left him there to be raised by Greek men (kindly men, doting and indulgent, quite a different household from Agamemnon's; and yet in the end it will come to the same thing: the sons, whether abused or coddled, are raised for war, and will be sent off by the fathers to murder and be murdered in their turn). Thetis knows Zeus won't change this fate, or Achilles's fateful choice. Nor will he grant a full Trojan victory. All he will concede to the goddess who stood by him when his own wife and brothers betrayed him, is that without Achilles, Troy will prevail for a time, sweeping battle after battle, pressing the Greeks against the beach, ultimately setting fire to the ships themselves. And that Agamemnon and all the others, humiliated and desperate, will beg Achilles's pardon, and sue for his return to battle at any price.

In other words, Achilles is going to get basically everything he thinks he wants. If the point of a strike is to force the capitulation of the other side, his victory will be total (within the terms of his destined choice). And yet—something else is happening, something completely unforeseen. Perhaps it's the other side of Achilles's nature, what we might call here the "Trojan" side, which is part at least of all of us, stirring and waking for the first time. Perhaps it's that like any young ruffian of a gang culture (which is what the Greek camp is), he's simply never really taken a moment for reflection before. Forced into it now by circumstance, for the first time in his life he begins to *think things over*. And the more he thinks, the more he begins to see through the veil of the culture myths and values he was raised on, the gigantic fraud perpetrated (on men and women alike) by what we now sometimes call "the patriarchy," whose real truth is that *it eats its own young*. Confusedly, hesitantly at first (this is all new to him, to say nothing of his companions)—and then with a stronger, clearer voice:

> ... *Why must we battle Trojans,*
> *Men of Argos? Why did he muster an army, lead us here,*
> *that son of Atreus? ...*
> *for Helen with her loose and lustrous hair?*
> *Are they the only men alive who love their wives,*
> *those sons of Atreus?*
> *...I loved that woman with all my heart,*
> *though I won her like a trophy with my spear...*

—meaning Briseis, the concubine Agamemnon has wrested from him. Most unGreek words—but there's more:

> *I say no wealth is worth my life!*
> * ...Mother tells me*
> *that two fates bear me on to the day of death.*
> *If I hold out here and I lay siege to Troy,*
> *my journey home is gone, but my glory never dies.*
> *If I voyage back to the fatherland I love,*
> *my pride, my glory dies...*
> *true, but the life that's left me will be long...*

And then, most alarmingly of all, when the embassy of Agamemnon visits him on the beach, beseeching him to reconsider,

> *tomorrow at daybreak, once I have sacrificed*
> *to Zeus and all the gods...—watch, my friend,*
> *if you'll take time and care to see me off,*
> *and you will see my squadrons sail at dawn,*
> *my crews manning the oarlocks, rowing out with a will,*
> *and if the famed god of the earthquake grants us safe passage,*
> *the third day out we raise the dark rich soil of Phthia.*
> *There lies my wealth, hoards of it, all I left behind...*

One thing more. To the rest I'd pass on this advice:

sail home now! You will never set your eyes
on the day of doom that topples looming Troy.
Thundering Zeus has spread his hands above her—
her armies have taken heart!

The desperate embassy offers him virtually all the wealth and honors to be had in the camp, plus more at home, bevies of women, even the hand of Agamemnon's eldest daughter Iphegenia and an equal share, one day, in his kingdom (this last at least is disingenuous, of course, since the girl is already dead—as we know but the Greeks don't, except for Agamemnon himself, who had her ritually killed on his way out of town, a human sacrifice in exchange for a favorable breeze). Still the young hero holds firm, spurning bribes and entreaties alike. He vows again he will defend his own ships with his own men if need be through the night, and no more. And with that the dejected embassy has to go back empty-handed to Agamemnon, to give him the bitterest news of all: tomorrow the High King himself will have to lead the heavily outmatched army.

But of course the skygod has other plans. The Trojans will reach and torch the ships; Patroclus—"best and gentlest of the Greeks" —will beg Achilles's armor, and impersonating the hero, rally the Greeks and drive the terrified Trojans all the way back to the walls of the city. There Hector will face and kill Patroclus, whereupon Achilles, blind with rage and impotent grief, will return to battle to hunt Hector down, heaping insults and abuse on his dead body, then slaughtering further scores of Trojan youth in his rampage. His rage finally spent, he will hold great funeral games for his beloved friend, at which he will give away essentially all his wealth as prizes, like the dead man walking he now is. Old King Priam will brave the lines to petition Achilles for his son's body, still unburied, and Hector himself will finally have his funeral, which ends the *Iliad*. The war is a complete stalemate, most of the heroes on both sides are dead; Troy still stands. But the will of Zeus has not yet worked its way to its inevitable, bitter end.

And the rest, as they say, is history—or in this case, is legend. With Hector dead and the old king mad with grief, Paris becomes regent, returning to the strategy of ambush, archery, and attrition which was winning the war for them just a few days or weeks ago, before hotter heads insisted on meeting the Greeks on their own terms, head-on in battle. Paris himself will dispatch Achilles with one of his unerring arrows, thus accomplishing from a safe distance what a battalion of armored men has failed to do for ten years. At this point Troy has won the war; the few tattered Greeks still standing are aging and wounded; no doubt illness and their own internecine quarreling, with the help of the occasional arrow, will pick them off.

But then the Trojan way would live on, the old values of peace and harmony; the slight to the skyqueens' power would go unavenged. And Zeus is not going to let that happen. Thus the treachery of the Trojan horse, the sack of the city, and departure of the remaining captains, laden with treasure and women. Significantly, not a *single one* of them will arrive home to safety— except of course Odysseus, eventually, minus ten years and all his men. Odysseus is supposedly the sagest and most strategic of all the Greeks, but his decade of wandering will be entirely due to his own ego and hotheadedness, and his first act on reaching Ithaca will be the wholesale slaughter of a generation of his own subjects, who are jockeying for his throne. By the end of Homer's great second volume of this tragic tale, not a one of the Greek heroes, alive or dead, including Odysseus, will have learned anything (except for Achilles, too late, in the Underworld). Thus the ethic of Zeus, the glory of heroes and the blood of the children, will prevail, as it still prevails, tragically unaltered, down to our own day.

Homer's Legacy

And so Troy falls, not by defeat but because the skygods demand it. And thus a great cultural vision falls with it, an integrated whole of values, social relations, and self-experience, the last fleeting glimpse we will get of that degree of harmony and balance, at least in a high urban culture, anywhere in written history. But what was that ethos and ethic, exactly, that underlying set of deep cultural assumptions and values about who we are, and how we relate to the world, each other, and ourselves? What fundamental, underlying assumptions divided it from that of the Greeks—or from our own culture today?

A simple way of summing up the Trojan system, at least as Homer characterizes it for us, is that it was founded in an *ethic of belonging*. Like any ethic, any organized system of values, this one has to rest on and presume a particular anthropology—in Goodman's sense of that term, meaning a particular vision of human nature. That is, who we consider ourselves to be, what we are *like* in our essential human nature and condition, always contains and implies certain ethical propositions, of how we therefore need to act, in relation to each other, ourselves, our natural environment. This may seem obvious, but still it's a proposition in need of defending, inasmuch as it was long questioned and finally rejected by Western philosophy in modern times—a fundamental tenet of scientific modernism being that *who we are* and *how we ought to act* are utterly separate things, with nothing to do with each other. A Gestalt understanding of human nature, by contrast, enables us to see this separation itself as culturally conditioned, and not finally valid—more on this below.

The anthropology of Troy, its underlying vision of human nature, as with any nature-deity and spirit culture, is an *anthropology of participation*: in Gestalt terms, a *holistic* field model and vision, of who we are and how we relate to ourselves and the world around us. When we define and see ourselves as participating in the world, partaking of both nature and others in and as ourselves, and thus *interpenetrating* in essential ways with our social and natural surround, then *taking care of self* and *taking care of the other or the environment* are no longer two separate things, in zero-sum relation to each other. Rather, the relationship becomes *complex, ecological, and figure-ground in nature*. Potentially at least, when I care for you I am enhancing my own field of belonging and liveliness—and vice versa. Thus an ethic of belonging—the Trojan way—implies an ethic of *relationship, responsibility, and care*. In our terms, we may call this a *Gestalt field ethic*, a view of ourselves and our individual nature as emergent in and of a relational field—and not as essentially apart from, prior to that field. In such a system, the Western dichotomy of self versus other tends to fall away: it makes no sense to take care of only myself and not extend that care to the whole field of other selves in some way (in principle if not in every moment)—because without a vibrant, nurtured field of caring, there is no place for me to stand and flourish and grow. The simplistic reduction of "me *versus* you" is replaced, again in principle, by the greater complexity of our co-responsibility for our mutual, interpenetrating field. All this follows, naturally and seamlessly, from the Gestalt (or Trojan) foundation of *holism*, the primacy of the whole field.

The contrasting ethic—the Greek way—is what we may call an *ethic of individualism,* which is of course the organizing cultural paradigm of Western civilization, since the time of the Greeks themselves and on down to our own day. That is, in this view our fundamental self-nature, the essence of our human condition, is that *the essential core of our being exists somewhere apart from everything around us,* the natural world and other selves alike (for discussion of this and the following points, see Wheeler, 2000). We find this deep assumption in the Western view of the individual soul, created and migrating through the world in some way utterly, ontologically distinct from other souls (and even from its Creator: this may be a hard point to get our bodyminds around, but to question it is to commit the mystical sin of pantheism, long a heresy in *every* mainstream Western religion). And we find it, raised to perhaps its highest possible philosophical expression, in Leibniz's monadology (1713), the world as "windowless monads," or soul-atoms, irreducibly distinct created bits of spirit/matter, changeless, eternal, and utterly without relationship to one another, beyond the mere reactive effects of bouncing off each other in a Newtonian mechanical universe.

In an individualistic ethic, the highest value, by definition, has to be individual achievement in some form or fashion, the realization of the *potential powers of the individual* (even with a religious/individualistic system, it is the achievement of individual salvation or pilgrim's progress of the individual soul that counts). That is, the ethic inherently is one of *assertion and conquest:* even where the immediate goal is conceived as donative or disinterested, still the achievement will be measured in terms of mastery of knowledge, conquest of nature, achievement of an artistic breakthrough, conversion of the infidel, the defeat of poverty, or disease, or even war itself. In the Homeric Greek spin on this ethic, all this is summed up in terms of *glory*. The sole achievement that can last, for an individual who is so utterly alone in the universe, so ontologically cut off from membership and participation in his/her world, is *reputation and fame*: the hero whose exploits are sung the longest, wins. This is commonly referred to as the Homeric or Glory Ethic—though the synonymy is perhaps unfair to Homer, whose unsentimental and even jaundiced view of war and warriors has often earned him the charge of Trojan sympathies, ever since classical times.

But an individualistic system, by the terms of our Gestalt perspective of affect and emotion, outlined at the beginning of this essay, is also by definition a system that rests on *shame and shaming*. This follows from our Gestalt understanding of shame, which is at its deepest level *a rupture in the field of belonging* (see Lee & Wheeler, 1996). The very hallmark of any individualistic system is the *absense* of belonging, as the fundamental assumption of the worldview. This is true both *ontologically* and *epistemologically*, which is to say, both as a description of what is real, or essential, about our nature—and also of how we know things, which is understood to be analytically, from the outside, not through participation in their nature. Again, that is, we know things by conquest of our ignorance, and of the thing-to-be-known itself.

Thus a Glory Ethic is also, inherently and by definition, shorthand for a *Shame-and-Glory Ethic*. Again, this is the opposition between the Greek and the Trojan ways of life—the one founded in connectivity and membership, or holism, and the other in "dualism," that series of dichotomies that define our world and ourselves, in the Western model, separating self from other, individual from relationship, person from nature, science from values, male from female, master from slave, and so on and so on (significantly, there is no evidence of slaves in Troy). Our Gestalt model teaches us to be suspicious, at the very least, of any such imagined dichotomies, in our experiential field or in the real nature of things.

In the end, this is why the theme of *infanticide* looms so large in the Greek myths and heroes' tales: because at least metaphorically, this is the ultimate rupture, in the natural field of care and belonging. If there is no natural bond, no inherent identification between parent and child, then there is no resting place, no locus of comfort and belonging anywhere in the world. Heidegger's vision, of man as "thrown" onto the shore of a world to which he does not, in "his" essence, belong, is already foreshadowed in the Greeks. In such a world home is by definition a place of danger, for which conquest itself becomes a temporary, imagined relief. And of course such a home will tend to expel or consume its own young (war accomplishes both of these nicely), keeping the reciprocal whole of culture on its self-perpetuating spiral. When Odysseus visits the spirits of the underworld later on, in the Odyssey, the shade of Achilles appears and speaks bitterly of the emptiness of fame and the ethic of glory—the same insight he gained on the beach, lost at Zeus's manipulative hands, and regains now, only of course too late. (Zeus, in sacrificing Patroclus on the altar of war, prefigures the same gesture in historical times by King Frederick William I of Prussia, father of the Enlightenment king known as Frederick the Great, who summoned his son before him together with his lover, and had the lover slaughtered on the spot before the boy's horrified eyes. That's how you toughen up a son, under the terms of the Glory Ethic).

Ethics and Natural Science

Since Hume's day, it has been commonplace in Western philosophy to argue that the two great branches of knowledge, "natural philosophy" (or science) and moral philosophy (or ethics)—what is and what ought to be—lie in unbridgeably separate domains, as entirely different kinds of "knowledge." The one, science, is "positivist," in the sense of being objective knowledge of a world which "positively" exists, and likewise posits itself to us in a direct, objective kind of way, suitable for analysis, beyond the murky realm of human interpretation. The world is just "there," in a positive sense, and knowing it is a matter of *discovering the objective facts of it*, and then stringing them all together. Bertrand Russell (1936), a century and a half or so later, pronounced this division to be firm and final, a cost of the enlightenment of science—much under the combined influence of his student Wittgenstein and, earlier, his mentor Moore. That is, objective, final, and absolutely dependable knowledge about the natural world is achievable (including, ultimately, the world of psychology, our own minds and behavior)—this kind of "conquest" is after all the great achievement of modernism. But alas, the same can never be true of the subjective realms of morality and ethics. In the end our ethical preferences are just that—preferences, different perhaps in effects but not in nature from our preferences in art, lifestyle, or anything else. To be sure, we should work and even fight for our principles (Russell went to jail in his 40's for opposition to World War I, was an early supporter of nuclear disarmament in his 80's, and in his later 90's led worldwide opposition to the Vietnam War). Still, none of this can be grounded in any natural view of human nature and human process—because those things belong to the other, "scientific-materialist" realm of knowledge (you could of course connect up the two things by bringing God into the picture, but here Russell agreed with Nietzsche, that that was a coward's way out of the dilemma). Thus Russell announced the end of the quest in philosophy to give an answer to Nietzsche, whose doctrine it was that all morality is relativistic and equal in value, each system being no more than the cover story of some particular interest group, in their drive for dominance and power (small wonder, of course, that the Nazis found in Nietzsche's writings a justification for their own ideology).

What Russell failed to see, of course, was that Nietzsche's dogma, far from *proving* the separateness of our ethics from our ideas of human nature, was rather *an example of their deep connection* (see discussion in Wheeler, 1992, 1996, 2000). That is, the modernist Western position, that ethics is distinct from scientific knowledge, *is itself a consequence of an individualistic view of human nature.* If we are outside the world, distinct from it, and not participating and interpenetrating with it, then the highest value (absent God) will indeed be individual striving and will, as Nietzsche says. The Nazis (or any other group) may strive for their agenda, Russell may strive for his—but ethically it's all equal. If, on the other hand, we belong intimately within that world, which also exists within us, in our "essential" being, then we may give Russell's moral vision and politics a deeper, more lasting foundation than he himself could give, from within the limitations of his modernist perspective. It is Gestalt that enables us to make this argument, and this reply; but Troy lived it, long ago.

Conclusion

Today Achilles's choice is our choice: the fork in his destiny lies immediately before us now in our own. Which will we choose: the familiar Greek way, separating person from relationship, parent from child, science from ethics, humans from nature, self from the living field of other selves? Or the Trojan way—which is also the Gestalt way, of holism, belonging, identity, and care?

Like Achilles, if we don't choose, we're still choosing. Zeus knew how to play the impetuous young hero, tormented as he was with grief and shame; but still he had a choice, even to the very end. When he gave way reactively to rage he wasn't avoiding his choice: he was making it.

The Gestalt model offers us a new perspective, from which to view our own culture, and ourselves. In a darkening world, perhaps we still have a bit of time on the shore of the future, to think it over.

References

Damasio, A. (1994). *Decartes's Error: Emotion, Reason, and the Human Brain*. NY: Putnam.

Darwin, C. (1872). *The Expression of the Emotions in Man and Animals*. London: John Murray.

de Waal, F. (1982). *Chimpanzee Politics: Power and Sex among Apes*. Baltimore: Johns Hopkins University Press.

de Waal, F. (1996). *Good Natured*. Cambridge MA: Harvard University Press.

Ekman, P. (ed). (1983). *Facial Emotion*. Cambridge: Cambridge University Press.

Fagles, R. (transl). (1990). *The Iliad*. NY: Viking Penguin.

Goldstein, K. (1939). *The Organism*. Boston: American Book Co.

Heidegger, M. (1962). *Being and Time*. London: SCM Press.

Kaufman, G. (1980). *Shame: The Power of Caring*. Rochester VT: Shenckman.

Lee, R. & Wheeler, G. (eds). (1996). *The Voice of Shame: Silence and Connection in Psychotherapy*. San Francisco: Jossey-Bass.

Leibniz, G. (1714/1965). Monadology. In P. Wiener, (ed.), *Leibnitz*. NY: Scribners.

Nietzsche, F. (1956). *The Birth of Tragedy and the Geneology of Morals*. Garden City NY: Doubleday.

Russell, B. (1972). *The History of Western Philosophy*. NY: Viking.

Tomkins, S. (1962). *Affect, Imagery, and Consciousness*. NY: Springer.

Wheeler, G. (1992). Ethics: a Gestalt perspective. In E. Nevis, (ed.), *Gestalt Therapy: Perspectives and Applications*. NY: Gardner Press.

Wheeler, G. (1994). Tasks of intimacy: Reflections on a Gestalt approach to working with couples. In G. Wheeler & S. Backman, (eds.), *On Intimate Ground: a Gestalt Approach to Working with Couples*. San Francisco: Jossey-Bass.

Wheeler, G. (2000). *Beyond Individualism: Toward a New Understanding of Self, Relationship, & Experience*. Hillsdale NJ: The Analytic Press/GestaltPress.

Wheeler, G. & Jones, D. (1996). Finding our sons: a male-male gestalt. In R. Lee & G. Wheeler, (eds.), *The Voice of Shame: Silence and Connection in Psychotherapy*. San Francisco: Jossey-Bass.

Editor's Note:

In the following chapter, Nigel Copsey shares with us the exciting work that he is doing in conjunction with marginalized ethnic and spiritual communities in the East End of London. In a single group format, he brings together members of vastly different cultural communities in a manner in which they not only co-exist but come to value one another. We learn how a relational ethic can yield a methodology for multi-cultural encounter and intervention, even under the most challenging circumstances. Here, the program is founded on the basic relational ethical injunction: that commitment to giving everyone a voice and remaining in relationship will support the exploration of difference, and the emergence of new intercultural possibilities in the field. This chapter also illustrates what Philip Lictenberg writes about in Chapter Ten of this volume, in that these communities tend to maintain isolation from one another, and thus may often be limited to projective fantasies to form an image of each other.

13

•••••••••••••

Finding A Voice:

Listening to the Mental Health

& Spiritual Needs of the New

Communities of East London

Nigel Copsey

The ideas which I will be presenting in this chapter have their origins in discussions with Sonia Nevis. And I want at the outset to honour her and her original thinking, for her support was a major factor in enabling me to develop a training programme in inner London which was both innovative and true to Gestalt principles.

The setting that accompanied my initial consultations with Sonia was the opening of Sonia and Edwin Nevis' Gestalt International Study Center (GISC) on Cape Cod. In retrospect, I realise just how important it has been for me to secure the support that I have needed to take this radical and risky step of faith. A rich combination of the presence and influence of Sonia, friends I have found on the Cape, a very dear and special therapist who sadly died recently, and the beauty of the Cape itself have together provided for me what Robert Lee so aptly refers to as the 'healthy village' that is needed for individual growth.

There are some important parallels between my experience at that first Individual Affiliates weekend of the GISC and the atmosphere I was later able to set in my training programme in inner London. At GISC that weekend, I was a member of a 'Spirituality and Gestalt' study group. I was moved to find myself alongside a group of colleagues, a dozen or so in number, who shared a common commitment to the spiritual path and to a sense of how Gestalt theory fits with and enables that journey. At the same time we were all very different in our respective spiritual quests. We spent considerable time that weekend listening to each other and learning from one another how we each experience our spiritual path. As we shared our stories, I realised that the task we were jointly embracing was a reflection of the theme of the whole gathering. Here we were drawn from different parts of the USA and the world, possessing a wide variety of clinical, organisational, and other backgrounds, working in an equally wide variety of settings, united in the common goal to discover and form our community. I saw that underlying the success of our venture here was a deep desire to know each other with all our differences. As I write, we are continuing in that venture through our respective home projects; it is an exciting prospect. But as with our experience together in the initial weekend, it will only be successful if each of us shows a deep respect and genuine interest in the others of our group. This has been and continues to be our relational ethic. This is not an ethic that has been imposed by an outside authority, and in fact we have not referred to it as an ethic. Nevertheless it is an ethic that has been ever present, an ethic which to some extent we carried with us in the form of our yearnings for connection when we arrived and which has been modeled by Sonia Nevis and nurtured through our interactions with her and each other. This relational ethic would also become a cornerstone in my building a radical training programme in inner London.

Travel with me now from Cape Code to my place of work and my home in inner London, a very different setting from the natural beauty of the Cape. The 'East End' of London is an exciting place to live and work. To orient you, when visiting London, most visitors arrive at Heathrow which is to the west of the city or at Gatwick to the south. London is built around the Thames. The East of London (or downstream) is the area where industry was developed. It was the area with the largest docks in the world. It was the place which Hitler sought to destroy in the blitz, and most importantly it was the place where waves of incoming communities have settled. The centre and the west of London were the areas where those with higher incomes lived. The East End of London was the province of the poor. This is still largely the case today although there has recently been a process of 'gentrification' as the City of London has extended into the old dockland area. It is very difficult to predict how such extremes of wealth and poverty living side by side within the same vicinity will impact this locality in the next decade. Our nearest neighbours in the heart of the docklands are from Africa, Asia, Turkey, Greece, the West Indies and London. This mix reflects the cultural diversity that is now characteristic of the inner city of London. We live in an area which now has the largest Bengali, Jewish, African and Pakistani populations in the UK. At one time this place was simply a slum for racial minorities. Over the last fifteen years it has been transformed into a rich culturally diverse community.

Two years ago I was asked to establish in this area a Department of Spiritual, Religious and Cultural Care for the mental health services of the National Health Service. The NHS (as it is known in the UK) is the state provider of healthcare. The aim is to provide care, free at the point of delivery, solely determined by need. Many in the USA find it hard to believe that the duration of psychological therapies is decided solely on clinical need. For example, I am currently supporting two clients as their key worker and have been doing so for three years. It is government policy that the NHS should provide spiritual care to all that use the service. Hence, in this richly diverse area of inner London I was asked to establish a department whose aim was to ensure that any user of mental health services, whatever their spiritual and cultural background, should have their needs not only recognised but also respected. In addition, our task is to ensure that mental health professionals recognise and respect the diverse spiritual and cultural traditions of the area. These goals will take many years to achieve as the psychiatric services' world view is often directly opposite to that of the Faith Communities represented in the district. At the same time the Faith Communities themselves are deeply suspicious of the psychiatric services, often with very good reason. They would see the western dominated world view as being at variance to their own understanding of mental health. For example, the Faith Communities across East London do not see a divide between the secular and the sacred: life is sacred. Our task is to ensure that the Faith Communities of East London can be open to the understandings of psychology and psychiatry and at the same time to encourage mental health professionals to widen their world view to include spirituality.

I would like to return at this point to Sonia Nevis, for it was as a result of conversations with her that I began to glimpse a framework in which the goals of my project might be achieved. The context of the conversation, which first prompted my thinking in this area, was the need to establish a radical training programme. The cost of training in both counseling and psychotherapy is becoming prohibitive. Further, the majority of training programmes prepare participants primarily for one activity, namely, therapy. My own interest has been to discover ways in which it would be possible to 'give away' the insights of Gestalt theory so that communities can be productively changed in accordance with their human needs while respecting their spiritual and cultural imperatives. For me, the power of Gestalt theory lies in its description of how change can take place through the quality of relationships. Why restrict that wisdom to a psychotherapeutic elite who happen to have the necessary resources to fund a training?

I had come to see that the Faith Communities of East London provided a rich resource within the East London populace as a whole, particularly with regard to two of my most basic aims. My hope was to be able to create a training programme that was accessible to the 'ordinary person.' I wanted to ensure that no one would be excluded because of cultural background or because of financial situation. Further, my hope was that members of the programme would reflect the ethnic/spiritual mix of East London. My own spiritual journey within the Christian tradition has led me into a deep conviction that God cares deeply about those who are marginalised and powerless. For the last twenty-five years I have been committed to working and living alongside those in such situations, seeking to support them. On many occasions this has meant an active political involvement with the aim of securing humanitarian and ethical change.

It was with this sense of mission that I approached Sonia to ask her if she were interested in supporting me in the creation of this training programme. I was thrilled when she agreed, as I needed the assistance of someone who knew at first hand the initial radical Gestalt agenda as developed by Goodman. I had been attracted to Gestalt theory because of its early commitment to social action.

The Faith Communities of East London all have very distinct cultural identities. As a result people's lives revolve almost totally around and within their own Faith Community. Because of this my initial idea was to work with each community separately. Sonia's response was to suggest bringing together representatives from all the faith groups to form a pilot training group. The aim, she advised, was to facilitate learning from each other. Using a phenomenological approach, my aim was to ensure that the members of the training group asked questions of each other to discover the differences that existed between them. Following that initial discussion, a group was invited together which consisted of white Christians, black Christians, Hindus and Muslims.

Participants of this pilot training group were located by reaching out to the Faith Communities in the area, attending their worship, meeting with their leaders, and in general devoting substantial time in building relationships. A large percentage of those invited to the group were also mental health workers or leaders of the Faith Communities, as we wanted people that were not only interested in our endeavor but who also were in contact with others in their community that might need mental health services. As this and subsequent training programmes have evolved, we have discovered that all those who have attended have themselves in some way been touched by mental distress.

The Christians were drawn from the indigenous white community of London known as 'Cockneys.' The Cockney community grew up in East London as the docks were developed. They see themselves as the true London community, possessing their own rich cultural traditions. This group has always proved very difficult to encourage into higher education or any endeavor that is considered to be 'middle class.' The community grew in an area of high unemployment, deprivation and poverty. They have always felt powerless as decisions have been taken concerning the area without their true consultation. It was impossible to find trained mental health workers drawn from this community since such professionals are seen as 'them.' The Cockney community also possesses a deep fear that 'their' London is being taken over by the new communities and is being lost in the process. The racist groups have exploited this fear. The combined result of these and other influences is that this strong, rich cultural tradition has lost its voice.

The black Christian community is now the largest Christian community in inner London. In recent years there has been a revival within this tradition; it is now possible to drive along a street in this area of London and be unable to find a place to park as there are so many churches! The largest church in London is a black majority church with over seven thousand members. The tradition is Pentecostal which means that there is a strong belief in the power and immediate presence of God.

The Muslim community has also grown significantly in number. In a relatively small area, close to where I live, there are fifteen Mosques. In one area of East London there are more Mosques per head of the Muslim population than anywhere else in the world!

All of the above groups have a fundamentalist belief system in that they believe that the fundamentals of their faith or way of being in the world are non-negotiable. They are not groups that would engage in dialogue. Our initial meetings were not good examples of good listening! However, we persevered and tried gently to explain the ground rules that emanated from our relational ethic: that our aim was genuinely to listen to one another. I was able to use our experience as it unfolded to explain some of Gestalt theory and how it supported our process. Very slowly we moved from entrenched, polarised positions to a willingness to learn from each other. To use Sonia's phrase, those in the group had begun to 'join' with each other. As the following weeks unfolded, they revealed a moving willingness to be vulnerable and to learn from one another. As we journeyed together, I could not help but marvel at what I was witnessing: a group of men and women, who would not normally engage with one another, beginning to see differences as important. We did not seek to change each other. Our aim was to celebrate and honour the differences in one another while remaining in relationship. Again this was the core of our relational ethic which supported our journey together. There were moments of strongly held disagreement but these took place while remaining in relationship.

We had begun the journey of what Sonia described as 'giving a voice' to each person. To return to the initial conversations with Sonia that gave birth to this experiment, her challenge to me was to bring together a group of men and women who all came from very different cultural and spiritual backgrounds. The challenge was to respect and work with the initial defensive behaviour with the aim of facilitating a true dialogue where participants could experience the miracle of remaining in relationship while exploring differences. The aim was not to minimise the differences but to celebrate them. Sonia encouraged me to think 'out of the box.' I did so by bringing together men and women from four very different backgrounds. The initial sessions consisted of each group seeking to convince the others of their own rightness. There was no listening. It was in those initial sessions that I sought to 'coach' the participants to reach out to one another by asking questions. Sonia had encouraged me to train group members in the asking of questions. She said that they would start with a limited awareness but with the use of questions, they would reach out, be curious with each other and so enlarge their field. In those early meetings, I realised how difficult this was for group members. All of them were carrying both individual and community stereotyped images of outside cultures and of how they should act in response to other cultures (known as introjects in Gestalt theory) which were preventing them from truly showing a real interest in one another. We had to explore many of those introjects before it was possible to go beyond them. I learned how hard it is truly to give everyone a voice when our received introjects are so strong, especially in the areas of culture and spirituality.

Let me underline again that it was this fundamental belief, this relational ethic—to give everyone a voice so that differences could be explored while remaining in relationship—that underpinned both the training programme and the establishment of the Department of Cultural, Spiritual and Religious Care.

Sonia also provided me with a number of other foundational beliefs, correlational actualisations of our underlying relational ethic, which underpinned the process. The first of these was to develop this group into a resource team that would model the value of remaining in dialogue while holding differences. This new community would then become the basis for changing first the psychiatric community, and then the wider community. The repeated challenge to me was to see this group (which included myself and my colleagues) as a community which was to model a different way of relating. Sonia would say, 'Train them to teach each other. Encourage them to tell stories.' I could see that my goal was, by increasing awareness, to help all of us in the group to speak a language which was both spiritual and psychological.

Sonia's second major challenge to me was to always think relationally, to encourage members of the group to join with each other so that we could move to an 'us' experience. The relationships that were established within that first group illustrated to me that it was possible for people with very different backgrounds and carrying archaic introjects, to join with one another in a shared vision.

Sonia said that 'time invested in another person can be miraculous.' It was that very simple truth that we sought to create together in that first group—to provide the safe setting where each person could genuinely be interested in others. As with my experience in my group at GISC, the ethical stance of being interested in others could not be forced or imposed by an outside authority. This ethic can only flow with the experience of sufficient safety and support. So the first implication of relational ethics for us in bringing together this pilot group was the ethical precondition/ injunction to establish sufficient relational safety. Providing that safety allowed us to model and explore with the participants how it is only possible to give everyone a voice when all are committed to being interested in each other.

These were the foundational principles which underpinned the formation of the programme. I am grateful beyond words to Sonia for pointing me in this direction with her deep yet simply expressed wisdom. True wisdom is always expressed simply; it does not need jargon. To illustrate how these principles guided our effort, I am going to tell you some stories.

Giving Voice to Cultural Taboos

The members of the group spent a great deal of time exploring the ways in which each Faith Community lives by deeply held stigmas relating to mental illness. The local Cockney Community sees psychiatric wards as the 'nuthouse.' There is a fear in the local population that they will be attacked by the patients who are described as 'nutters.' To my surprise, this stigma was also expressed by those from the Asian Faith groups. The Muslim and Hindu members of the group saw mental illness as being linked to spells. Many from the Bangladeshi community wear charms to keep the evil spirits away. To them mental illness is seen as a spiritual problem needing spiritual care. A rite of exorcism is therefore required to expel the spirit. Oil, Holy Water and texts are all used to bring healing. In all these communities an individual's mental illness is experienced as deeply shaming by his/her family. So much so that Asian family members would not visit the psychiatric wards in case the community discovered that one of its members was in the 'madhouse.' The fear is so great that there is a belief that the illness can be transmitted to other family members. One of the Muslim members of the group described how her mother believed that if she had a nightmare it was due to having caught an evil spirit by working in such a place. Among all members of the group there seemed to be a strong belief in the connection between mental illness and evil spirits. Another member of the group, from Nigeria, described how family members would be kept in a room, isolated from the wider community. When the group went on to discuss the more specific conditions such as suicide and depression, members of the group said they were unable to mention such states within their community.

By giving a voice to the thoughts and feelings of the group members' cultural sense of emotional/mental problems, for the first time, members of the group felt able to 'join' with each other in discovering that although they had very different interpretations of the various mental conditions, they could listen and learn from each other. Such conversations led to an awareness of how essential it is to break down the stigma of mental illness within the community.

Having become aware of the power of what Robert Lee calls 'ground shame'[1] in the example cited we have decided that as we move to the future we need to prioritise our time and energy to reduce the power of this shame. Unless we can achieve this it will not be possible for us to facilitate the necessary field conditions for those suffering from mental distress to experience real support. We need to invest heavily in supporting the communities of East London as we try to encourage them to become part of the healing process. As part of that needed investment, we have recently employed a member of our team to focus just on this area. She will be going to the Faith Communities with the aim of forming close working relationships with them with the goal of creating a genuine dialogue.

Initiating a Dialogue Between the Faith Communities and the Mental Health Services

Since there is such a clear link within the Faith Communities between mental illness and the spiritual dimension of life, it is necessary to facilitate a dialogue between mental health professionals and the different faith leaders. There is a need to give voice to those who hold very different world views. We have started this process within the training programmes with the beginnings of a dialogue between mental health staff and local faith leaders. Our difficulty so far is that we have been unable to attract the interest of the majority of the doctors to join in this dialogue. We are, as I write, organising

---

[1]See Chapter One of this volume.

a day conference for both doctors and faith leaders.

The resource teams emanating from the training programme will have a pivotal role both in the psychiatric services and also in the community. We have a very high mountain to climb. On the one hand we provide services in an area of London which has the largest and most diverse population anywhere in the UK. On the other hand, our mental health system is anchored in a world view which is predominantly Western and euro-centric.

A vivid example of this tension is illustrated by unilateral changes that occurred during the construction of a recently opened mental health facility. It is the most modern of its kind in the UK. At the planning stage, we ensured that a prayer room would be made available for all faiths. To highlight and respond to the importance of this function within the spiritual communities that this building would serve, the prayer room was to be placed at the centre of the building. When the new centre opened, we discovered that some project manager had taken the decision to move the prayer room, without consultation, to the rear of the building. That decision illustrated the unwillingness of the system to give voice to the majority of the population. In stark contrast to this lack of awareness and appreciation of the significance of this function, when the new facility was visited by a leading local politician, the first question she asked was, 'Where is the prayer room?'

This illustrates the gap that exists between the management community which controls the resources and the Faith Communities of the area who do not have an adequate voice. Not only do the Faith Communities fail to provide adequate support for their members suffering from mental distress, but also the system which is charged with providing the necessary support fails at such a fundamental level. It is little wonder that those suffering who most frequently also have a deep sense of the spiritual are unable to feel supported in their often very isolated journey.

Giving Voice to the Spiritual and Cultural Needs of Service Users

Over the last two years we have run three training groups. The first two were pilot groups to which we invited a total of sixteen participants. Using our experience with the pilot groups, we then developed a one year course in partnership with a local university, employing the same style of learning as in the first courses. As with the initial pilot groups, the university-associated course consisted of mental health workers, members of Faith Communities who had themselves suffered from mental distress and leaders from those communities who had been touched by mental health problems.

From discussions within the training groups around member's experience of receiving mental health services, it became clear that members did not feel that their spiritual and cultural needs were respected or even recognized during that process. For example, black service users wanted to read the Bible and pray in a way appropriate to their tradition. Muslim service users regarded it as important to have a sacred place where they could pray in private. And Asian women wanted their need for separateness to be respected. The culture of the wards did not reflect or recognize the importance of these and other Faith Community practices, especially in the areas of prayer rituals and dietary customs. As these needs were given voice, we realised that it was necessary to engage with the staff teams in the mental health facility to raise their awareness of the importance of these needs and to encourage them to empathise with and respond to service users in these crucial areas. We sought to achieve this by establishing regular sessions with staff teams, in which they could dialogue with group members who had had the experience of being a patient on the ward. Our hope was that the 'ordinary person' would begin to be seen as the primary expert. To our surprise, many of the staff 'came out' and shared their own spiritual journey for the first time. They were being given permission to voice their own spiritual path to their colleagues.

At the same time, bringing these needs to light brought resistance from the staff teams, for responding to such an important agenda would mean a greater sensitivity combined with extra work. This is illustrative of the pace and rhythm of our journey. While we have made progress, I do not want to give the impression that we have solved this problem. We are seeking to include a range of mental health workers in the training groups so that we are able to enlist partners within the mental health teams. This will take a number of years. I have been encouraged that by adopting the model outlined in this chapter, something significant can happen. The aim must be to create an awareness training programme at many different levels, all emanating from our basic set of relational ethics.

And again our underlying goal in this regard has been to fashion an environment where all of us can together learn from each other and truly understand one another. I believe that if we are successful in this project we can together create a 'healthy village.' Again, this is a high mountain to climb as we are seeking to change the culture both in the mental health system and also in the wider communities. We wish to ensure that people suffering from mental distress are supported in the hospital by the whole organisation and in the community by their own Faith Communities. At present, there is insufficient support in either. We were encouraged this year by Diwali and Eid celebrations in one of the hospitals which were attended by the whole community.

Giving Voice to Important Basic Language Needs

We quickly discovered that being able to communicate in the native languages of the Faith Communities was an essential element to the success of the groups. There were a number of members for whom English was not their first language. As such it was important to ensure that there were appropriate language skill resources within the team to communicate with all members in their language. Additionally, this required group members to be able to empathise with those who experienced isolation through an inability to understand due to language differences. In time this process worked well.

However, in the development of the training programme with the local university, I was challenged by members of the validation committee who said that English had to be the only language used in the programme. I fought against this requirement as I argued that we needed to give voice to all sections of the East London community, which was impossible without the use of each individual Faith Community's own language. This was particularly relevant for us at the time as a Tamil-speaking community worker had recently joined the group. He was working with asylum seekers who were suffering from a high level of mental distress. That worker was crucial to the preventive work being done with one of the most marginalised groups in the area.

At the end of the discussions, a compromise was agreed upon which allowed for freedom to be given to members if they were seen as course tutors. My original request could not be fully implemented for fear of litigation! Again this is one of the realities of the pace of change that we have encounter in this project. However, in order to provide the necessary support for those who want to join us in this journey we need to invest heavily in ensuring that there are some radical support structures available which do not necessarily fit with the traditional western academic paradigms. Unless we can achieve this, those who we most need to join us will be unable to do so.

Support for Service Users

Another fundamental need that emerged in the first groups was that of basic human emotional support. Those service users who had themselves experienced mental distress, described in detail their isolation. This was due to a number of reasons, most notably because of the aforementioned stigma attached to mental illness within their communities. We agreed that the training group itself should become the foundation for a resource team to support individuals, not only while in the hospital, but as they returned to their communities. One member of the group was determined to initiate a coffee morning for Muslim women who had no support structures. Others saw the importance of befriending individuals once they had left the hospital. We also agreed that an educational programme needed to be initiated with the Faith Communities across the district so that, by raising awareness, individuals would not feel so isolated. As stated earlier, every individual needs to feel that someone else is genuinely interested in him or her. Isolation is a terrible evil, an ethical wrong as well as a psychological injury.

Conclusion

My own spiritual journey within the Christian tradition has stirred within me a passion to change structures for those who are most marginalised and who have no voice. This journey has led me to live and work in the inner city of London. My deeply-held spiritual beliefs join with what I have come to understand as unique about the Gestalt tradition: that it is possible to do something different at a structural level by changing the level of contact between people.

I was first introduced to this realm, that Lee describes as Gestalt's ethics of connection, whilst in a therapy group for six years. There, with an exceptional psychotherapist, I witnessed a new community being created and saw how true contact in relationships can effect miraculous change. I have also come to see the importance of awareness. Living these values, I have a vision that it is possible to change social structures, especially within the mental health system. With the generous support and inspiration of Sonia Nevis, I hope that I have illustrated how this dream has begun to become a reality within the communities of East London.

Editor's Note:
As the final chapter in our exploration of the values of connection, Gordon Wheeler, who has written on the topic of the Holocaust previously from a Gestalt point of view (1993), brings us an eloquent analysis of the dynamics of courage and the fragility of goodness, in which he relates the remarkable, little known story of how no Jews of Bulgaria were lost to a Nazi concentration camp during WWII. This is a story of how not one but myriad, often unconnected, acts of heroism, emanating from and supported by the Bulgarian culture as a whole, together were sufficient to delay, forestall and finally block the deportation of Bulgarian Jews, saving millions of lives. It is a story of hope, showing how internally shared values of connection can flourish even in the harshest of times.

14

The Fragility of Goodness: How the Jews of Bulgaria Survived the Holocaust A Gestalt Field Perspective

Gordon Wheeler

Introduction

At some six decades after the horrors of the second World War, the collection of persecutions and exterminations known as "the Holocaust" (as if, alas, there were only one) continues to mesmerize our gaze and haunt our imaginations. That these events revealed a colossal and tragic flaw in the culture of "the West" goes without saying: gone is the smug moral superiority of European culture in the Victorian Age, and with it, the facile assumption of universal human progress—led of course, again, by "the West." But what is that flaw exactly? Our Western cultural tradition has given the world both unprecedented technological advances, and an unmatched flowering of *interiority*, the deep and wide exploration of subjective consciousness—including the space of ethical and moral activity, impulse, emotion, and behavior. What is missing in this great worldview, that could account for things going so horribly wrong—to the point where today, it is not just one or another people or culture threatened with genocide, but the entire human race, and with it perhaps most or all of complex life on the planet?

Those who do not remember the past, said Santayana, are condemned to repeat it. Compelled to repeat it—Freud insisted, in one of his more holistic, "Gestalt" moments—out of an obsessive need to return again and again to old unresolved problems of attachment and aggression, love and hate and fear, even without benefit of any new awareness, any clear understanding of the problems themselves, or the workings of those dynamics in our relational nature. Thus the unresolved problem itself becomes the pattern and organizing dynamic of our lives, our relationships, and our very selves. And thus too we find, again and again, such familiar, disheartening phenomena as the perpetuation of abandonment and abuse down through generations of the same families (or societies, or whole cultures), the echoes of the unresolved issues of founders or previous generations in the life of an organization (or a theory), the ceaseless renewal of prejudice and oppression in societies, and the numbing repetition of cycles of conflict and destruction among nations, religions, and other ideologies.

Surely nowhere are we in the West more acutely aware of the menace of Santayana's dictum than in the history of the years 1933-45 in Europe. But what exactly is it that we are to remember and understand out of the Medusa-like horror of that particular past? Which memories, which lessons and conclusions are the ones which might free us from the philosopher's curse, and give us some hope of setting a new course now and in the future? These are questions that concern us all, as therapists, as consultants to organizations and programs, as members of the currently dominant (and currently besieged) EuroAmerican world culture, and as citizens and custodians of this endangered, embittered world. So many lessons, so many conclusions are possible. Which ones are key, if we want to avoid yet another repetition of these horrors on a world scale?

That mankind is capable, as we know, of unspeakable cruelty and evil? That "Western Civilization," so-called, far from being a reassuring bulwark against the worst of that evil, turns out to be one of its chiefest perpetrators? That most people, here as elsewhere, are basically pretty decent and fair-minded, yet often reluctant to risk their safety and comfort, or especially that of their families, for anybody but their nearest and dearest? That only a relatively few people can ever be recruited to actually do unspeakable deeds—and even those few generally require active, intense brainwashing and still show severe stress reactions—but that many more will look the other way while they do it, or avail themselves of our seemingly limitless capacities for denial? That self-interest and expediency may steer people either toward evil or away from it, as the winds change? That within all these other truths, a remarkable number of people will nevertheless "stick their necks out" for total strangers, often completely unpredictably and at least on occasion successfully? That people in positions of great power and security may often squander that position needlessly when they could have used it far better—or then again sometimes use it quite nobly, without regard to personal cost? That to get most people to be horribly cruel to their fellow beings, even passively, you first have to harden them up with quite a bit of propaganda and lies—and that such lies do tend to work, to some extent, at least for awhile? That even with all that, if you happen to want to kill a whole lot of people, you absolutely have to put a justifying cover story on it, and do it somewhere far away and as out of sight as possible—because if you surprise their neighbors and onlookers with the truth, many of the latter's first reactions will be troublingly, subversively moral?

All these and more are potential lessons we may draw from this agonizing history. Which ones are key? Even more urgently, if all this repertory of gestures and responses is part of our potential, then what are the underlying conditions—the attitudes, beliefs, and specific actions—that favor one outcome, one response over another?

To explore these questions, and in the quest as well for renewed heart and hope, we turn to all those events of the period, large and small, which stand out as exceptional, cases where people *did* turn away from the safest, easiest course, often at considerable risk of personal exposure and reprisal. Many cases of individual or group resistance, subversion, and/or heroism did of course exist, and over the years many of these have been documented, from great acts of public courage of the type exemplified by anti-Nazi martyrs like Dietrich Bonhoeffer and others, to countless smaller acts of risk and kindness, most of course undocumented and now lost but very many of them as well finding their way into archives and print down through the intervening decades, as the great silence that descended over these times has been partially lifted (see for example many such instances in Heimannsberg & Schmidt, 1993).

To a great extent these cases of moral courage are individual acts, or those of small networks such as the White Rose. National underground networks of resistance to the Nazis of course existed as well, and accomplished great things, including many acts of sustained, organized courage. But when we turn to the public arena, the picture grows much bleaker. France, the heart and home of the European Enlightenment, collaborated officially in mass deportations, in both occupied and unoccupied sectors of the country. Italy, known for centuries for tolerance, allowed deportations, even before the fall of Mussolini and German occupation. Switzerland, fiercely democratic and independent, was not above official policies of profiting from the victims of the Nazis. The United States, a nation of immigrants and refugees, turned away thousands of desperate seekers of asylum—and not out of fear, but xenophobia and selfishness. The King of Denmark was public in his sympathy for Jews; yet alone he could do nothing to prevent the deportation of thousands from occupied Denmark. The Catholic Church, for its part, will likely never recover the moral authority it gave up through its supine and accommodating relationship with the Nazis (though to be sure, many individual clerics and local orders offered courageous exception, at times in defiance of their own superiors).

And so it goes, a bleak and deeply disheartening record. Indeed, of the more than twenty countries of Europe either allied with Germany, or occupied or annexed by Germany, only a single one stands out, as having lost *none* of its Jewish citizens to the Holocaust. This country was, of all places, Bulgaria—a monarchy with a fascist government, quite distant from the center of the liberal tradition in Western Europe. The story of this exceptionalism—a story even now not widely known in the West—sheds a different light on our understanding of the dynamics of courage itself, as a condition and an event of a whole social field.

Precarious Hostages: the Jews of Bulgaria

Bulgaria, a small, deeply Catholic nation on the Black Sea, pinched at the outbreak of the War between the two expansive, anti-Semitic empires of Hitler and Stalin (soon to be at war with each other), would seem the least likely of all places to emerge at the end of the War as the sole wholly successful Continental resister, from Madrid to Moscow, to the extermination of the Jews. The majority party of the Bulgarian parliament was fascist; moreover, King Boris, the reigning monarch, was a public anti-Semite who had supported and signed Bulgaria's 1940 law stripping Jews of most of their rights as citizens. Worse still, in the checkerboard of shifting power politics of Eastern Europe, the Bulgarian government had allied itself with Germany, against Russia (its traditional protector against the Ottoman Empire), in expectation of recovering the provinces of Thrace and Macedonia, which had been lost in World War I

However, by 1942, the midpoint of what was to be a six-year War and after the failure of the Nazis' Moscow offensive, German victory was no longer a foregone conclusion. In the face of military setbacks (and thus unable to realize Hitler's latest plan, of resettling the Jews in Madagascar), the Nazis began to embark on what would become an official program of mass extermination. When the first orders came from Berlin, for the roundup of 20,000 Bulgarian Jews, the King temporized; anticipating public reaction, he declined to authorize arrests on Bulgarian soil, but still made no objection to the deportation of some 12,000 from the "lost" provinces, which were Nazi-controlled. Even so, public reaction was negative and considerable, and clearly problematic for the government.

In the face of growing Nazi insistence, he then agreed to the further removal of Jews from Bulgaria proper. It was only the unexpected ferocity of minority opposition in the otherwise collaborationist National Assembly—and above all the vigorous, courageous, and sustained pressure exerted publicly and privately by the Christian Bulgarian Orthodox Church—that delayed and ultimately dissuaded the King, who put Berlin off with the thin excuse that Bulgaria's Jewish citizens, no longer allowed in the armed forces, were therefore essential to the war effort at home as domestic road crews.

Evil delayed is suffering that hasn't happened, and may not happen. As fortune had it, each further delay brought further dimming of the Nazis' military star (and with it, increasing odds that Stalin, not Hitler, might yet emerge as master of Bulgaria's fate; at the time it was not yet clear how little that would likely have helped the Jews). Eventually the King traveled personally to Berchtesgaden, to explain to the Fuehrer that Bulgaria's Jews, being largely Sephardim, were racially "different," and somehow less threatening to the purity of the Reich than those of Western Europe (Hitler was unmoved—a Jew was still a Jew; but he was increasingly preoccupied elsewhere, and again valuable time was gained). Meanwhile, the minority petition to block all deportation eventually gained over forty co-sponsors in the Assembly—not nearly a majority, but enough to give the government considerable pause, affording crucial time for the development of much more effective action, from a much more resolute and powerful quarter.

This quarter was the Bulgarian Orthodox Church, to which much of the credit must go for the salvation of the Jews of Bulgaria. From the time of the first racial laws in 1940, the Church's protest had been energetic. In 1943 the Metropolitan Synod (the council of Bishops) stepped up their protest, now demanding government protection not only for their own parishioners of Jewish heritage, but for all the non-converted Jews as well. When the Metropolitan Bishop of Sofia was threatened with arrest and treason charges, his response was to announce that the doors of every Bulgarian church and monastery of his district would be opened to Jews if necessary, and that any arrests would require violation of the sacred principle of sanctuary. The Bishop of Plovdiv, for his part, assured the Jews of his city that he would take them into his own residence in any numbers possible, and vowed as well to lie down personally and bodily on the tracks in front of any deportation train bearing Jews from Plovdiv.

These announcements, coming from such a source, alarmed the

government and electrified the country. Protests spread; newspapers weighed in, in defiance of government censorship. Demonstrations broke out; petitions were circulated; the widow of a revered former Prime Minister led a public delegation to the government. The Swiss ambassador (an official neutral) took it on himself to represent the protest and pressure of the Allies, distant as they were. To make a comparison, imagine if the Pope of the western Catholic Church had protested publicly to Hitler (or Mussolini, or Franco) with anything like equal force and courage. Imagine the outcry and consequences, if he and the Bishops of Italy, Germany, Austria, and other countries had faced the Nazis (or the local police, who in many countries collaborated) with the shocking necessity of violating holy sanctuary in order to arrest Jews, and running trains over the bodies of priests to deport them. Imagine the tonic support to literally millions of anguished and fearful Catholics and others across Europe (and the United States), hesitating to raise their own voices in protest against the crimes they saw around them (even at a time when the full magnitude of those crimes was still not at all widely known)—crimes which certainly were troubling the hearts and minds of millions, privately, as we now know from contemporary letters and other sources, many of whom were looking at the time to their own local pulpits and parish priests for inspiration and guidance—largely, alas, in vain (though there were still local exceptions, in defiance of their own Church government).

Imagine, finally, the moral authority of the Church in the world today, as a force for peace and justice, had the Pope (who after all was in a much more powerful, more protected position than local Bishops in the Eastern Churches) shown anything like this moral voice and vision. That world—our world today—would be literally a different place. To what extent it would be different we cannot know, for want of that squandered opportunity.

Implications for Today's World

Thus it is that we may draw one more lesson from the tragedies and failures—and the courage and accomplishments—of those dark times, for our own equally dark times today. That lesson is this: that even in the face of powerful, organized evil, the reactions of everybody do count, great and small, near and far, dramatic and behind-the-scenes, even when those reactions may seem hopeless and quixotic at the time. Even when we don't know it, even under conditions of great oppression and fear, it may often be that we actually have a good deal more "wiggle room" than we realize, for a gesture, at least, in the right direction. And that gesture, even if small itself, may be a dynamic, energizing part of a much larger whole.

The public resolve of the Bishops of Bulgaria in 1943 galvanized the country, completely changing the situation and saving millions and millions of innocent lives. But these acts of great public courage came more than a year after the first deportations (from outside Bulgaria proper)—more than three years after the passage of laws stripping Jews of their legal rights and protections. Without the strong protests, publicly and in the Assembly, to the earlier deportations, delaying the situation and throwing it into doubt, the Bishops would likely never have had time to reflect so deeply, to persuade the reluctant among themselves, and to act so resolutely (but some Bishops were protesting individually from the start, which in turn set a climate for both public and political resistance). Without some forty cosigners in the Assembly, those legislative protests themselves would not have carried the weight that they did with the King, who was no democrat and no particular friend to the Jews. Without the climate of public and press protest, many or most of those Assembly co-sponsors might not have dared sign on, in the face of political ruin or even arrest (the minority leader himself was deprived of his seat for his pains). It even helped that the King himself, while at best indifferent to the fate of some of his subjects, was at least not personally, rabidly a hater of Jews (passive evil is still better than active evil; opportunism is at least more open to influence than fanaticism).

The picture that emerges from all this is not of some long linear chain of causation, any single link of which, once broken, would lead to certain disaster. Nor is it one of any singular, individual act of courage which changed the fate of the country. Rather, what we can see is a great interactive tissue of reciprocal causes and effects, a whole, delicate web of contributing acts and conditions—acts creating conditions, and conditions favoring and supporting acts. A hole in that tissue in one place might be made up by strength in another; that strength in turn might serve to repair a weakness someplace else in the fabric. A majority of the Assembly might have joined the resolution; they didn't. The Bulgarian Church might have issued its ultimatum sooner, perhaps affecting their brother Bishops in the occupied provinces; they didn't. The King could have registered protest to the context-setting racial laws of 1940; he certainly didn't. And yet the cumulative effect of all the actions that did take place—some late, some partial, some calculating—was to achieve a tipping. Great evil was delayed, then opposed, then forestalled—then prevented. The Church stands out; yet no one action alone sufficed, no individual gesture accomplished the goal. Rather, the singular result in the Bulgarian case—again, alone of the more than twenty nations allied with or occupied by the Nazis (or both)—was the outcome of myriad acts, large and small, each energizing and contributing in some small or large way to the others, recursively, in a great beneficent circle.

This is the action of a field, through the agency of many individual hands, each of them affecting that field dynamically and positively (just as other actions affect the whole in the opposite, weakening direction). This is not the way we often think of courage in our Western tradition, steeped as we are in the romanticism of the individual, and the ideology of individualism. Looking over our world through this lens, we may see the holistic effects of a moral field, for good and for evil, all around us. Sometimes one individual—Gandhi or Mandela—does seem indispensable (if not sufficient—behind both of them were hundreds or thousands of others); more often a lone, exceptional individual seems plainly, tragically inadequate, for all his or her courage (think of Rabin in Israel, Bonhoeffer again in Nazi Germany, or many others). And yet even these "failed" gestures may serve to inspire others, then or later.

In the end the moral field, like any field dimension, is indivisible. Each part is affected dynamically, for good and for evil, by all the others, and by the whole. That whole is the world we live in, affecting and affected by all the parts, all the individual voices and points of consciousness. To those who say our world today is grown too big, too complex, for the actions of any individual to affect, and that everything is therefore futile, the answer must be: how can you be sure? True, we have lost the sentimental romance of the individual, like the aptly-named Han Solo of *Star Wars*, cowboying his outlaw way to saving the universe, in defiance of the technological megapower. What we gain is each other, each doing what we may, at times energizing others to do the same, or more. The salvation of the world today can lie only in the fact that people, while often selfish and fearful, are not always or only so—and that small acts cumulate, energizing others and the shared field. This is the fragility of goodness, and the hope of the world.

References

Heimannsberg, B. & Schmidt, C. (1993). *The Collective Silence: German Identity and the Legacy of Shame* (C. Harris and G. Wheeler, translators and editors). SF: Jossey-Bass.

Wheeler, G. (1993). "Translator's Introduction." in B. Heimannsberg & C. Schmidt, *The Collective Silence: German Identity and the Legacy of Shame* (C. Harris and G. Wheeler, translators and editors). SF: Jossey-Bass.

Epilogue

••••••••••••••••••

The message throughout this book is consistent. Gestalt field theory brings us a strong set of relational ethics—a platform on which we can build our treatment of patients/clients and our interaction with others. These values have long been inherent in the Gestalt model. At the heart of this ethics is the tenet of understanding others and ourselves from a perspective of their and our relational strivings. It is people's relational strivings that hold the key to understanding their behavior, offering avenues of connection that are not available from other perspectives.

Further, individual health and development is intimately connected to the health and development of the larger field. It takes a *healthy* field to foster and maintain *healthy* individuals across their life span. Both require paying attention to the relational strivings of the people involved. It only takes a glimpse at our present world condition to understand that without a field of healthy individuals, we all suffer.

Achieving this field condition requires a switch from the individualist thinking that is so prevalent in our culture. It has been difficult to make such a move in our society. Not only does individualism have its roots as far back as the ancient Greeks, but over the last couple of centuries many of our modern freedoms have been won by breaking loose from and discrediting hierarchical societal orders that often locked people into a given place, a role and station from which it was almost unthinkable to deviate (see discussion in Taylor, 1992). Thus, the pursuit of individualism has flourished in modern times. However, the price of individualism is enormous. As the philosopher Charles Taylor says: "the darker side of individualism is a centring on the self, which both flattens and narrows our lives, makes them poorer in meaning, and less concerned with other or society" (1992, p. 4).

We must get beyond the notion that "I can prosper by myself." How we view ourselves and our sense of connection with others is inextricably tied to how we will treat others and ourselves. Our beliefs in this regard constitute our internal ethical system, which is resistant to change unless our underlying felt beliefs about the real possibilities for connection, support, and belonging in our shared human field change.

The task is one of constantly enlarging our sense of what/who is "me" as opposed to "not me," continually expanding the province of "my world" as opposed to "not my world." In order to ignore, neglect or aggress on others—from "dissing" them to attempting to control, humiliate, exclude, or discriminate against them—we must first define them as "not me," part of "not my world."

With our clients/patients it means being able to facilitate new experience that will provide an opportunity to belong and will challenge their notion that true relationship is not possible for them, something that has long been a strength of the Gestalt model. This means not only providing limits when needed, but most crucially listening for and hearing the yearnings under masking/camouflaging behavior—again, understanding our patients/clients from the perspective of how they are trying to survive relationally. And it means supporting the other people in their systems.

For ourselves, as Lee Geltman shares with us, enlarging our sense of what/who is part of "our world" is an ongoing task. Like with our patients/clients, this task requires us finding sufficient reception in the field for our own needs for connection. As Lynne Jacobs so graciously shares with us of her own experience, it is when we are off balance without sufficient support that we start to define others as "not me."

As Philip Lichtenberg reminds us, we all have the potential to be an oppressor. In workshops that I offer, I invite people, after developing enough sense of connection in the workshop, to explore what they do—what strategies they employ that defines others as "not part of their world"—when they are off balance without sufficient support. Such learned behavior and strategies are usually automatic and out of awareness. The list that comes back is always extremely creative, imaginative, and diverse, enlisting some element of protecting oneself without regard to the effect on another. To do otherwise, to not employ such strategies, requires us knowing when we are off balance and developing a sense that sufficient support is possible at such times, either internally or most importantly from our environment. It means investigating the possibility that the values of connection can work, testing whether it is possible for our voice to be heard. And if not, helping to build a field where it can be heard, learning from and appreciating difference while maintaining a relational connection as discussed by Nigel Copsey, employing the practices of care, inclusion, and openness to dialogue as presented by Lynne Jacobs, harvesting the power and importance of mutually-invested-in intimate relationships as described by Chuck Kanner, and the list goes on.

In short it means understanding the development of responsibility from the Gestalt notion of cultivating the ability to respond, which by definition sits in a field context. It means appreciating the subtle yet vital connections between reception/belonging and our having access to our ability to respond to ourselves and others in the fullest manner in our shared human experience. We can reflect on the many examples this book has brought us of people's deflated, deadened ability to respond and the field solutions of connection and belonging that have brought revitalization.

So many of us (our patients/clients are often prime examples), have had experiences—trauma, abuse, neglect, discrimination, poverty, significant loss, hardship and so on—which has resulted in defining significant parts of our self—our affects, needs, desires, ways of being in the world, and so on—as "not me." As demonstrated throughout this book, these disowned/shamed segments of self/other require a relational approach to heal. Healing necessitates the opportunity to develop a sense of the possibilities of respectful, trustful, wanted connection as opposed to a sense that one must do unto others before one is done unto.

When people are offered this opportunity, for sufficient time to get through their belief that this is not possible, they are freed to actualize a fuller way of being in the world. Their desires to get what they need are transformed from those of an isolated individual who has learned to not pay attention to the effect on others to those of a valued member and co-architect/caretaker of their field. And this becomes a self-perpetuating way of life. This is more than an altruistic response based on the "goodness" of people; it is a natural response emanating from the experience of belonging. When people taste this way of being in the world, to the extent that they can believe it is truly possible, they love it—it gives them joy, a sense of connection and completion and belonging and a support for a sense of themselves and their worth, and they hunger for it.

There is much work to be done. The world is in desperate shape. We have to shift to a field focus to understand and deal with our problems. This is not just dry theory. This will change our world.

May, 2004   Robert G. Lee
                                               Newton, Massachusetts

References

Taylor, C. (1992). *The Ethics of Authenticity*. Cambridge, MA: Harvard University Press.

Appendix

••••••••••

All of the chapters in this book, with one exception, are original material that were written for this book. The one exception was updated by the author from a previously published article and also contains original material. We are honored that several of the chapters have subsequently been published in journals. The following is a list of chapters that have been co-published or previously published in journals.

A version of Chapter One, "Ethics: A Gestalt of Values / The Values of Gestalt," by Robert G. Lee, appeared in the *Gestalt Review*, 2002, 6(1), 27-51.

A version of Chapter Two, "Ethics of Context and Field: The Practices of Care, Inclusion and Openness to Dialogue," by Lynne Jacobs, appeared in the *British Gestalt Journal*, 2003, 12(2), 88-91.

A version of Chapter Four, "The Story of Daniel: Gestalt Therapy Principles and Values," by Sandra Cardoso-Zinker, appeared in the *Gestalt Review*, 2004, 8(1), 80-95.

A version of Chapter Five, "The Relational Ethic in the Treatment of Adolescents," by Chuck Kanner and Robert G. Lee, will appear in the *Gestalt Review*, in press.

In Chapter Eight, J. Richard White updated his award winning article "A Special Case for Gestalt Ethics: Working With the Addict," which originally appeared in *The Gestalt Journal*, 1995, 18(2), 35-54.

A version of Chapter Thirteen, "Shame and Belonging: Homer's *Iliad* and the Western Ethical Tradition," by Gordon Wheeler, appeared in the *International Gestalt Journal*, 2002, 1(2), 95-120.

Selected Titles from GestaltPress